Pioneers of Social ~~~~

London's Cosmopolitan Methodism

Brian Frost
with
Stuart Jordan

✛ EPWORTH

Copyright © Brian Frost and Stuart Jordan 2006

The Authors have asserted their right under the Copyright, Designs
and Patents Act, 1988, to be identified as the Authors of this Work

British Library Cataloguing in Publication data

A catalogue record for this book is available
from the British Library

0 7162 0603 X/978 0 7162 0603 3

First published in 2006
by Epworth
4 John Wesley Road
Werrington
Peterborough PE4 6ZP

Printed and bound in Great Britain by
William Clowes Ltd, Beccles, Suffolk

Contents

Foreword   ix
Preface   xi
Introduction: The Social Passion of the Methodists   1

Part 1 Urban Missioners

Introduction by Stuart Jordan   15

1 *To Those Who Need You Most*   17
   Thomas Jackson, Peter Thompson and Pioneer Urban
   Mission

2 *Christian Audacity*   31
   Hugh and Katherine Price Hughes and the West London
   Mission

3 *God Cares Also for Minds*   45
   John Scott Lidgett, the Bermondsey Settlement and
   Methodist Educationalists

4 *Partners Not Passengers*   60
   James (Jimmy) Butterworth, Vic Watson and Clubland

Part 2 Social Providers

Introduction by Stuart Jordan   75

5 *April Weather . . . Shadow and Shine Alternating*   77
   Thomas Bowman Stephenson and the National
   Children's Home

6 *A Divine Imperative*   91
   Walter Hall, Hilda Bartlett Lang and Methodist Homes

7 *Life Abundant*   103
   William Kyle and the Westminster Pastoral Foundation

Part 3 Community Builders

Introduction by Stuart Jordan   115

8 *As Unchurchlike as Possible*   117
  Joseph Rank and Central Halls

9 *The Richest Woman in the World*   131
  Hilda Porter and Methodist International House

10 *Living on a Large Map*   143
  Douglas Griffiths, Youth and Community Work

11 *Working With, Rather than For*   158
  George Lovell, Catherine Widdicombe and AVEC

Part 4 Public Advocates

Introduction by Stuart Jordan   173

12 *The Magnificat Puts the Communist Manifesto in the
   Shade*   175
   Donald Soper and Christian Socialism

13 *A Small Cog in a Big Anti-Apartheid Wheel*   189
   Pauline Webb, David Haslam and End Loans to South
   Africa (ELTSA)

14 *Only One Race – The Human Race*   202
   Sybil Phoenix and Racism Awareness

Postscript by Stuart Jordan   215
Select Bibliography   224

Dedicated to
Bishop David Sheppard (1929–2005),
pioneer of new city ministries

London Methodism:
it's a challenge, it's a problem, it's a joy
Wilfred Wade[1]

1 *Methodist Recorder*, 8 July 1954. Wilfred Wade was a many gifted Methodist minister and District Chair who worked in London (Harrow, Kilburn and Hampstead), Birmingham and Luton and also shared in the early stages of ecumenical institutions, including the World Council of Churches. As secretary of the Methodist European Relations Committee he learned German in order to do his work better. A one-time Chair of the British Council of Churches' Youth Committee, from time to time he helped promote Religion and Life Weeks. As in his final job when he chaired the Nottingham and Derby District, he stamped all work with his personal authority. He died in 1968.

Foreword

This book chronicles a cavalcade of Methodists whose tireless commitment to Christ caused them to roll their sleeves up and tackle human misery. It is a record of which every living Methodist can be proud, while the rest of us look on with admiration and deep gratitude that for the sake of our Saviour they knew him, shared in his suffering and desired to become like him.

Methodists' work with children and young people is legendary. But housing associations, chiropody clinics for older people, cinemas showing decent films, racism awareness courses, psychotherapeutic counselling, homes for older people – the list is endless – have also been products of their concern to bring wholeness to people in need. Church buildings have been adapted to serve as soup kitchens, air raid shelters and centres for homeless people. Methodism is active worldwide, so its reach in the UK naturally embraces people from newly arrived ethnic minorities as well as the longstanding indigenous population.

Even in the most progressive social service state there will be the need for inspiration, innovation and volunteers. Christian disciples know that the Lord who said that 'human beings do not live by bread alone' also fed the 5,000. They will go on bringing hope to those whose hope is lost, voice to the voiceless, listening to the unheard, for they will hold on to their vision of the bright Kingdom of God in the earth's darkest places. Like their predecessors, they will continue to pioneer social passion – always looking to Jesus, the ultimate pioneer and perfector of a holistic wholeness.

The Most Revd & Rt Hon Dr John Sentamu
Archbishop of York

Preface

Pioneers of Social Passion can be read at different levels. It can be understood as the story of more than 20 remarkable personalities who made things happen. Clearly they had certain gifts, which helped them overcome considerable difficulties and tensions, but they also had staying power. Such strength of character surely stemmed from both their genetic inheritance and their environment, but was also sustained by a deep faith and conviction that what they were doing had been given to them as a vocation.

This book can be read, too, as the story of Methodism responding to key issues over 100 years of its London life. First, there are personal issues – care for very young children in distress, for the elderly, and for those with emotional and personal problems, some of which have resulted in organizations that have survived their pioneer founders. Second, there are city-wide issues like poverty, education and the needs of young people and overseas students. Third, there are political and economic concerns. Finally, there is the need for action to help marginalized peoples.

Pioneers in Social Passion can also be read as an account of how Christians, and others, have responded locally to the needs of often deprived neighbourhoods; or sought skills to develop communities that are increasingly multicultural in one of the most diverse cities of any continent.

Clearly the pioneers who grapple with such matters have special gifts and a capacity to open up paths where others may follow. Some had their counterparts in other denominations or secular movements. Though on occasion there was co-operation with others, essentially the pioneers described here were often lonely, sometimes with edges to their personalities that made it difficult for others to get near them or help them. There is something surely about singlemindedness that both attracts and repels.

A further way in which *Pioneers of Social Passion* can be viewed is as a particular form of being a disciple, through the prism of God's love seen in the actions of Jesus of Nazareth, who was open to all, identified with those often on the margins or who were ostracized, and willing to suffer for the good of the community. This does not necessarily mean that the pioneers in this book were 'saints' in any traditional meaning of the word. Indeed, often they found they had to deal with dynamics almost too strong for them. But it does mean they possessed certain graces that enabled them to stay on the journey they had undertaken (sometimes despite ill-health), and see it through, even though there was heartbreak, despair and failure on the way.

The question posed by their lives is this: If they saw clearly what had to be done in their contexts, no doubt despite their weaknesses and fears, what are the issues now with which we ought to be grappling? And what will our successors say of us and how we responded in the different contexts in which we have to live our lives in the capital?

This book does not pretend to be a history of Methodism in the capital. Rather, in 14 chapters, it tries to describe the work of pioneers, and what happened to the movements in which they were involved. Mainly it is concerned with Methodist responses to social issues in an ever-changing, restless urban and suburban context.

In 1995 a group called the London Pride Partnership produced a London Prospectus, which drew attention to the fact that of the ten local authorities in England with the highest deprivation, seven were in London. These were Newham, Southwark, Hackney, Islington, Tower Hamlets, Lambeth and Haringey.[1] Inevitably, therefore, areas such as these have shaped Methodism as it has tried to respond to the complexities of communities in them.

The same document also put the size of the metropolis in the context of other cities and conurbations, as the map in Figure 1 shows in a startling way.[2] This is the second fact to be considered when assessing Methodism in London.

Clearly, London cuts all groups down to size by its immensity, which is increased daily by the thousands who commute from the south-east region and beyond to work in the capital. But its very size can provide sponsorship for a wide variety of initiatives, as well as providing Londoners themselves with a rich experience of urban life. Indeed, in 2005 a newspaper produced a map of the capital's ethnic centres and main concentrations of faith communities (Christian, Hindu, Moslem, Sikh, Jewish, Buddhist), and it described the metropolis as 'the world in one city'.[3]

But London is not only complex and mobile. It is often without faith, as Lord Soper indicated at the celebration of the centenary of the London Mission in 1961, when he urged the Mission to seek to understand its work in the perspective of the first secular age in human history. Ironically, since then this has become less true, for as well as being

Figure 1. Population comparisons of London boroughs with major towns and cities.

a city of unbelief, London's increasing cultural diversity has brought with it the regeneration of mainline congregations, the founding of many independent churches, and a growing presence of Islam and other traditions, making it once more a city of faith.

'Methodists have a duty and obligation to bear witness against racial discrimination, economic poverty, religious intolerance, political exploitation,' Dr Irvonwy Morgan once observed.[4] In the lives of the pioneers described in this book – set as they often are in the context of urban deprivation, and impacted on by a restless fast-moving environment – some of the issues to which Dr Morgan has drawn attention have been addressed with particular energy. Clearly, these pioneers have been both shaped and moulded by a tradition. In the introduction I try to show how their responses have roots stemming from the Wesley brothers' work, which is then traceable in the nineteenth and twentieth centuries in the lives of individuals, even when they did not themselves found movements.

I am well aware, however, that I have not been able to consider the inner sacramental and devotional life of congregations across London, as they have waxed and waned, as London grew partly because of the development of transport networks. Nor have I addressed the significant preaching of many ministers or laity, including Drs Sangster, Weatherhead, Soper and Morris. Further, when considering the social impact that Methodists have made on London, it is impossible to trace, let alone document, the Monday to Friday lives of the laity, dispersed as it is in secular employment across the city, or the impact of specific initiatives, such as the Christian Commando Campaign of 1947, run by William Gowland and involving some 3,000 lay men and lay women in its outreach.[5] Perhaps another book could draw some of these threads together.

Almost as complex as some of the work I have tried to consider has been the fact that over a period of 100 years, boundaries and names have changed, and Methodism has altered as well. Life in London began to look very different in 1964, for example, when the 32 London boroughs began their work and the Greater London Council was inaugurated, though it followed on from the work of the London County Council. As you might expect, some contemporary situations will have changed since the interviews and research for this book were undertaken in 2004–05. Money itself has changed value continually, and the respective value of figures from previous decades are shown in Table 1.

Table 1. The purchasing power of the pound
(£1 in 1830 would have been worth £55.80 in 2000).

1830	£55.80	1920	£26.60
1840	£52.00	1930	£42.20
1850	£70.00	1940	£——
1860	£56.70	1950	£20.80
1870	£59.00	1960	£15.00
1880	£64.00	1970	£10.55
1890	£78.90	1980	£3.00
1900	£75.30	1990	£1.60
1910	£72.50	2000	£1.00

Source: Based on figures compiled by E. Barry Bower and supplied by Sir Jeremy Morse, one-time head of Lloyds Bank.

Sometimes material in one chapter recurs in another. This is inevitable, for life – unlike a book – is never tidy, and a number of topics straddle different headings. This seeming confusion is made even more complex when not only circuits – and indeed boroughs – change their names, but when issues beyond London impinge on the capital and the churches in it. Thus many ministries in London reflect the London dimension, the south-east region and also have national overtones. This threefold sociological fact is highlighted in some of the 14 chapters more than others and, in one case in particular, reveals the international economic pressures that the City of London experiences.

For myself, London became a passion when in 1964 I was appointed Greater London Area Secretary for Christian Aid. Before then, I had only known London as a place to visit, a city full of history and famous landmarks. Now I went all over the 32 boroughs and came to understand, at least in part, some of their problems and possibilities. I was also made sensitive to London's national role, epitomized in my life by three events staged in Trafalgar Square. The first, in 1965, was the final of a beat and folk festival of songs on human need that Christian Aid let me run, when the best ten from the competition were presented and Sydney Carter's 'When I Needed a Neighbour', specially written as the theme song, was first sung. According to police estimates, the event was attended by over 20,000 people.

The second event was in 1973, the culmination of a week-long worship and prayer celebration called 'That's the Spirit', which the Ecumenical Centre, of which I was director, promoted. With BBC TV cameras live, Bishop Colin Winter, the exiled Anglican bishop from Namibia, celebrated the Eucharist and it moved not only the crowd present in Trafalgar Square, but also viewers at home. It is, to date, the only time Holy Communion has been celebrated in Trafalgar Square.

The third event was the finale of an annual ethnic arts festival, called London Entertains, which I with others pioneered, running from 1978 to 1988. In the 1978 festival, African drums beat out from St Paul's Cathedral steps, and events took place over one weekend in Covent Garden. In subsequent years the finale was in Trafalgar Square where many diverse groups showed how multicultural London – and indeed the UK – had become, with music, song and dance from Continental Europe, from Britain and Ireland, and from Africa, Asia, the Americas and the Middle East in particular.

Working or living in, or near, central London from 1973 to 2000 I was able to experience the city's diversity and the possibilities for a range of ministries, but was also made aware of how quickly moods and fashions, as well as people, change. Nevertheless, I came to believe that the Churches must work ever more diligently ecumenically and develop new ministries because, as a recent United Nations report has indicated, 60 per cent of the world's population will live in cities by the year 2030.[6]

In researching and writing *Pioneers of Social Passion* I have relied on many eyes and ears. I would like to thank all those, too numerous to name individually, who have helped me with specific chapters and their personal reminiscences, sometimes verbal, sometimes in written form. I am particularly grateful to the Revd the Lord Griffiths and the Revd Dr Ron Gibbins, with whom I discussed the idea for this book at an initial stage, and to the London Committee and its staff, especially the Revd Dr Stuart Jordan, my collaborator in the task, who has helped to give shape to the material and has written the brief Introductions to each section, as well as the Postscript. I am also grateful to the Revd Dr Henry Rack for finding out information lodged in the Methodist Archive in the John Rylands Library in the University of Manchester, and to the Revd John Munsey Turner for initial encouragement and for references from Methodism's early years.

I thank also Sheffield University for permission to quote from Dr Maurice Barnett's unpublished thesis on 'Holiness in the Bible' and the following individuals for help with photographic material: Deryck Underwood Adams; Gordon Ashworth; Peter Dawe; Keith Ellis; David Haslam; Kath Humphreys; Tony Holden; Hilda Marsh; Ken Newbury; Sybil Phoenix; Geoff Ridgway; Frances Smart; Ernest Willis. I would also like to thank the following groups for the use of photographs: Clubland/Walworth Methodist Church; London Mission Committee; Methodist Church/MAYC; MHA Care Group; National Children's Home; South London Press; United Nations; Westminster Central Hall (Archives). All reasonable attempts have been made to locate copyright holders, but I am aware that as some photographs come from early years, I have not been entirely successful. This can be corrected in any future edition.

I hope *Pioneers of Social Passion* will help the new London District of the Methodist Church, launched in 2006, both to celebrate and understand its history and learn from it as it looks forward to a renewed but different future. Some may wonder if it is wise to put in such a modest book the life and work of many of the giants of Methodism, but unless some record is attempted at the start of a new era in Methodism in London, how else can its history be recalled?

I hope too that readers from other Christian traditions can realize more fully through this book the contributions to urban ministry that Methodists have made as, with them, they struggle to find new roles and to respond to new and often different realities. The starting point for each of us, however, must surely be our answers to questions asked recently by one central London minister: 'How does God reach me in the distinctive context of the modern city and how do I engage in the work of God there?'[7]

Notes

1 *London Pride Prospectus* 1995, p. 7, issued by the London Pride Partnership, comprising the Association of London Authorities, the Confederation of British Industry (London Region), the Corporation of London, the London Boroughs Association, the Chamber of Commerce and Industry, London First, the London Planning Advisory Committee, London's Training and Enterprise Councils, the London Voluntary Service Council and Westminster City Council.

2 *London Pride Prospectus*, p. 11.

3 *The Guardian*, G2, 21 January 2005.

4 Irvonwy Morgan, *'Twixt the Mount and the Multitude, the Relevance of John Wesley to His Age*, Peterborough, Epworth Press, 1957, p. 56.

5 David Gowland and Stuart Roe, *Never Call Retreat, A Biography of Bill Gowland*, London, Chester House Publications 1990. The Gowland papers are lodged in the Wesley Study Centre at Oxford/Brookes University.

6 UN-Habitat, *The State of the World's Cities 2004/2005*, Earthscan, 2004, p. 3.

7 Geoff Cornell, 'A Living Spirituality and Theology for the City', 2005, available at www.wlm.org.uk/churchatthecentreofthecity.html.

Introduction:
The Social Passion of the Methodists

When you leave platform 11 at Victoria Station you pass first Boots, then W.H. Smith's, not realizing their Methodist connections. Nor that Jesse Boot was a major benefactor to Nottingham University and W.H. Smith's family was involved with Central London Methodism in the nineteenth century, with one Smith becoming MP for Westminster and in 1871 a member of the first London School Board.[1] They exemplified John Wesley's advice to earn, save, give all you can, and this led them, as others, to become more prosperous as they excelled in commerce and business. With the development of the railways, this produced strong congregations on the edges of Britain's cities as those who prospered sought better living conditions in the suburbs. Initially this movement depleted many urban congregations, though more recently African–Caribbean groups have emerged in inner London, an unexpected bonus from the ambiguities of colonialism.

Methodists have often been respected in their community, as even the *London A–Z* indicates, for listed there are the Meakin and Creasey Estates, named after two South London Mission staff. Nearby (John) Scott Lidgett is commemorated in a Crescent bearing his name and also a school. More recently, Sybil Phoenix Close has been created in Deptford and (Walter) Finch Mews named after a microbiologist who was a governor and chair of a local school and was associated for 60 years with Peckham Methodism.[2]

In East London, F. W. Chudleigh, from the East End Mission, is recalled in Chudleigh Street, and on the site of Harold Hill Methodist Church is Harkness Close, recalling one of the Mallinson family, another of whom founded 30 chapels.[3] Charles Wesley, who lived near Marylebone High Street, is recalled in Wesley Street, and John Wesley Court, in Queen's Road, Twickenham, is built on the site of a former Methodist church. Two plaques commemorate other Methodists, one in Exton (formerly Church) Street, near Waterloo, where Thomas Bowman Stephenson began the Children's Home, the other near Tower

1

Hill where, in 1927, Donald Soper began open-air speaking. But probably the most unusual public notice is in multicultural Thornton Heath,
where a bus stop is called 'Parchmore Road Methodist Church', an indication of its significance for the local community.

Both Wesley brothers are buried in London, which is appropriate
because – though they also had centres in Bristol and Newcastle, where
an orphanage was established – London was their base. Susannah
Wesley lies in Bunhill Fields, opposite Wesley's Chapel, behind which is
John's tomb, while Charles was buried in Marylebone Parish Church
cemetery, though he has recently been re-buried in its Garden of
Remembrance. From London, John promoted social Christianity,
Christ's gospel knowing 'no religion but social, no holiness but social
holiness',[4] which even included the founding in Dublin of a home for
20 elderly widows.[5] This was congruent with Scripture, as Maurice
Barnett, who studied biblical holiness, wrote, 'even those turned away
at the Last Judgment being rejected for not doing good'.[6] Holiness thus
encompasses personal, social and civic life, a new relationship with God
leading to love that takes initiatives. 'Because of this it is the fire of social
righteousness,' Barnett has explained. 'Love cannot tolerate those things
in society which mean other members of the family are crippled by
social distress.'[7]

Both Wesley brothers demonstrated this love. While John was in
Germany, Charles prayed with condemned prisoners in Newgate Prison
(now the site of the Central Criminal Court), accompanying them to
Tyburn where they were hung.[8] On one occasion John found 57 sen-
tenced to death there. 'While they were coming in,' he recorded, 'there
was something awful in the clink of their chains.' Sometimes he was not
allowed access, but he and his colleagues persisted in their work.[9]
'Shame to those who bear the name of Christ, that there should be any
prison at all in Christendom,'[10] he raged.

The Wesleys also campaigned against slavery, with John issuing a
tract against it that had a wide circulation. In the last days of his life he
read the story of Olaudah Equiano, known widely as Gustavus Vassa,
and his slave experiences in a book that Equiano published himself with
help from many donors, of which John Wesley was one. Indeed his last
letter, to William Wilberforce, urging him on in his anti-slavery work,
quoted from the book;[11] and Elizabeth Ritchie, his companion latterly,
read extracts to him.[12]

In Wandsworth, where John Wesley's wife, Mrs Vazeille, had lived,
he preached in a house in the High Street at a gathering attended by
Nathaniel Gilbert, Speaker of Antigua's House of Assembly, who had
been impressed by Wesley's *Earnest Appeal to Men of Reason and
Religion*, published in 1744. Two of his black servants in attendance

were converted and later baptized by John Wesley. Back in Antigua, Gilbert called his slaves together and told them what Christ had done for everyone, and so began Antigua's Methodism, before even the first missionaries arrived there.[13]

John Wesley's passion for freeing slaves, which he shared with his brother Charles, who had seen their suffering in Georgia, also led him to want English people to have adequate education. Already an old man in 1780 when Robert Raikes opened his Gloucester Sunday School, John regarded such places as one of the noblest institutions 'seen in Europe for some centuries'.[14] Indeed, in the 1785 *Arminian Magazine* there was an appeal for Sunday Schools.[15] John also took a keen interest in a girls' school in Leytonstone and Lambeth, run by Mary Bosanquet and two women friends, which in 1768 moved to Leeds.[16]

John sought advice from Philip Doddridge, who had opened a Dissenting Academy, and having preached on a derelict site of the former Government Foundery building near Moorfields, bought its lease with a loan, borrowing further money to rebuild it. In its back room, where 66 Methodist class meetings providing spiritual and counselling help were held, John set up a day school, with two masters and 60 poor children.[17] Elsewhere there was a book room, stocking John Wesley's abbreviated classics in his Christian Library series, provided partly to educate preachers. He also issued a *History of England*, a compendium of natural philosophy, and many grammar books.[18]

The Foundery was also a lending bank. John collected £50 from prosperous members, appointing two stewards to meet weekly to loan money, to be repaid within three months. In its first year (1747), more than 250 were helped, which later included James Lackington, who used his loan to establish a bookselling business, which eventually achieved annual sales in excess of £100,000.[19] Moving to Finsbury Square in 1794, dubbing himself 'the cheapest bookseller in the world', he was originally critical of Methodism, but by 1804, regretting his earlier attitude, recanted in his *Confession*.[20]

At the Foundery, which was John Wesley's headquarters from 1739 to 1785, the first free dispensary was opened, and an apothecary was subsequently employed there. In 1747, John Wesley published *Primitive Physic*, which gave advice on illness and possible remedies, including 'that old, unfashionable medicine, prayer'.[21] It ran into 23 editions in his lifetime.[22] He also stressed the importance of hygiene, favouring preventive medicine, of which he was a pioneer. John Wesley understood the role that passions play in health, arguing, 'Till the passion which carried the disease is calmed, medicine is applied in vain.'[23] Most controversially, in 1776 John obtained an electrical machine, which still exists. He 'ordered several persons to be electrified who were ill of various disorders; some of whom found immediate, some gradual cure'. 'Two or three years later,' he remarked, 'our patients are so numerous that we are obliged to divide them; so part were electrified in Southwark, part at the Foundery, others near St Paul's, and the rest near Seven Dials.'[24] 'Wesley and Robert Lovett,' one writer has judged, 'were the first two who made a serious attempt to use electricity in medicine and their names should not be forgotten.'[25]

John Wesley was also enough of a pioneer to use secular buildings and the open air, writing to a friend: 'I should hardly have expected any increase of the word of God in Launceston, but probably it would be enlarged by preaching in the Town Hall, for many would come hither who would not come to our preaching-house.'[26] He was also sensitive to people affected by the early stages of the Industrial Revolution. 'I began visiting those of our society who lived in Bethnal Green Hamlet,' he wrote. 'Many of them I found in such poverty as few can perceive without seeing it.'[27] Alexander Mather, who went to Wesley's Chapel in 1798, was equally sensitive to nearby poverty, setting up a house in Golden Lane, especially for children, that became a centre for outreach.[28]

To help the many in distress, John Gardener and others at Wesley's Chapel in 1785 founded the Benevolent Strangers' Friend Society,[29] which still operates, though not as significantly as then. 'I like the design and Rules of your little Society,' Wesley wrote, 'and hope you will do good to many. I will subscribe three pence a week, and will give you a guinea in advance, if you call on me on Saturday morning.'[30] Members toured the attics and cellars of Spitalfields and the East End, aiding and befriending the widowed and unemployed, as thousands flocked to London seeking work. Soon large numbers were helped, partly through Adam Clarke, Wesley's London colleague.[31] 'So this is one of the fruits of Methodism,' Wesley noted.[32] Though it was aid without strings, spiritual help was offered, recipients encouraged to understand duty to God and neighbour and, like their helpers, to become 'frugal, thrifty and hard-working'.[33] Such was the scheme's influence by 1832 that the late King William had donated £186, and by 1840 his Dowager Queen had given £50.[34] In the twentieth century, of course, this concern for the poor led people like Patricia Layen in Clapham to spearhead Christian Aid in the area for many decades, and John Tanner to chair the World Development Movement.

Wesley's stress on lifestyle was a key to his social passion as he urged Methodists to use money wisely, first in their own families, then in the Church and also for the poor.[35] He was certain, too, 'we are to gain all we can without hurting our neighbour'.[36] He also preached on dress habits and sobriety.[37] By dressing simply and living on modest fare, in one year he gave away £1,400.[38] Wesley was a living example of how to handle old age, keeping his mind active and alert and remaining punctilious about practical matters. 'For upwards of eighty-six years,' he wrote, 'I have kept my accounts exactly. I will not attempt this any longer, being satisfied that I save all I can and give all I can – that is all I have.'[39] When, therefore, in recent years, Wesley's Chapel has explored lifestyle issues involving waste disposal, electricity consumption and First World/Third World imbalances, it is following in a twenty-first century context, ethical approaches being deeply rooted in its tradition. So, too, is Chelsea Methodist Church, which has encouraged its members to embrace a more green lifestyle. In 2006 it was accredited as London Methodism's first eco-congregation.

Pioneer that he was, John Wesley was no revolutionary, nor did Methodism – which had only 70,000 members by the time of his death – prevent revolution as some have maintained. Believing there was 'most liberty in a limited monarchy, less under an Autocracy and least under a Democracy',[40] Wesley nevertheless understood the state must act for the good of all, a view that later encouraged many Christians to support the creation of a Welfare State and a minimum wage. But though Wesley organized collections for the poor in 1772, when the harvest failed, appealing through the press for help,[41] he seemed unable to analyse the long-term effects of his beliefs, though with S. E. Keeble, the Methodist socialist of a century later, he certainly considered 'Christianity works like leaven and not like dynamite.'[42]

Wesley knew about the unreformed Parliament and the two MPs sitting for Old Sarum, a place with no people, yet did not condemn the situation. Perhaps he was fearful that Methodists, already causing substantial controversy, would be judged as anti-patriotic if he were too outspoken. He did, however, speak out against smuggling, though his attitude to the American Civil War was only to urge restraint, judging America to be 'like a house on fire'.[43] Not here at his best, he yet had an understanding that peace-makers rejoice to deal 'bread to the hungry' and cover 'the naked with a garment', and extolled the injunctions in the Sermon on the Mount.[44]

Clearly an innovator in his use of lay preachers, could John Wesley have operated without his brother Charles, despite their disagreements? Sometimes in history *two* people emerge – like George Fox and his wife, Margaret Fell, Francis and Clare of Assisi, or even Eberhard Bethge and Dietrich Bonhoeffer – and vast energies for good are unleashed. So it was with the Wesleys, and later with other original Methodists like Catharine and William Booth. It was John's uniqueness, however, that enabled him to combine the radical, the evangelical and the sacramental, each influencing the other, which then, and now, gives the social passion of the Methodists a depth and impetus.

Later developments

Only eight years after the building society movement had spread to London, in 1848 Methodists at Wesley's Chapel were creating the Planet Building Society,[45] which by 1871 was the third largest, though by then it was in financial difficulties.[46] It was not the first building society, which had started in Birmingham in the 1770s, but was a significant player.[47] In 1975, however, Planet merged with Magnet, begun in 1868, then became part of the Town and Country. In 1992 it joined the Woolwich, which itself soon was owned by Barclays Bank. Magnet had been merged with Shern Hall Building Society, started in Walthamstow by Sir William Mallinson, where it was based. A pioneer in the manufacture of plywood, this timber merchant had always lived in the East End, using his money partly to provide recreational opportunities for thousands through the playing fields he bought.[48]

Methodists were also involved in building societies at the national level, often as vice-presidents, with Sir William McArthur, Thomas Burt, the MP with strong Primitive Methodist roots, Sir Josiah Stamp from Beckenham Methodism, Sir Kingsley Wood, MP, and Lord Ammon, being high profile.[49] For several decades, Sir Harold Bellman headed the Abbey National and was involved nationally and internationally in building society politics.[50] More recently, London Methodists have continued this housing concern through the Paddington Churches Housing Group, the Springboard Housing Association in Bow, where Kenneth Start, a sector minister, was director for 20 years, and the National Housing Federation, whose director, Stephen Duckworth, served for the same length of time.[51] Locally, Chelsea Methodists redeveloped their site, co-operating with Servite Housing Association to provide sheltered accommodation. It was opened in 1984 by Cardinal Hume. From 1996 it has also been helping homeless people, creating – along with others – Chelsea and Kensington Homeless Concern, whereby churches each provide shelter and meals one night weekly throughout the winter.[52]

Since John Wesley's time, there has also been growing concern for a range of people who suffer disadvantage. In 1831, when Jamaican slaves revolted, missionaries informed British Methodists of injustice there, and by 1853 Wesleyan petitions had 229,426 signatures from 260,491 members – all the more remarkable because a Wesleyan 'No politics' rule prevailed for several decades under Dr Jabez Bunting, which had led to political quietism.[53] In 1992, a further petition was organized. The Petition of Distress from the Cities emerged from an Urban Mission consultation which was taken in July to the Methodist Conference, which backed its demand that the government initiate action to deal with urban problems. It was then taken to Buckingham Palace by leading Methodists, including that year's president, Kathleen Richardson, on 23 April 1993. The Petition urged the government to establish a Royal Commission on the Cities, reiterating the call made by the 1992 Conference.[54] It came at a time when Methodism, through its Mission Alongside the Poor Programme, raised £2.8 million between 1983 and 1993 from an appeal authorized by the Methodist Conference and later continued in another form until 1999. The concerns of the programme then became part of general Methodist policy.[55]

Methodists were also keen to identify with all engaged in industry, focused for them on the Luton Industrial College, founded in October 1957 by the Revd William (Bill) Gowland. Several Methodist chaplains, backed by the Home Mission Division, worked in the Southwark Diocese South London Industrial Mission (SLIM) and the London Industrial Chaplaincy (LIC) in the Diocese of London. Here contacts ranged from the East London Docks to Heathrow Airport.

In 1954 the Revd J. Clifford Adams took part in Bill Gowland's Christian Commando Campaign in Manchester. The link came to full fruition when Clifford joined Bill at Luton to help run courses after working with SLIM in the early 1970s at the Charlton Sainsbury's and in two other smaller chaplaincies.

After Luton (1977–83) Clifford joined the LIC, exchanging places with the Revd E. Roy Putnam. He was there from 1983 to 1986, working from West Acton, as Roy had done before him, with specific Underground lines and a car components firm. Roy himself had worked full time for the LIC team from 1973 to 1983 across north-west London, inheriting from the Revd David Wright links with the engineering apprentices and secretarial trainees, building on contacts David had made during his seven years (1966–73) in Acton.

The training manager and his staff at the Brent and Harrow Engineering Training Association worked consistently to facilitate regular meetings of chaplains with the 120–130 apprentices in their first years of foundation training at its purpose-built engineering training centre in Kingsbury. This gave chaplains links with many firms supporting the Training Association – including Hoover, Lucas, Osram, Marconi and Frigidaire.

Roy Putnam also developed strong links with the new London Transport Engineering School by Acton Town tube station. Besides its 100-plus annual apprentice intake, he also met regularly with other young trainees, who were learning typing and shorthand skills. He also often went into factories to meet employees on the factory floor, listening to their personal concerns amid the hum of machinery. He spoke, too, at meetings across London about industrial chaplaincy work; and was invited to attend joint management and trade union committees, sometimes being asked to comment about matters raised. An annual service was held by the London Industrial Chaplaincy, and was attended by many of the team's contacts.

Sometimes, of course, in the flow of history it has been individuals not groups who reflect Methodist social awareness – men like George Makippe, a former slave from equatorial Africa, who became a Christian through David Livingstone, then in 1886 was one of the bearers of his coffin at the state funeral. Staying on and marrying in Britain, Makippe worked as a gardener for over 50 years, living in the Chislehurst area where he was a well-known Wesleyan both in London and beyond.[56]

Another visitor to London, Kamal Chunchie, who like Makippe stayed and married, developed a remarkable personal ministry among seamen and their families. A former Ceylonese Muslim, educated at Kingswood School, Kandy, and formerly head of 800 police in Singapore, he fought for Britain in World War One and was twice gassed and wounded. Converting to Christianity on the Flanders battlefield, he worked initially for the Seamen's Mission, but then Chunchie and his wife, a woman from the Women's Army Auxiliary Corps from a Walthamstow Methodist Church, moved in 1922 along with their daughter, to a rented room in Poplar and from there developed a shared ministry. They also rented a dance hall in Docklands to develop their work among Christians, Muslims and those of no faith.

Initially supported by Wesleyan Methodism as his Sunday School grew, by 1926 the Chunchie family moved to Canning Town, where he set up the Coloured Men's Institute, which flourished until 1930, when road widening caused its demolition. Chunchie toured Britain seeking funds, but in the 1930s Methodism parted company with him over his lifestyle and his refusal of a job outside London, though Lord Soper knew and respected him. Chunchie continued on his own, though the Institute itself did not survive and harassed by money worries, Chunchie continued working from his home in south London until 1953, his wife surviving him until the late 1990s.[57]

In March 1922, the year Chunchie began his work, Lt Col Stuart Mallinson, DSO, MC, founded the League of Young Laymen. Its aim was to help churches across London give effective witness in the United Methodist Church, including those in Tottenham and Pimlico – the latter now being flats for sale built for Chelsea Methodism through Methodist Homes. Visiting 24 congregations in 1924, Mallinson's enthusiasm was fired afresh by the needs of Canning Town, Hoxton, Battersea and Camberwell.[58]

Mallinson and Chunchie, from very different backgrounds, epitomize

Methodism's attraction for many diverse personalities, though significantly in the 1930s it showed it had clear boundaries when it came to drinking and clubbing, with class sensitivities being revealed by Sir George Chubb, who once remarked to Lord Salisbury: 'Wesleyan Methodists belong to a much higher class than used to be the case.'[59] This became clear in the family of George Macdonald, one-time minister at Chelsea and Hinde Street, whose daughters married socially upwards – one to the pre-Raphaelite painter Edward Burne-Jones; one to the President of the Royal Academy, Edward Poynter; one to J. L. Kipling, whose son Rudyard became a novelist and poet; and another to Alfred Baldwin, whose son Stanley became Prime Minister. All the daughters left Methodism way behind.[60]

At the other end of the spectrum socially, Methodism touched radicalism, with the wife of the eighteenth-century agitator James Wilkes being Methodist, as were the Tolpuddle Martyrs. Ironically, Jack Dash, the dockers' leader, as a boy – while queuing for pictures on offer from the East End Mission – listened to communist agitators and so became one himself.[61] But it is more likely to attract a Peter Jones, founder of the Sloane Square shop,[62] or a Tom Moullin, a Guernsey man living in Stepney who became involved with Pearl Insurance. It is able to retain, too, the loyalty of women like Mrs Chippingdale from Poplar, whose devotion Wesley commended as he refused to consider closing his work there, though small,[63] and a Buckingham Palace servant, whose Methodism so upset others that Queen Victoria went to a class meeting to learn firsthand about Methodists, returning home to commend it to the objectors.[64] But it seldom attracts aristocrats or artists.

The overall picture is complex. Some, like Dame Thora Hird, stay Methodist, while others, like Sir David Frost, do not. Some, like Vincent van Gogh, who preached in the Richmond area while in London,[65] pay but a fleeting visit, while others, like Neil and Glenys Kinnock, retain only Methodism's social fire, as does Michael Foot, from his West Country Methodist family background. The poetess Kathleen Raine and the QC Norman Birkett are but two of many who come to London but leave Methodism, perhaps finding it insufficiently sophisticated for their tastes. At the artistic level, while Frank Salisbury – whose paintings of Chelsea artists for the Town Hall, royal events and five American presidents and British prime ministers – stayed,[66] jazz artists like Courtney Pine and John Dankworth have not. Nor did Hugh Burnett, son of a *Methodist Recorder* editor, though his cartoons often reflect a religious fascination.[67]

Most interesting are former Methodists who often become Anglicans. The travel agent Sir Henry Lunn was one; Janet Lacey, Christian Aid's dynamic director, was another. Margaret Thatcher, the product of

Grantham Methodism and who was married in Wesley's Chapel, is influenced by the Church of England. Another significant person is Dame Cecily Saunders, foundress of the Hospice Movement, who worked as a volunteer at St Luke's Home for the Dying in Bayswater, the creation of Dr Howard Barratt, Katherine Price Hughes's brother. Its impact led her to challenge conventional medical wisdom, so that at 38 she trained as a doctor, then set up her first hospice in south London.[68]

In contemporary London, the work of Julian Joseph, whose Methodism was confirmed while studying in Boston, where Methodists supported him, stands out in both jazz and classical areas. Sometimes hosting BBC jazz series or working with orchestras at the Proms and elsewhere,[69] his link with Methodism is through the Wandsworth church that cradled Lord Soper.

Among the many less well known is the policeman from Harlesden Methodism who, through his membership of the Black Police Officers Association, helps to recruit more officers from minority ethnic groups; a social worker involved in a management role in Lambeth Child and Family Welfare Services;[70] and a member of the West London Mission who works with hospitals in the patient liaison area. In the legal field, a group in Muswell Hill Methodism opened a Centre of Access for parents, either separated or divorced, so their children could see the parent not involved in their daily care. Begun in 1989, with trained volunteers, it belongs to the 300-strong Child Contact Centres in the UK, more than 15 of which are in Greater London.[71] At the political level, four Methodist ministers have been appointed to the House of Lords, two of whom, Lord Soper and Lord Griffiths, have taken the Labour whip, and one, Lord Roberts, the Liberal Democrat. The fourth, Baroness Richardson, sits on the cross-benches. Also at the political level are Methodists who work for the Greater London Authority and others who are elected local councillors – all part of the Methodist kaleidoscope in the capital. They are part too of the hidden history of the laity, who make up 99 per cent of the Church, stretching back to Christ himself. Deeply affected by Jesus' social passion, they embody and continue the work of the pioneering John Wesley.[72]

In the chapters that follow, Wesley's willingness to innovate and encourage others to follow where he has led, both essential ingredients in the personality of a pioneer, are demonstrated in the lives and work of over 20 men and women who all seem to have been seized by John Wesley's stress on love working out socially, and his view that it is important not always to be bound by traditional boundaries in work structures or concerns. This perhaps is the core meaning of his famous phrase 'the world is my parish'.[73]

The pioneers in the four sections of this book, grouped together under certain key themes, have taken further what the people in this Introduction have exemplified, even though they were not founders in their own right. The spirit in which they have all worked, however, following John Wesley, is the same spirit of love expressed in and through society because that is God's nature, revealed in the New Testament in both the gospel story and the early Church.

Notes

1 John A. Vickers, ed., *A Dictionary of Methodism in Britain and Ireland*, Peterborough, Epworth Press, 2000, pp. 36 and 323.

2 See John D. Beasley, *The Bitter Cry Heard and Heeded: The Story of the South London Mission 1889–1989*, South London Mission, 1990. For Henry Meakin, see pp. 18–40, 69. For James Creasey, see especially pp. 45–6.

3 See Sir William Mallinson, Bart, JP, *A Sketch of My Life*, Peterborough, Epworth Press, published privately in the late 1930s.

4 See John Wesley, Preface to the 1739 Hymn Book, quoted by J. Wesley Bready, *England: Before and After Wesley, The Evangelical Revival and Social Reform*, London, Hodder & Stoughton, 1938, p. 229.

5 In 1771 and 1789, John Wesley gave Holy Communion to the residents of the home. For the history of the home, see Dudley Levistone Cooney, 'Twenty reduced widows', *Dublin Historical Record*, vol. XL, no. 1, Spring 1997. In recent years it has become Eastwell Residential Home, and now not all residents are widows.

6 Maurice Barnett, 'The biblical concept of holiness, with special reference to its social aspect', unpublished PhD thesis, Sheffield University, 1959, 207764, serial no. 1062, p. 248.

7 Barnett, 'Biblical concept', p. 508.

8 Robert Southey, *The Life of John Wesley*, 1920, abridged and newly edited with notes by Arthur Reynolds 1903, p. 142.

9 See Frederick C. Gill, *In the Steps of John Wesley*, Cambridge, Lutterworth Press, 1962, p. 46.

10 John Wesley, 3 February 1753, cited in Bready, *England*, p. 131.

11 John Wesley, letter to William Wilberforce, 24 February 1791. For text, see John Wesley, *Journal*, vol. 8, p. 135.

12 'Miss Ritchie attended Wesley during his last days and took over as a reader to him from one of his preachers. The last four days of his diary (which continued later in the *Journal*) shows that she read Equiano to him on 22 February 1791. On 23 February he read it to himself (apparently) and it seems again on 24 February, though there is no entry for that day (nor indeed any later). He says in the letter to Wilberforce (dated 24 February) that he was that morning reading what is clearly Equiano's book (though he is not named) and is shocked at what he says about lack of justice for blacks as their oaths in court count for nothing against whites . . . There is no indication of how much Miss Ritchie read to him either in the Wesley diary or in the biography of her by Agnes Bulmer (*Memoirs of Mrs Mortimer*) which includes her letters and extracts from her account of Wesley's

last days written for Dr Whitehead. (This is printed in full in Vol. VIII of Curnock's edition of the *Journal*, but not in Ward's new edition. Both have Wesley's diary.) This looks to be as far as we shall get.' The Revd Dr Henry Rack, letter to author, 20 September 2005.

13 Norman Taggart, *The Irish in World Methodism*, 1760–1900, Peterborough, Epworth Press, 1986, p. 19.

14 *Wesleyan Methodist Magazine*, quoted in M. G. Jones, *The Charity School Movement 1938*, p. 143, cited in Josephine Camm, *Hope Deferred, Girls' Education in English History*, London, Methuen & Co., 1965, p. 97.

15 Cited in Maldwyn Edwards, 'John Wesley', Rupert Davies and E. Gordon Rupp, eds, *History of the Methodist Church in Great Britain*, vol. 1, Peterborough, Epworth Press, 1965, p. 67.

16 Davies and Rupp, *History*, p. 304. See also F. C. Pritchard, *The Story of Westminster College, 1851–1951*, Peterborough, Epworth Press, 1951, p. 1.

17 Gill, *Steps of John Wesley*, p. 42.

18 Davies and Rupp, *History*, p. 67.

19 'John Wesley in London', information sheet provided by Westminster Central Hall for the use of tourist guides, 2004.

20 For information on James Lackington (1746–1815) and the issue of loan stock, see Richard P. Heitzenrater, *Wesley and the People Called Methodists*, Nashville, Abingdon Press, 1995, pp. 166, 251, 321. For James Lackington generally, see Vickers, *Dictionary*, p. 195.

21 John Wesley, *Primitive Physic*, Peterborough, Epworth Press, 1960, para. 15.

22 Vickers, *Dictionary*, p. 282.

23 Wesley, *Primitive Physic*, 1747.

24 John Wesley, *Journal*, 9 November 1756, *Standard Edition, vol. 4*, pp. 190–1.

25 A.Wesley Hill, *Introduction to Primitive Physic*, p. 20.

26 John Wesley, letter to Samuel Bardsley, Otley, 21 July 1789, cited by George Sails, *At the Centre, The Story of Methodism's Central Missions*, Home Mission Department 1970, p. 11. See John Wesley, *Letters*, vol. 8, ed., John Telford, Peterborough, Epworth Press, 1931, p. 155.

27 John Wesley, *Journal*, 15 January 1777.

28 See Ronald C. Gibbins, *Methodist East Enders*, Peterborough, Foundery Press, Methodist Publishing House, 1995.

29 John Gardener, *The Grain of Mustard Seed, or an account of the Rise, Progress and Extreme Usefulness of the Benevolent Strangers' Friend Society*, founded 1785, London, Christie's, 1829, cited in Timothy S. A. Macquiban, 'British Methodism and the poor, 1785–1840', unpublished PhD thesis, University of Birmingham, 2000, p. 73.

30 John Wesley, *Letters*, vol. 7, p. 308.

31 Macquiban, *British Methodism*, p. 132.

32 John Wesley, *Journal*, 14 March 1790. See also letter to Adam Clarke, 9 February 1791. *Wesley XIII*, p. 105; also Maldwyn Edwards, in Davies and Rupp, *History*, pp. 66–7.

33 Macquiban, *British Methodism*, pp. 134–5, citing 'Evangelical Sects', *Quarterly Review*, no. 1810, pp. 489–90.

34 Report of the Benevolent Strangers' Friend Society in the year ending 31 December 1841, published 1842. London Mission Committee files.

35 John Wesley, On the Use of Money, in 44 *Sermons*, Peterborough, Epworth Press, 1956, p. 586. John Wesley also preached sermons on the Danger of Riches and on Dives and Lazarus.

36 Wesley, 44 *Sermons*, p. 580.

37 Maldwyn Edwards, *After Wesley, A Study of the Social and Political Influence of Methodism in the Middle Period 1791–1847*, Peterborough, Epworth Press, 1955, p. 143. For the sermon on Dress, see John Wesley, *Works*, vol. VII, p. 21. Later the 1806 Conference declared that the rules relating to dress would be enforced.

38 See John Telford, 'John Wesley', in the *Encyclopaedia Britannica*, cited in Bready, *England: Before and After Wesley*, p. 238.

39 John Wesley, *Journal*, ed. J. Curnock, vol. VIII, p. 80.

40 John Wesley, Observation on Liberty 1776, cited by M. Edwards in Davies and Rupp, *History*, p. 64.

41 Edwards, *After Wesley*, pp. 66–7.

42 S. E. Keeble, *The Idea of a Material Life*, 1908, p. 8, quoted in Michael Edwards, 'S. E. Keeble and Nonconformist Thinking 1880–1939', unpublished M.Litt thesis, University of Bristol, 1969, p. 109.

43 John Wesley, 'Seasonable Address to the more serious part of the inhabitants of Great Britain respecting the unhappy contest between us and our American brethren with an occasional word interspersed to those of a different complexion', 1776.

44 John Wesley, Sermon 18 ('Upon Our Lord's Sermon on the Mount' Discourse Three), 44 *Sermons*, p. 225.

45 *One Hundred Years, 1848–1948, The Planet Building Society*, Barclays Group Archives, Dallimore Road, Wythenshawe, Manchester M23 9JA.

46 See Seymour J. Price, *Building Societies and Their Origin and History*, Franes & Co. Ltd, 1958, p. 130. See also E. J. Cleary, *The Building Society Movement*, London, Elek Books, 1965, p. 66.

47 Cleary, *Building Society*, p. 12.

48 For Sir William Mallinson, see Vickers, *Dictionary*, p. 221.

49 Price, Appendix IV, pp. 579–83.

50 Vickers, *Dictionary*, p. 26.

51 Stephen Duckworth, Notes on Methodists in Housing, June 2005.

52 Klaus Huber, *A Ministry of Open Doors*, Chelsea Methodist Church 1903–2003, published by the church at 155a Kings Road, Chelsea, London SW3, 2003.

53 David Hempton, *Methodism and Politics in British Society, 1750–1850*, London, Hutchinson, 1948, p. 209.

54 *A Petition of Distress from the Cities*, published by the Urban Theology Unit and Urban Mission Committee and the Methodist Church, Methodist Home Mission Division, 210 Abbeyfield Road, Sheffield S4 7AZ.

55 See Tony Holden, *MAPPGuide, An Annotated List 1983–94*, London, Home Mission Division, 1995, p. 17.

56 See June Okokon, *Black Londoners 1880–1980*, Sutton Pub Ltd, Phoenix Mill, Thrupp, Stroud, Glos GL5 2BU, 1998. There is a good photograph of George Makippe in the National Portrait Gallery near Trafalgar Square.

57 John Slader, 'A Champion of London Docklands', in *Contemporary*

Review, April 1991, pp. 208–10. See also *Walworth Road Methodist Magazine*, December 1924 and January 1925, in Southwark Borough Local Archives. Further details about Kamal A. Chunchie can be found in Rozina Visram, 'Kamal A. Chunchie of the Coloured Men's Institute: the man and the legend', *Immigrants and Minorities*, March 1999, vol. 18, no. 1, pp. 29–48. Also, Geoffrey Bell, 'Kamal Chunchie and West Ham's early black community', 2002: An Eastside Community Heritage Publication, in 'The Other East Enders' series, The Old Town Hall, Stratford E15 4BQ.

58 See *Sunday School Chronicle*, 1, January 1926.

59 Sir George Chubb, letter to Lord Salisbury, 15 July 1885, Salisbury Mss, cited in James Munson, *The Nonconformists*, London, SPCK, 1991, p. 335.

60 For the story of the Macdonald daughters, see Judith Flanders, *A Circle of Sisters*, London, Penguin, 2002.

61 The Revd Dr Ron Gibbins, interview with author, 8 February 2004.

62 Huber, *Ministry of Open Doors*, p. 24.

63 W. H. Lax, *Lax His Book*, Peterborough, Epworth Press, 1937, pp. 199–200.

64 Huber, *The Ministry of Open Doors*, p. 24.

65 Vickers, *Dictionary*, p. 362.

66 Frank Salisbury (1874–1962), *Oxford Dictionary of National Biography*, Oxford, OUP, p. 703.

67 See Hugh Burnett, *Top Sacred, Sacred and Confidential, Beware of the Abbot*, cartoons, many of which first appeared in the *New Statesman* in the 1950s, but were then published by the Merlin Press.

68 *The Times Register*, 15 July 2005, p. 62.

69 Julian Joseph, interview with author, 2 October 2005.

70 See Pride and Prejudice, Committee for Racial Justice, Methodist Church Racial Justice Unit 2000.

71 Mrs Jean Hughes Smith, Notes on the Contact Centre, Muswell Hill, 20 April 2005.

72 For the laity, see Mark Gibbs with Ralph Morton, *God's Frozen People*, London, Fontana, 1964.

73 See John Wesley's letter to James Hervey of 20 March 1739, reproduced in A. Outler, ed., *John Wesley*, Oxford, OUP, 1964, pp. 70ff.

Part 1

Urban Missioners

Introduction by Stuart Jordan

The extent of social need in Victorian London is well known, documented as it is in a range of sources from Charles Booth's detailed survey of poverty to Charles Dickens's novels. From the 1851 religious census onwards, moreover, the low level of church attendance in Victorian London was also often noted, especially once the development of public transport encouraged an extended drift from inner London, and its churches, to the new suburbs. This double phenomenon led to a wide range of initiatives in the second half of the nineteenth century and beyond by Christian agencies and individuals such as the London City Mission, University Settlements, the East End priests inspired by the Oxford Movement, or the Salvation Army – all seeking to meet both the physical and spiritual needs of London.

As the chapters in this section reveal, the distinctive challenge of urban mission was one to which London Methodism also responded in a variety of ways. The story begins with the individual work of Richard Chapman and Thomas Jackson and their commitment to the needs of seafarers and the homeless. But soon there was a wider, institutional response when, in 1883, the Wesleyan Conference agreed to create a network of London Missions dedicated to what we would now call 'new ways of being Church'.

This was achieved by exempting the mission centres from certain established Methodist practices and supporting them with additional resources. The normal pattern of three-year ministries was suspended, for example, allowing greater continuity and longer periods of service for the development of leadership and the creation of new ways of working. New forms of worship were encouraged, often using bands and other types of popular music in order to make it more accessible. Social-care programmes were also given a high priority, as was the development of cultural activities. All this created freedom for innovation for missioners, and doubtless encouraged those who were instinctive pioneers.

Peter Thompson and Hugh Price Hughes represent two of the earliest of such missioners, though very different in their focus. Thompson was firmly rooted in East End realities, while Price Hughes used his West End base as a platform for a high-profile engagement with national and even international issues. John Scott Lidgett and, later, Jimmy Butterworth at Clubland, created models of mission each with a strong sense of location, and programmes designed to develop human potential. In the case of the Bermondsey Settlement, the residential experience reflected Lidgett's wider commitment to education. In the 1920s at Clubland, as a traditional Methodist Church was redeveloped as a youth centre, the active participation of young people encouraged aspirations to personal achievement.

These examples reflect a wide range of innovative responses to social realities. In some respects the earlier accounts suggest a desire to 'rescue' individuals from their situations that is shared with many of their contemporaries, although even in those terms they are remarkably varied and innovative in response to the raw human need for food, shelter, companionship, advocacy, legal and medical assistance, rudimentary education, slate clubs, employment agencies and the like. What is significant in this is to note how the work evolved with changing circumstances, honouring the proud traditions they inherited while retaining a spirit of innovation in response to new situations.

While moved by individual needs, however, the gifted urban missioners described here also show a consistent engagement with the wider community: campaigning for new social provisions or union rights; as elected civic representatives to local councils or university senates; speaking out on public issues or recruiting the support of public figures. While many others were engaged in faithful urban mission, it was this ability to create and use a public profile for the furtherance of their work that sets these missioners apart.

I

To Those Who Need You Most
Thomas Jackson, Peter Thompson and Pioneer Urban Mission

Christmas 1902 looked like being bleak for many in Poplar and Bow so Sisters from the Bow Deaconess House, opened in 1898, made plans for a cheerful Christmas Day. Some 250 tickets were issued to fatherless children, or those whose fathers were unemployed. Christmas Eve itself was occupied with preparing mounds of bread and butter and huge clothes baskets full of oranges and bags of sweets. Another gift, a joint of beef, arrived at 11 p. m. On Christmas Day, guests arrived at 9 a.m. for breakfast and had finished by 10 a.m.[1]

The deaconesses were some of the many women who over the decades were to serve London Methodism. At the Leysian Mission in Finsbury they shared in medical work, and at Shern Hall in Walthamstow Sister Constance was secretary to the doctor. One deaconess was responsible for the Slate Club, and in Acton another began a crèche. In Islington, Sister Lottie did visiting in Holloway Prison, as Sisters from the United Methodist Church Institute in Pimlico stood in police courts as character witnesses, sometimes persuading magistrates that those before them were 'trying to do better' and that they would have the support of church members. In Rotherhithe, Sister Clare organized 'play' hours for poor children and guilds to enable them to read books and see lantern shows.[2] Elsewhere in south London, James Flanagan, who built St George's Hall on the site of 'The Old Kent Tap', organized many philanthropic activities and created a Women's Settlement where, after nine months of training in medicine and nursing, Sisters began working with him and other churches connected with Primitive Methodist outreach.[3]

Women also played a prominent part in developing the Seamen's Mission, begun in 1843 to spread the gospel to seafarers and their families. One, Mrs Bilson, an elderly sailor's widow, in 1860 became a 'Bible Woman', whose task was to meet sailors on arrival in port, offer the Bible and tracts, and invite them to the Seamen's Chapel in Cable Street. Between 1860 and 1861 she distributed 7,000 tracts and made

1,168 visits to 'the most respectable' lodging houses and shipping offices. Miss Wright replaced her in 1867, and for five years visited coffee shops and beer houses.[4]

The Seamen's Mission had begun informally with Richard Chapman's work in 1845 as he collected money for tasks that eventually involved him visiting 2,400 ships, distributing 4,700 tracts, and selling 83 Bibles.[5] He also uncovered the social problems of seamen and their families, who were often left alone for months on end, and tried to solve them. Over a number of decades the Mission buildings and staff changed, but the work he began remained constant. By 1892 there was even an employee of African–Caribbean descent at the Queen Victoria Seamen's Rest, as it became in 1901 when King Edward VII gave consent for the name change. Like many missions it had a clinic and dispensary, with magic lantern shows for the children while the deaconesses worked to help seamen's families.[6] There were country holidays too for the sick and vulnerable, and Christmas parties for the homeless.[7]

Post-1945 there was a Centenary Extension,[8] followed by more renovations in 1968. However, though 3,000 men were accommodated in 1970, bookings were declining as docks closed and the Thames ceased to be a major shipping waterway. Now the Mission recruited marine engineering students,[9] though even as recently as 1974 some 145 seamen, from 55 nations, used its hostel nightly. As shore leave was extended, the Seamen's Rest found itself providing a home for those with nowhere else to stay. Thus its social and pastoral work was intensified, helped by the nearby Poplar Mission.[10] By 1982, Princess Alexandra, who had succeeded her mother as patron, had opened a new medical suite as residents came from the Merchant and Royal Navies and former dock workers without family. Also resident later were large numbers of Somalis.[11]

If Richard Chapman was the first Methodist 'London Missioner', Thomas Jackson of Whitechapel was the second. Entirely self-educated, and beginning work at the age of six, straightening nails in his father's shop, he studied hard and became a Primitive Methodist minister. He married Annis Ramsden from Sheffield in 1872,[12] and she soon shared a joint ministry with him on their arrival in Bethnal Green in 1876. Seven years in Walthamstow followed, where four of them lived on about £1 a week.[13] Moving to Clapton in 1884, Thomas established a dispensary, employed a doctor, and set up a legal bureau and a rest home in Southend, where the neediest stayed free of charge.[14]

Most dramatically, one evening Thomas visited Trafalgar Square with a colleague, finding there hundreds settling down for the night. At dawn he invited them to a service in front of the National Gallery, a gesture repeated on following mornings to large crowds and that was noted by the press. Thomas now made new contacts, one of whom provided free breakfasts as questions were asked in Parliament about the workhouse conditions that caused people to sleep rough. An enquiry into dormitory provision soon ensued and improvements followed.[15]

In 1888, when Thomas and a colleague were holding meetings in a thieves' kitchen off Ratcliff Highway,[16] he knew he needed to return to Whitechapel by buying a suitable property there. By October 1896 Thomas had found one by Whitechapel Station, and so began the Primitive Methodist Mission – Home for Friendless and Orphan Lads.[17] Soon it was home to hundreds, who profited from the evening classes for further education alongside the church activities. Men on probation were encouraged to join this Christian community that emerged under his magic touch. Thomas and Annis – who had organized work for women – eventually lived in two rooms in the Whitechapel Mission and soon were helping newly released prisoners, sometimes opening their home to them for many months on end. Annis Jackson was as strong as her husband spiritually at the start of their work, pawning valuable property to obtain money for their first free breakfast,[18] and was unperturbed when she needed to superintend breakfasts for 300 children, taking her young daughter with her.[19] She relished her role as matron of the Home, and when asked about her self-sacrifice would simply say, 'We are better off than our Saviour when He was on earth.'[20]

Her husband soon gained powerful backers, including several Lord Mayors and the QC Charles Russell, who was later an MP and, as Lord Russell of Killowen, Lord Chief Justice.[21] By 1906 Thomas had created the Whitechapel Mission in a derelict Congregational Church near the London Hospital, giving destitute men supper, lodgings and breakfast. For women, there was a 'Women's Bright Hour' that attracted 300. Thomas fought for women in the 'sweated trades', lobbying MPs for better wages for them and founding the Garment Workers' Trade Union, which united the anti-sweating movement. By 1910 the Trades Boards Act was passed and a Wages Board established to fix pay rates that now exceeded former remuneration.[22]

The date of 18 October 1926 was a red letter day for the Jacksons when the Mansion House was open to them and their supporters for the celebration of Thomas's jubilee as a minister.[23] Thomas died in 1932, but by 1939 his work was still flourishing, with the addition of 'Windyridge', at Thorrington near Colchester, a farm colony and hostel for young men on a 'conditional residence' as they served out a probation order. This was Thomas's idea, but was brought to fruition by J. E. Thorp. Under a successor, A. E. D. Clipson, there was manual work and classes for social readjustment in the family. Refurbished, it was reopened in 1958 by the Duke of Edinburgh.[24]

Energetic work was also developed at the Leysian Mission (which was united with Wesley's Chapel in 1989), as Dr W. F. Moulton inspired former pupils at the Leys School in Cambridge to work in the inner city, staying in a hostel for businessmen begun there in 1900.[25] Like Poplar and Grove Missions, among several others, it set up a Penny Bank that by 1895 had 600 accounts.[26] There was medical work, too, as in Missions in Clerkenwell, where Edward Smith was a notable pioneer, Deptford, Greenwich and Islington. At Deptford and West Ham, special help was available for those who were blind or crippled, while the Leysian Mission made home visits to those who had disabilities.

During this period, the East End Mission itself was created by Peter Thompson when, after a period in Wood Green and Redhill, in 1885 he went to St George's, Cable Street, as Superintendent. Like Thomas Jackson, Thompson was largely self-taught, and his mother's ambition for him to become a Methodist minister now came to fruition. His congregation contained sea captains, small city traders and clerks, but already they were moving out to the suburbs. Alarmed, others also left, and those remaining watched closely what Thompson was going to do. Soon he was visiting the sick, making contacts in brothels and thieves' dens, and starting soup kitchens and secondhand clothing stores. His fighting spirit was especially evident when he took on ring leaders of prostitution and drinking shops, exemplifying John Wesley's dictum to go 'to those who need you most'.[27]

Most strikingly Thompson bought two gin palaces, Paddy's Goose and the Old Mahogany Bar (see illustration), which included Wilton's, the first and most successful London Music Hall.[28] He turned them into Christian Missions, and even as late as 1916 they were very active, surrounded by a mainly Jewish population.[29] By 1919, work among West Africans had developed,[30] so three years later the Superintendent could report that as many as 40 to 60 were attending worship 'and using Mission facilities daily'.[31] The Old Mahogany Bar's work reached its peak under the famous lay pastor G .F. Dempster, whose *Finding Men for Christ* was first published in 1935 and had been reprinted 20 times by 1956, when a demolition order was served on the Bar. Fortunately, by 1964 the poet and conservationist John Betjeman had saved it and the British Music Hall Society bought Wilton's, soon to be finally refurbished with backing from prominent figures including the Prince of Wales.[32]

Thompson's work also involved him in the 1899 Dockers' Strike, with his Mission providing alcohol-free meeting halls and soup kitchens for the dockers. In the longer term, he and another Mission member also became union treasurers. He was also on the Board of Guardians overseeing poverty relief and helping to promote the Anti-Sweating

The Old Mahogany Bar as it was in 1871

League.[33] No stranger to illness, as by 1900 his wife was an invalid, Thompson arranged for three doctors to attend to Mission patients, one of whom dealt with 2,000 a year either through visits or surgery attendances.[34] At Blackheath, Thompson created a shelter for girls in trouble and arranged places in institutions in Redhill and Sunningdale for those needing support through illness. He also energized young people to sign the pledge against alcohol and to recruit others,[35] contacts that led him to help young mothers with childcare – in particular educating them about diet.[36]

By 1905–06, the Mission's Christmas Goose Club had 800–900 members – more than the pubs did, he gladly reported![37] The following year he opened Stepney Central Hall as the Mission's headquarters. Here a Mission led by Joseph Nix, a former colleague of Hugh Price Hughes, produced 800 pledges and 150 professed conversions.[38] Yet Thompson was feeling the strain. 'The financial burden is enormous and heavy,' he wrote. 'We are at the end of our wits, but not of our prayers.'[39] What lifted his spirit above such problems, however, were individuals whose lives changed – like a former African slave who gained spiritual as well as physical freedom. Now a market porter, this man testified 'to the power of Christ in Spitalfields and Billingsgate often,' Thompson noted.[40]

In 1919 when F. W. Chudleigh became Superintendent, Mission

work was not going well. Peter Thompson, who remarried after his wife's death, himself died in 1909. Chudleigh, who had returned to the East End from south London in 1916, had set up the first wartime community canteen with soup, stews and puddings available for 2*d.* each, reaching 2,000 daily. Soon his idea was copied by the Food Ministry as similar canteens began in other cities. After World War One, and indeed right through to the 1930s Depression, children going to school were able to get free breakfasts at the Mission.[41] But now Chudleigh had a situation where the Central Hall was threatened with closure. As a bachelor who lived at the Hall in two modest rooms, Chudleigh was available at all hours, and his belief in people soon led to a thriving community there.

An early scout master and good with young people, Chudleigh was also an excellent organizer. Thus he began restoring Thompson's medical work.[42] He also created Children's Cinema, an idea that Aldom French had earlier instituted at Tooting Central Hall,[43] which spread to other areas including St Helier, Deptford, Hackney, Poplar, Bow, Islington, Canning Town and Dagenham. Severely criticized at its start, Chudleigh won over his critics once they had attended his picture services – which regularly attracted 1,000 children and several hundred adults. By 1932, however, a year after his sister's death – which greatly upset him – Chudleigh died, struck down in his mid-fifties, just like Hugh Price Hughes. When Chudleigh's coffin was placed in its grave, 'The only flowers on it were bought with the half-pennies and pennies of East End children,' Ensor Walters recorded, calling him 'a St Francis of modern London'.[44]

Thomas Tiplady regarded Chudleigh's death as 'martyrdom in the service of the poor'.[45] It was Tiplady, beginning in 1928, who had developed a cinema ministry above all, using secular commercial films and a 35mm projector. Starting in Wensleydale and tempered by war experience on the Somme, Tiplady's life now came to fruition when in 1922 he was sent to the Lambeth Mission. Here he twice organized visitations of 5,000, yet saw no response. He decided, therefore, 'to use the cinema for religious purposes'.[46] Judging it immoral not to use church property fully in overcrowded Lambeth, he noted wryly just as 'the invention of locomotion has emptied the church', it was possible 'the use of another invention – the cinema – might fill it'.[47]

Accordingly, Tiplady renamed his church 'The Ideal'. Within weeks, Lambeth Mission was crowded for Sunday evening services which used hymns he wrote specially and visual presentations followed by a film.[48] The weekday Ideal had a staff of ten and was professionally run with some 8,000 passing through at its peak. Girls and boys were separated in the special services put on for them, work run by Len Bradbrook, probably Methodism's first black youth worker, who had an amazing way with them. A former member of the Mission's Sunday School, he taught them to respect the Bible and that church could be a kind and happy place, as tough Lambeth children came to both respect and love him.[49] Thomas Tiplady also reached out to those sleeping rough on the Embankment, who also attended film services and joined a club he inaugurated for them. There was, too, a brotherhood for men with no church link and a medical department, as well as holidays away for over-burdened families and Christmas treats, work that was featured in a film made about the Mission's work in the late 1930s.

In 1933 a Guild of Light, aiming to monitor film contents, was begun by a barrister member of Ealing Methodist Church, on whose board Tiplady sat, which now linked up with J. Arthur Rank and his growing interest in religious film. The group renamed itself the Religious Film Society and appointed Rank as treasurer.[50] The youngest of Joseph Rank's three sons, Arthur Rank had caught the vision of the Christian faith from his parents and became a Sunday School Superintendent in Reigate, Surrey, where he lived. He worked in the family firm, but knew that his elder brother would run it after his father had retired, and, though conventional in politics, had an unconventional streak that was met by interest in the cinema. 'I am in films because of the Holy Spirit', Rank would claim.[51]

By 1932 Arthur Rank had persuaded an employee, Walter Knights, to take an interest in religious films and soon this new work was flourishing. Rank's first venture was *Mastership*, the story of Lax of Poplar,[52] followed by *Inasmuch*, about St Francis, in which Greer Garson played her first film role.[53] Two more films, of better quality, were made before Rank abandoned Merton Park and Elstree for his own studios in an adapted Gypsy Hill cinema.[54] Religious Films, as it was called, was to have a long innings, surviving beyond Arthur Rank, who died aged 83 in 1972, having given away an estimated £100 million to various good causes.

After 1945, Rank had become more interested in secular films and bought a cinema chain to show a series of outstanding British films that the Rank Organization made. He also had 300 religious 'shorts' prepared, a new one shown every three weeks. Donald Soper has recalled one that suggested 'I shall pass through the world but once, any good therefore I can do or any kindness I can show, let me do it now.'[55] If such a 'short' were unavailable, ministers took the stage, a practice in operation for many years, especially on Good Friday. Derrick Greeves, at Westminster Central Hall, spoke at the Odeon, Marble Arch, finding the experience harrowing, but Soper, more adept at handling crowds, even had the back row's attention.[56] So did Arthur Bird, who spoke one

Good Friday in cinemas in Kensington and Victoria on the meaning of Easter.[57]

In 1952 Arthur Rank's eldest brother, Jimmy, died and he returned to milling full-time, remaining involved with the Church's mission. Judging its ministers unskilled in handling television, at Tooting Central Hall, he set up the Churches' Television Training Centre, moving it to Marylebone, then to Bushey, where it remained for 40 years before relocating to central London in 2005 as an independent television and radio production company. Arthur Rank also chaired the Rank Trust, which supported projects as in his father's time, though Arthur's faith was broader than Joseph Rank's. Indeed, he even had a crucifix in his dressing-room that he would kiss 'as part of his prayer routine'.[58]

Opening a major extension to Battersea Mission, with which he had been involved since its inception, Arthur declared: 'This mission is faith triumphant', suggesting John A. Thompson, its founder, 'had the secret of Christian living'.[59] Rank's family also became involved, with his wife providing money for a Milk Centre and Nursery Section, and with his daughter Ursula at one point being the girls' club leader.[60] Not officially opened until 1946, like many Methodist churches it had been a rest and air raid shelter in the war, and also a first aid post and canteen.

In its founder, the Mission had a person to match the hour. After all, had Thompson not even camped outside Downing Street to get the necessary authorization for supplies when restrictions were severe? Indeed, his project began in the 1930s without consulting anyone outside his prayer circle when he bought a property for £12,250.[61] Fortunately, the elder statesman, Luke Wiseman, who piloted Thompson's scheme through the Methodist Conference, backed him and was given pastoral oversight. Like Thomas Jackson, Thompson had a magic touch, involving public figures like Sir Malcolm Sargent, the cricketers Jack Hobbs and Denis Compton, singers like Anne Zeigler and Cavan O'Connor, as well as Queen Elizabeth and the Queen Mother, who patronized Sargent's Albert Hall concerts to raise funds for the Mission's medical work.[62] Thompson, however, died in 1953, though he saw his work that had begun in 1932 now include a day nursery, and he knew his clinics for ante-natal care and psychotherapy had been pioneering at the time.[63]

Arthur Rank's support enabled the Battersea Mission to build a third storey, and have a Jewish doctor's commitment for over 25 years at a successful leg ulcer clinic here. Yet by 1980 the congregation, many members from nearby estates, had dwindled as new Methodist churches continued to emerge in London's suburbs. Indeed, on hearing of Gordon Ashworth's sudden transfer from Brixton to Battersea, a friend remarked: 'You realize it will be all over in ten years?'[64] By now, Battersea was strongly multiracial and Gordon briefed parents when baptizing their children on Christian responsibilities. Being a computer buff, he mailed them regularly about events, so when he left 14 years later, the Mission had grown into a lively multiracial family.

During his time there were 50 courses on chiropody at the Rank Teaching Centre for doctors and students and a day course for district nurses, run jointly with the London Borough's Joint Training Committee.[65] Later, with government help, the former air raid shelter became the Battersea basement studios and an Alternative to Custody Scheme started, with a television studio available for making videos for elderly and disabled people and community groups. Some now learnt keyboard and computer skills, though each person had a worker to help lifestyle reviews and was required to take part in group work, obligations on which the Magistrates' Courts and the Crown Court insisted.[66] Further developments at Battersea Mission have been a Cancer Resource Centre, which offers support, information and complementary therapies, and a Greater London Chiropody Clinic, backed by the local health authority. The day nursery, with minimum fees, still provides a service, while Sound Minds is a daytime project engaging young people in music-making as a means of overcoming their emotional problems. If in previous decades Missions provided poor men's lawyers, Battersea Legal Services is a natural development of this. But all such projects are seen as independent partners if what they offer is congruent with the Church's objectives.

Little could Alexander McAuley have realized when he set in motion work in 1858 in Brick Lane, Spitalfields, with responsibility for Poplar, then a middle-class area, how Mission concepts would change. Yet he laid the foundations for what came later when, despite acute family tragedy, he created the Bow Mission Circuit and also five other new ones, extending his work to Upton Park, Barking and beyond. The peak of work in Poplar and Bow occurred when W. H. Lax was Superintendent. A minister there for 35 years, he boasted that his was the only Nonconformist church Queen Victoria ever entered.[67] But its claim to fame rested more on its creation of the first foot clinic and another for cancer control. Lax's pastoral skills were abundant, even reaching the Chinese community through membership of Poplar's Public Health Committee.[68] In 1918 he became Poplar's mayor, inaugurating street parties, which then spread more widely.[69] Even three days before Lax's death in February 1937, the Duchess of Gloucester was opening the Queen Mary Day Nursery, an indication of the respect his work had generated.[70] Lax was, Ensor Walters wrote, 'great in heart, in vision and in power; great in speech and great with the pen'.[71]

In 1955 W. E. Clapham – a founder member of Poplar's Old People's Welfare Committee and chair of its primary schools work – who had worked with Lax for 14 years, looked back. 'Our Church here in Bow,' he wrote, 'was another piece of pioneer social work, and we had a doctor, a dentist, an optician and a physiotherapist',[72] though with the arrival of the NHS only the chiropody and physiotherapy had continued. Four years later the Bow Mission, now crowded with teenagers in gangs, was in trouble as they treated their club as a cheap café, some jeering at the Epilogue as others broke telephone wires and light switches or threw records out of windows. Inevitably the club closed, and when it reopened gang members were banned.[73]

The Mission now began work with single homeless men, many on methylated spirits and living on bomb sites. Pioneered by James Martin, at one building there was a short-stay assessment facility, at another there was a permanent home for eight very damaged alcoholics, and at a third a detoxification unit, with provision for long, but not permanent, stay.[74] Later, the Bow Mission developed another single homeless project, B-Sharp, for recovering alcoholics. Begun in the summer of 1976, it helped clients regain dignity and to attempt independence beyond both addiction and institutional support. Arriving perhaps from a detoxification centre, a hospital bed, a prison or a day centre, they were helped to move on and upwards. 'As a project we went all the way,' its creator, David Moore, has explained.[75] With the free rein that London Mission staff were allowed, he also became a founder member of Crisis at Christmas (now the charity CRISIS) and CHAR, the Campaign for the Single Homeless. In addition, the Bow Mission offered space for southern Africa exiles like Bishop Colin Winter of Namibia and Cedric Mayson, a Methodist minister from South Africa.

'We live as survivors here,' wrote one minister of his East End experience.[76] Moreover, as another observed, some church members were neither local nor attached, though determined to retain a link from their new suburban base. This made work difficult, exacerbated by an 'over-emphasis on social work' which had 'almost detracted from our essential work'.[77]

Perhaps sensing this, Ron Gibbins, originally from Shoreditch, took a new tack when appointed to Stepney Central Hall in 1968. Severely burned from an air crash that left him needing plastic surgery, after war service he trained for the ministry and worked on a Middlesbrough housing estate and in Basildon New Town. With a keen interest in education and sociology, he instituted an enquiry centre in Brick Lane, Spitalfields, the focus for a community of some 30,000 Muslims. Backed by Trevor Huddleston, then Bishop of Stepney, he employed an American minister with community development skills. Soon underprivileged

Bangladeshis were seeking help, but the centre closed when Bishop Huddleston accepted a senior Anglican appointment in Mauritius.

With help from a Tower Hamlets youth officer, a Methodist layman from south London, Ron soon gained the support of borough authorities, the Inner London Education Authority and the government, for a Social Studies Centre, attended by pupils from two large schools, one grammar, one comprehensive. Released for half a day to attend the Centre's year-long course on religion and sociology, at its height some 600 to 700 came weekly, served by a staff of three, all ministers and qualified teachers, who aimed to shape better citizens as they studied marriage, the trades unions, law and personal responsibilities. The Centre also arranged courses for 18–20-year-olds who had dropped out of school, but now wanted to gain professional qualifications. Adults came, too, from the local tenants and community associations, to study what was called 'the community challenge'.[78] There were also five youth clubs with a full-time youth worker which met three times weekly, and at weekends National Association of Youth Clubs personnel came as visitors to learn about the Centre. Black students from former Rhodesia also benefited from courses, some of whom are now leaders in Zimbabwe.[79] Sadly, in the early 1980s funding for the Centre was no longer available, which also ended the Urban Studies Centre through which students from St Mark and St John's College of Education, Plymouth, learned about the inner city.[80] Stepney Central Hall itself finally was sold in 2005 and its work incorporated into a major re-development scheme for the site.[81]

What motivated Ron Gibbins? Essentially a sacramentalist, he links worship and life, sees the Church as Christ's Body and everyone as being made in God's image. So the Eucharist, which he celebrated weekly, was the focus for building Christian life and faith. 'We look at each other's faces in worship,' Bryan Rippin has reflected, 'and know ourselves as our greatest possessions.'[82] It is Ron's view also, as East End congregations seek to remain a 'faithful remnant', in solidarity with one another and the community, while new congregations, often African–Caribbean, replace others in sharp decline.

One congregation that has seen new life emerge is at Bryant Street in Stratford where, in 1975, half its members commuted over five miles. With experience of Lancashire and South Wales Methodism behind him, Tony Holden, its new minister, found a church that was small, fragile even, with a sense of near-failure in an ever-changing community.[83] Undaunted, Tony put up signs saying 'Welcome' in several languages and encouraged participatory styles of both management and worship, which reflected the congregation's multiracial composition. Premises were made available for community use, which involved 25 groups.[84] A shared ministry also evolved, with full-time youth workers and a worship group.[85] The Prayer for Peace was used regularly, an emphasis the congregation espoused partly because one member worked with Amnesty International and another at the national level ecumenically with the Churches' international concerns.[86] The Stratford church also supported Wesley House for overseas students, begun in the mid-1960s. Most importantly, in 1977 work started in the circuit on a Christian Youth and Community Project called E15.[87]

David Moore, Ron Gibbins and Tony Holden are examples of people responding to urban mission creatively, for which there can never be an overall blueprint, only trial and error. Clearly, the days of huge congregations and massive social enterprises are largely over. It remains to be seen if Methodism has both the will and the energy to sustain new, if more modest, work as city life continues to change, often in alarming and sometimes unexpected ways. Indeed, as Bishop Huddleston wrote while Bishop of Stepney, recognizing the complexities of urban mission, the task is 'to come to grips with the challenge of secularism, of deprivation-in-affluence, of rapid social change, of immigrant cultures and inner city identity itself'.[88]

Notes

1 E. Dorothy Graham, *Saved to Serve: The Story of the Wesley Deaconess Order 1890–1978*, Peterborough, Epworth Press, 2002, pp. 282–3.

2 Graham, *Saved to Serve*, pp. 37–8.

3 For James Flanagan, 1851–1918, see R.W. Russell, *The Life of James Flanagan*, 1920, cited by Graham, *Saved to Serve*, pp. 363–4.

4 See the Queen Victoria Seamen's Rest 1843–1995, 150th Anniversary Brochure, 121 East India Dock Road, Poplar, London E14 1DF, 1998.

5 The Queen Victoria Seamen's Rest, Brochure, p. 4.

6 The Queen Victoria Seamen's Rest, Brochure, p. 23.

7 The Queen Victoria Seamen's Rest, Brochure, p. 25.

8 The Queen Victoria Seamen's Rest, Brochure, p. 28.

9 The Queen Victoria Seamen's Rest, Brochure, p. 30.

10 The Queen Victoria Seamen's Rest, Brochure, p. 31.

11 The Queen Victoria Seamen's Rest, Brochure, pp. 33–4.

12 William Potter, *Thomas Jackson of Whitechapel, a Record of Fifty Years of Social and Evangelistic Enterprise*, Working Lad's Institute, 1929, pp. 16–17.

13 Potter, *Thomas Jackson*, pp. 37.

14 Potter, *Thomas Jackson*, pp. 48–54.

15 Potter, *Thomas Jackson*, pp. 55–7.

16 Potter, *Thomas Jackson*, p.57.

17 Potter, *Thomas Jackson*, p. 61.

18 Potter, *Thomas Jackson*, p. 143.

19 Potter, *Thomas Jackson*, p. 144.

20 Potter, *Thomas Jackson*, p. 143.

21 Potter, *Thomas Jackson*, p. 113.

22 Potter, *Thomas Jackson*, pp. 128–9.

23 Potter, *Thomas Jackson*, p. 156.

24 See *Methodist Recorder*, 16 June 1958.

25 London Wesleyan Methodist Mission Report 1900, p. 60.

26 London Wesleyan Methodist Mission Report 1895, pp. 22–3.

27 John Wesley, *Twelve Rules of a Helper, 1744*.

28 John Singleton, *Methodist Recorder*, 13 May 1999, p. 17.

29 London Mission Report 1916, p. 11.

30 London Mission Report 1919, p. 3.

31 London Mission Report 1922.

32 Singleton, *Methodist Recorder*, p. 17.

33 Ron Gibbins, *Methodist East Enders*, Peterborough, Foundery Press, Methodist Publishing House, 1995.

34 Peter Thompson, Wesleyan Methodist Mission Report 1895, p. 14.

35 London Mission Report 1903, p. 20.

36 London Mission Report 1902, p. 12.

37 London Mission Report 1906, p. 7.

38 London Mission Report 1908, p. 5.

39 London Mission Report 1908, p. 5.

40 London Mission Report 1909, p. 13.

41 Harold Finch, *The Tower Hamlets Connection*, A Biographical Guide, Tower Hamlets Library Service and Stepney Books, 1996, p. 50, where a number of Methodists who have been involved in the borough are listed and their work briefly described.

42 R.G. Burnett, *Methodist Times*, March 1932.

43 See David Lazell, *What's On at the Pictures?*, Evergreen, 1995, available from PO Box 52, Cheltenham, Gloucs GLY 51YQ. Also, *Sixty Glorious Years 1910–1970*, Tooting Central Hall Jubilee Celebrations Brochure.

44 E. M. Walters, *C. Ensor Walters and the London He Loves*, Peterborough, Epworth Press, 1937, pp. 32–3.

45 The Revd Thomas Tiplady, *Methodist Times*, March 1932.

46 The Revd Thomas Tiplady, *Spiritual Adventure: The Story of the Ideal Film Service*, The United Society for Christian Literature 1935, p. 41.

47 Tiplady, *Spiritual Adventure*, p. 19.

48 Tiplady, *Spiritual Adventure*, p. 27.

49 Tiplady, *Spiritual Adventure*, p. 40.

50 Tiplady, *Spiritual Adventure*, p. 45. See also Michael Wakelin, *J. Arthur Rank, The Man Behind the Gong*, London, Lion, 1996, p. 46.

51 Tiplady, *Spiritual Adventure*, p. 207, citing Alan Wood, *Mr Rank: A Study of J. Arthur Rank and British Films*, London, Hodder & Stoughton, 1952, p. 66.

52 Wakelin, *J. Arthur Rank*, p. 47.

53 Wakelin, *J. Arthur Rank*, p. 49.

54 Wakelin, *J. Arthur Rank*, p. 47.

55 Wakelin, *J. Arthur Rank*, pp. 66–7.

56 Wakelin, *J. Arthur Rank*, pp. 66–7.

57 Arthur E. Bird, *Adventure in Evangelism*, Henry E. Walter, 1968, p. 60.

58 Wakelin, *J. Arthur Rank*, p. 206.

59 J. Arthur Rank, *Methodist Recorder*, 4 November 1968.

60 *Forward with Christ: the Story of Battersea Central Mission*, compiled by Pat Ashworth, 1992, p. 34.

61 Ashworth, *Forward with Christ*, p. 6.

62 Ashworth, *Forward with Christ*, p. 17.

63 See Robinson Whitaker, Synod Obituary, quoted by Ashworth, *Forward with Christ*, pp. 19–20.

64 The Revd Gordon Ashworth, interview with author, 25 February 2005.

65 London Mission Committee, Joseph Rank Benevolent Fund files 1982.

66 Ashworth, *Forward with Christ*, p. 24.

67 W. H. Lax, *Lax of Poplar, by Himself*, Peterborough, Epworth Press, 1927, p. 22.

68 Lax, *Lax of Poplar*, p. 227.

69 W. H. Lax, *His Book, The Autobiography of Lax of Poplar*, Peterborough, Epworth Press, 1937, p. 189.

70 The Revd W. E. Clapham, *Methodist Recorder*, 4 August 1955.

71 Foreword, W. H. Lax, *Let's Go to Poplar*, Peterborough, Epworth Press, 1929, p. 29.

72 Clapham, *Methodist Recorder*, 4 August 1955.

73 London Mission Report 1959, p. 7.

74 London Mission Report for 1966 and 1970, p. 10.

75 The Revd David Moore, letter to author, 16 January 2005.

76 Bryan Rippin, *The Christian Juggler*, Peterborough, Epworth Press, 1985, p. 32.

77 Douglas Wollen, London Mission Report 1974, p. 12.

78 The Revd Ron Gibbins, interview with author, 8 September 2004.

79 Gibbins, interview.

80 The Revd Ron Gibbins, letter to author, 27 July 2005.

81 It is being refurbished with shops, as the front was in 1907, by Goldcrest Developers. The rear part of the site is to be pulled down and housing erected. A community facility will be available and also a new unit for the congregation.

82 Rippin, *Christian Juggler*, p. 32.

83 Tony Holden, *Keeping Faith*, Ten Years of Inner City Ministry, Methodist Church Home Mission Division, 1988, p. 33.

84 Holden, *Keeping Faith*, p. 37.

85 Holden, *Keeping Faith*, p. 58.

86 Holden, *Keeping Faith*, p. 63.

87 Holden, *Keeping Faith*, pp. 63–4.

88 The Rt Revd Trevor Huddleston, Preface to Ron Gibbins, *Mission for the Secular City*, Star Press, 1976. (The Star Press was part of the work of the East End Mission.)

2

Christian Audacity
Hugh and Katherine Price Hughes and the West London Mission

'What is morally wrong can never be politically right,' declared Hugh Price Hughes, the leader of the recently formed West London Mission at a packed Sunday afternoon meeting in St James' Hall, just off Piccadilly Circus, in November 1890.[1] He was speaking in the context of the movement for Irish Home Rule that William Gladstone, the former Prime Minister and eminent Victorian statesman, who was to regain office again in 1892, espoused as a key plank in his politics. Unfortunately, it had become public knowledge that the leader of the Irish politicians in the House of Commons, Charles Stewart Parnell, was embroiled in a divorce case involving Mrs Kitty O'Shea, with whom he was accused of committing adultery. In the presence of Mr O'Shea, Hughes explained that his support for Irish Home Rule remained firm, but it was impossible to separate the personal from the political. If politicians wanted the support of English Nonconformity – Hughes was now seen both as the leader of the Forward Movement, whose aim was to help Methodism connect with the non-churchgoing masses in the cities, and a Free Church crusader against poverty and immorality – then Parnell must resign. 'Of course Mr Parnell must go,' he wrote in the paper he founded and now edited, apologizing to his readers for 'even discussing so obvious a fact'.[2] 'There is,' he continued, 'no subject on which the Free Churches of this country feel so deeply as on Social Purity. And if there is any hesitation to supersede Mr Parnell, the Liberal Party in England will be shattered.'[3]

When Irish parliamentarians discovered the grave political difficulties his statement created, a majority, with the support of the Irish bishops, turned against Parnell and sought to remove him as chair of the Irish Parliamentary Party, which now split into two groups.[4] Nonconformity seemed more united than ever, with Dr John Clifford, the Baptist leader, supporting Hughes. Despite the fact that *The Times* ridiculed Hughes, suggesting adultery was a social and theological sin best left to social and theological punishment,[5] Gladstone broke with Parnell as Hughes became a household name in Britain. 'Is this Nonconformist conscience or Nonconformist cant?' asked the paper, reacting to Hughes's description of the sinner as 'unfit to govern or lead a constitutional movement'.[6]

'Hughes was committed to an impossible notion of Christian politics,' one biographer has judged, 'a politics that attempted to achieve secular ends through secular institutions without any compromise of moral principles to secular realities. The real response to "what is morally wrong cannot be politically right", is "what is morally right may not be politically possible".'[7] 'Could and should Gladstone have resisted the Nonconformist clamour?' Roy Jenkins has asked. Probably not, he cites another historian as saying, for when Gladstone had last ignored Nonconformist opinion over the 1870 Education Bill, it had led him to the disastrous 1874 general election.[8] Others, however, did think Gladstone took Nonconformist bluster too seriously, yet Parnell was finished. He married Mrs O'Shea in June 1891, and was dead, aged 46, by October. Irish Home Rule was kicked into the long grass,[9] and was never achieved.

Hughes's opposition to Parnell was not his first foray into politics. In 1869, as a trainee Methodist minister in Dover, he had opposed the drink trade, espousing the Band of Hope before it was even allowed on Wesleyan Methodist premises. For a number of reasons, he also took up reform of the Contagious Diseases Act (CDA) when the government set up medical arrangements for inspecting prostitutes in Garrison towns like Dover.[10] He had opposed, too, the 1870 Education Act because it promoted sectarianism, funding schools regardless of denomination and this lent support to 'popery'.[11] A meeting he attended with the radical Welshman, Alderman Rees, to hear Josephine Butler oppose the Act, even made Hughes cry.[12]

By autumn 1875, now in Tottenham, Hughes hoped Methodism itself would embrace the temperance cause when that year the Wesleyan Conference set up a permanent Temperance Committee, partly to watch legislation and evaluate information about it.[13] After 1878 he could point to the repeal of CDA and, thus emboldened, hoped for similar legislation in Parliament favouring Prohibition. First in Dulwich, and then in Oxford, he expounded his conviction that all Christians had a moral responsibility for social reform, using the power of the Church to change society.[14]

After three years at Oxford at the Wesleyan University Church, and where he was influenced in his thinking by the philosopher T. H. Green, Hughes was moved to Brixton Hill, where his destiny became clear. In 1883 the Revd Andrew Mearns, the secretary of the London Congregational Union, published *The Bitter Cry of Outcast London* about the city's poor, many of them living in slum property in inner London. 'My husband was stirred to the depths of his being,' his wife Katherine has reflected, 'and many discussions took place at our house and at the Sunday evening gatherings at Raleigh Hall.'[15] The Hall was the home of Sir William M'Arthur, the Liberal MP for Lambeth from 1868 to 1885, so from the start Hughes had the backing of prominent figures in public life. 'I believe that the term "The Forward Movement" originated at one of those gatherings, when Mrs Alexander M'Arthur said in reply to some remark, "We all belong to the forward Movement here", and the name caught and stuck,' Katherine Price Hughes has explained.[16] Surprisingly, in 2006 Raleigh Hall became high-profile again when Lambeth Council announced it had earmarked this Grade II listed building as the site for Britain's first Museum of Black History, the result of a 20-year campaign by the Black History Archive for a permanent base.[17]

Concern about the overcrowded conditions in Britain's cities, part of the Forward Movement's focus, led to the formation of an East End Mission, and some regarded Hughes as a natural for the job. The authorities, however, chose Peter Thompson to start the Mission. They 'feared my husband's ardent sympathies with the "left" and lived in constant apprehension of what he would do next,' Katherine has commented.[18]

Instead, Hughes created the West London Mission (WLM) where the Senior Chaplain to the Services, Richard Allen, told him there was need, though a 'different form from that in the east', and that Hughes was specially fitted for the task.[19] Church authorities were still concerned, however, about Hughes's social and political views expressed through his speaking and writing, even though in his ministry he also espoused a strong evangelical agenda, and was successful in gaining converts. But 'the rank and file of the "Forward Movement" hailed the idea rapturously and carried the day,' Katherine recalled, though such a job was a totally new idea to him.[20]

In the autumn of 1887, the Hughes family left Brixton for a central London home in Taviton Street. Mark Guy Pearse, artist, preacher, lecturer and searcher after holiness, whom Hughes insisted on having as a colleague before he would accept his new post, took the Sunday morning service, which was soon established in the rented St James' Hall, near Piccadilly Circus. Here he built up 'one of the largest morning congregations in London,' another colleague, W. H. Lax, observed.[21] Lax was a minister with Hughes for five years before 1899, at Hughes's request settling in Poplar, where he remained for over 30 years, 17 of them as an alderman on its borough council.[22] 'I had never seen Hughes before,' he wrote later, recalling his job interview. 'That tall striking figure, with slightly greying hair, the closely-bearded, almost terrifying fierce face simply held me.'[23]

Lax was put in charge of Craven Hall, near Regent Street, one of a number of places used by the WLM before moving in 1912 to its permanent home at Kingsway Hall. It was in Soho, through friendship with Dr Severs, a local doctor, that Lax met many music hall stars like Marie Lloyd, herself a former member of an East End Sunday School, Albert Chevalier and Dan Leno, who challenged Lax to appear with him at Drury Lane as 'Leno and Laxo'. Hughes used to say Lax was 'the Dan Leno of Methodism', Lax remembered.[24]

Hughes owed most to his wife, Katherine, whom he first met when asked to take a Bible class at Richmond Theological College, where he was a student. The daughter of Howard Barrett, the college governor, she used to meet him on walks in the garden and 'in spite of continuous teasing and quarrelling, got very friendly'. Before she left Richmond, through her father's ill health, her friendship with Hughes grew and 'deepened into a mutual attachment which we both felt very deeply, with all the force and passion of youth,' she recorded. Both sets of parents were told and Katherine was urged to wait for three years and not to see Hughes, exchange letters or arrange secret meetings. There was to be 'dead silence'.[25] Katherine, now studying at Laleham Boarding School in Clapham Park, founded by Hannah Elizabeth Pipe to provide a liberal education, obeyed the injunction. Here Katherine's natural intelligence at Richmond, once excited by the visit of the Italian nationalist leader, Garibaldi, was honed as she grew aware of East London's problems through the social reformer Octavia Hill.[26]

Katherine was 18 on 3 April 1871, and received the letter from Hughes she expected. 'My reply', she remembered, 'was unhesitating, and with my parents' consent we became formally engaged.' She went to Carmarthen to meet Hughes's parents, while he grew accustomed to getting to know a determined young woman 'with a will of her own and very rebellious ideas regarding the position of her sex'. They had differences of opinion, 'but God meant us for one another and we came through with a lot of give and take on both sides,'[27] Katherine has indicated.

While in Oxford she had become indignant about the lack of rights for women at universities, and again sensitized to the way thousands lived in London's poor areas. 'Gradually it began to dawn upon my mind that I was destined to take some part in the great struggle for the rights of the poor and the alleviation of their sufferings,' she decided.[28] Then two things converged in south London: the needs of the poor and the needs of the educated young women. With the help of Mrs M'Arthur and others, Katherine took a small house in Brixton Hill and opened a home for girls in need of protection, an issue that became national when W. T. Stead of the *Pall Mall Gazette* denounced the 'White Slave Traffic' at London's heart.[29]

Once in central London, Katherine decided to create a Sisterhood to involve educated and leisured young women seeking creative outlets for their energies.[30] They would wear a uniform – but not take vows like the deaconesses in the Order that Dr Bowman Stephenson was establishing. Katherine shared her ideas with others, especially her husband, who encouraged her to set up Sisters of the People, as they became known after their work began in 1887. The first to join was Katherine's old friend, Katharine Page, from the Brixton scheme,[31] who stayed for 40 years. Others soon signed up as Katherine discovered that, near St James' Hall, the pavements were crowded each night with men and women involved in the pursuits that W. T. Stead had described. 'One of our Sisters bravely volunteered to get in touch with these women between the hours of 11.00 p.m. and 2.00 a.m. and try to get into friendly conversation with any girl or woman who seemed to be alone,' Katherine reported.[32]

Sister Margaret became that friend at one point and the Sisterhood opened a home in Walthamstow where women could 'be kindly looked after till they could find more secure employment'. There were patrols off Piccadilly, Oxford Circus and Leicester Square, as she and others got to know by sight the agents of the prostitution trade during their attempts to rescue girls from their clutches.[33] A lawyer in Gray's Inn, who was a magistrate, was especially helpful to the Sisters by assisting them to trace men who seduced girls, and forcing them to pay towards their children's support.[34]

Eventually social workers and parents sought the Sisters' support in finding and helping their missing daughters. But the work was diverse involving many of the Sisters. Sister Margaret herself had the use of a flat near Piccadilly, paid for by the Victorian writer Hall Caine. Sister Emmelie, a Wesley deaconess, broke down under the strain of the work, yet was able to open a home for expectant mothers affected by venereal disease, a project further developed by Sister Faull.[35] Sister Katharine Page, for several years a Poor Law Guardian in Soho, took over a crèche already established, aided by Sister Hope, who joined the Sisterhood in 1892. She then made it her own, by building and adapting it until the Kingsway crèche, as it was called, became one of the best equipped in London.[36]

Some 60 women served as Sisters of the People during the first 15 years.[37] Some ran classes for spiritual development, with Sister Lily having one with 200 in it;[38] others did district visiting, or were nursing Sisters who ran dispensaries. Sisters also served in the Mission's convalescent home and in St Luke's Home for the Dying, founded by Katherine Price Hughes's brother, Dr Howard Barrett. This continued on two different sites for the next 50 years. Yet more Sisters formed a relief committee to help striking miners and their families during the 1889 coal strike or staffed an employment office, a clothes and food centre, and clubs for mothers, girls and boys. There were also temperance societies to organize, Slate Clubs to manage, and outings and social events for poor and often lonely people who lived near the Mission's heart.

Katherine was the focus for these labours, but at the start she had also to support her husband in his multifarious activities, including his growing sense that Methodism's different strands must unite, a Free Church Federation must be created to speak on national issues, and that Christian unity was a necessity.[39] In addition, there was his evangelistic work, his WLM responsibilities, including responsibility for a class meeting of 100 men, and his political engagement. Katherine also had to attend to her four children, listen to the Sisters' problems and run her own class meeting of 100 women. No wonder she and her husband worked from early morning to late at night.

Like Katherine, the Sisters were not only involved with philanthropic work. Some talked politics with men in their workshops; others took an interest in their trades and employment and knew what books and papers they read. They also tried to instruct women in social and political matters, especially relating to children. 'They interest themselves in the School Board election and the County Council and General Election,' Katherine wrote.[40] A few, like Sisters Ada and Emmeline, became suffragettes and 'endured imprisonment and other ordeals with a calmness and courage'.[41]

For her part, Katherine had to rest content 'with being a supporter of Mrs Fawcett in her strictly constitutional and calmer warfare for justice to women'.[42] With all this activity, and especially from the preaching of Mark Guy Pearse and Hugh Price Hughes, as well as the contribution of people like Dr Henry Lunn, the Mission grew substantially in numbers and influence.

But Hugh Price Hughes, who had reached his peak in the 1890s, when Liberalism and Nonconformity were strongly in tandem, was over-stretching himself. 'His life,' his daughter, Dorothea, wrote, 'was a continuous strife.'[43] From his 'trumpet-note of defiance' at Dover[44] to his 'Christian audacity', the phrase he coined to describe his approach to mission, personal and social,[45] and his awareness of the darkness of sin and Christ's power to overcome it,[46] there was an acute tension at the core of his personality. Even though he respected the Buddha,[47] he most admired those practically engaged like Father Damien, Catherine

Booth, St Francis, General Gordon, Cardinal Newman and his ultimate hero, John Wesley. Hughes felt he followed Wesley in his spirit of innovation and experiment and 'rejection of any authority . . . which contradicted experience enlightened by the Holy Spirit'.[48] In addition, Hughes possessed an extravagant personality, which was revealed on a visit to Jerusalem when he lay headlong at the place General Gordon had proclaimed the authentic site of Christ's tomb. 'My Master lay here,' he murmured; 'see I stretch myself where He lay!'[49]

Hughes lost considerable support, however, at the turn of the century when he and Katherine, who had relations there, supported British intervention in South Africa.[50] Here was another great moral issue to embrace, though this time Nonconformity was severely divided as Hughes backed the Imperial Liberal leader, Lord Rosebery, while John Clifford and W. T. Stead, among others, supported a committee aimed at stopping the war against the Afrikaners in January 1900. Hughes was not a pacifist, and felt Kruger's independent government in Pretoria meant licence for the drink traffic and no rights for Africans. 'I really cannot see your objection to conceiving of the British Empire as a humanizing and civilizing force,' Hughes told objectors.[51] 'While some shrugged and others raged, he charged oblivious of it all, caring supremely for what he would have termed "the soul of the Empire", just as he cared supremely for the soul of her citizens,' his daughter wrote.[52] The British did indeed win what became known as the South African War. This time Hughes had supported the 'winning' side, though seeds of bitterness against Britain were sown for decades to come.

By 1902 Hugh Price Hughes's health had began to worry those close to him, but he regained his strength and in November 1902 preached at St James' Hall with his former vigour. Next evening, however, 17 November, he became ill and died. 'The light of my life went out and darkness encompassed me, but God was there somewhere,' his wife recollected.[53] 'To Hugh from Katie', she wrote on his coffin's only wreath. 'I have fought the good fight, I have finished the course, I have kept the faith.' On its reverse side his children's names accompanied a quote from a poem by Robert Browning – 'He's for the morning'.[54]

Hughes had achieved more than any other minister of his generation, except General Booth, one paper declared. Ten MPs attended the funeral, including Robert Perks, then deeply engaged with the Twentieth Century Fund to raise a million guineas for new work in Methodism; William M'Arthur; David Lloyd George himself; and the chairs of the Welsh Liberal Party and the London County Council.[56] Yet surely he had never achieved his hope for an evangelical social activity, though he had inspired Methodists uniquely to embrace social and political action, reflecting the power of a growing middle class, which in the main supported the Liberal Party. For forces were at work compelling other loyalties, which on the whole Nonconformists never captured. 'The Forward Movement was at the end of its life in 1902,' his recent biographer has judged, 'still largely what it was in 1885 – Hughes himself.'[57]

Those who came after Hugh Price Hughes – C. Ensor Walters, J. Ernest Rattenbury, who oversaw the building of Kingsway Hall during a time of great difficulty for WLM, C. Francis Ream and Ira Goldhawk – did not achieve his social significance, though Ensor Walters was a St Pancras Borough councillor and very active on its housing committee. In 1936, however, when Donald Soper became head of the WLM, he was able, through his commitment to socialism and pacifism, to play a prominent role, not only within the large congregation that remained at Kingsway Hall until the late 1960s, but also through the media and his open-air speaking at Tower Hill and Speaker's Corner. Here he reached a wide audience, including the left wing of the Labour Party. In his open-air crowd were three future Prime Ministers: James Callaghan (the UK), Jomo Kenyatta (Kenya) and David Lange (New Zealand).

WLM's social work continued across these decades. So, too, did Katherine Price Hughes herself, who died in 1948 at the age of 95. 'Kingsway Hall is the headquarters of the West London Mission,' wrote J. E. Rattenbury in 1914, 'but if it did not exist at all the WLM would still carry on an important social and redemptive work.' In his view, this included Katherine's unremitting energy and service, 'the greatest factor in the Mission's efficiency'.[58]

In 1910 there were still Slate Clubs for men and women, a servants' registry, a poor man's lawyer service, the crèche, and numerous young people's groups. The Home for the Dying continued, leaving WLM's oversight in 1911. Rescue work and district and health visiting by qualified Sisters was developed. A women's shelter in Paddington was very active and the flat near Piccadilly still in use.[59] A new work had begun by 1913 among hotel servants, and for those new to London and lonely, a Kingsway Institute was established. Some Sisters were engaged in prison visiting.[60] In February 1915, the Queen herself visited the Emerson Bainbridge Home, a hostel for girls working in the neighbourhood, where a centre for unemployed young women and refugee foreign students had been created.[61] By 1919, Hopedene had been acquired as a holiday home for children, and during the 1920s and early 1930s on average there were 10,000 attendances recorded yearly at the crèche, with some 50 admitted daily.[62]

In her report of 1930s work, Katherine wrote: 'As never before all roads lead to London', but now there was no mention of temperance work, Slate or Boot Clubs or Penny Banks. Labour Exchanges had mostly made a servants' registry and the labour man's bureaux redundant. Health insurance caused the dispensaries to close and there were no more 'workhouse teas'.[63] Sisters of the People still cared for and visited the sick, disabled and needy, of course, and the crèche and secondhand clothing store was still valued. But prominence was given now to the Sister Mabel Hostel, begun in Drury Lane in 1921, which was for girls stranded in London and needing care and supervision; and the Parkhurst Maternity Hospital founded in 1923[64] for the protection of women with venereal disease, where, by 1936, 238 babies had been born, most of them healthy. Sister Faull was in charge, while other Sisters visited Holloway Prison, serving on the Discharged Prisoners Aid Committee.[65]

In 1937 the Katherine Price Hughes Hostel, with 15 rooms, opened in central London to provide more accommodation for girls in need of care and protection,[66] and the following year a Men's Hostel in Drury Lane for 50 discharged prisoners, who stayed for differing periods, was started. Help was also given to some 1,000 callers, so that by 1941 the Mission was claiming that, out of the 1,500 men housed there since it began, only 52 had returned to prison.[67]

Donald Soper had been at Kingsway Hall only for three years when World War Two started. The crèche was evacuated and members of the congregation and staff provided meals for those sleeping overnight in the Underground, and by day ran a Kingsway club for young shelterers. A Christmas dinner, started in 1887, continued for the needy, but in a limited way.[68] The Hall itself became a pacifist centre, with Soper often attending tribunals to vouch the authenticity of conscientious objectors seeking registration. Significant public and political meetings continued to take place there, as it was known as a centre for debating controversial issues, a tradition continued well into the 1970s.

During the war a number of groups ran the Hungerford Club under the Charing Cross Arches, which Soper took over in early 1945, with London County Council funding. By autumn it had granted Kingsway Hall use of a ward in the former Lambeth workhouse and the Hungerford Club moved there in February 1946, continuing to provide overnight shelter for some 60 to 70 people.[69] The post-war years saw more social changes, but the secondhand clothes centre, the Hungerford Club and the crèche survived – the Hungerford until 1977, and the crèche until 1980. A new young women's hostel opened in Drury Lane in 1948 in memory of the legendary Sister, Gertrude, and Emerson Bainbridge House, which had closed in 1945, was reopened two years later. Also in 1947, Fellowship House in west London opened for young people starting work in London. It lasted until 1971. A home for young mothers began its work in Islington in 1951 and then in 1958 became a hostel for young offenders, the home being revived in Aubert Park, surviving there for 27 years, when residence ended, and the next year an independent Highbury nursery began.[70]

Donald Soper oversaw much of this work and took decisions with colleagues about the projects, sometimes closing them down. Increasingly, though volunteers continued to be available, work was done by paid professionals. The number of projects with which the Mission was involved was various as it sought to minister to those at the hard end of society's pressures. In 1953 Alfred Hartley House opened for elderly men needing a home, with a further one opening in south London in 1958. But both only lasted until 1980.[71] In 1957 Katherine Price Hughes Hostel moved to Highbury, and from 1960 dealt with those with serious drink problems, mostly funded by the Home Office. Also that year the Hungerford changed to St Luke's and St Mary's, a rehabilitation centre for men and women with alcohol problems. Two second-stage houses were set up in south London in 1967, and a decade later a house that for five years had been a hostel for ex-offenders was made available as flats for ex-residents. A further development occurred when the Lambeth Mission allowed a large hall to be used on weekdays by St Luke's as an afternoon walk-in centre.[72]

By 1973 there was need for a day centre for the single homeless, which was begun at Kingsway Hall itself, but when the social work moved its base to Hinde Street Methodist Church in 1980, and the Hall was sold, it moved to a site in Marylebone. The Wednesday Club, set up after 1975 one evening a week to cater for homeless and lonely people, also moved to Hinde Street.[73] Hugh Price Hughes once wrote: 'It is impossible to deal effectively with the spiritual destitution of London unless you deal also with the physical and mental destitution.'[74] By selling Kingsway Hall for £2.5 million, then reinvesting the proceeds and arranging a leaseback for the work until the final move to Hinde Street, the social work's future was safeguarded, and Donald Soper's successors there – John Newton, Leslie Griffiths, David Cruise and Geoff Cornell – were able to develop and adapt the work according to changed circumstances. One innovation, introduced by David Cruise, has been the annual sponsorship of the Hugh Price Hughes lectures to consider political, social and artistic issues of concern to both Church and society.

But with the ravages of inflation and cuts in government allocations, the Mission itself has had to shoulder an increasing share of the running costs of the myriad projects. In 1980 there were some 40 medical and social workers, for example, working at St Luke's and St Mary's and beyond, with remand work at Emerson Bainbridge in its new role and with the residents in the Highbury probation hostel. There was also, as John Newton noted, 'the sharply increasing number of single homeless people, who find their way to our day centre in Marylebone'.[75]

Fast forward to 2005. Work among 'outcast London' continues, but now with an annual budget of £2.5 million. The West London Day Centre sees 100 people daily, either the street homeless or those precariously housed, but Westminster Council, after several years' support, withdrew its funding. WLM money was used temporarily to keep the service running. The Lambeth Walk-In closed in 2004 when that council withdrew support, but in 2002 the Big House opened in Southwark. Part of the Walworth Road Methodist Church site, it offered accommodation and training for ten street homeless to enable them to re-learn skills and to recover self-esteem.

In 2001, the Homeless Arrest and Reachout Team began, making contact with homeless people in trouble with the law, meeting them in police or court cells to 'advise, assist and befriend'. By 2005 it covered all of Westminster, employing ten staff. WLM also pioneers a therapeutic model for those recovering from drug and alcohol dependency through its 26-bed residential centre, St Luke's in Lambeth, and its Second and Third stage projects in Wandsworth. The Haven, acquired in 2001, is a residential centre for men severely and terminally damaged by drug and alcohol dependency, while Katherine Price Hughes House, an approved hostel for those on licence and bail, works with 20 male residents, the majority of whom are high-risk offenders. At King's Cross Methodist Church, an advice centre for Chinese immigrants operates, offering legal help, pastoral care, job opportunities, translation facilities and language classes. From there comes *Blessed News*, a gospel newsletter in Chinese for Chinatown and beyond, with a quarterly print run of 3,000.

WLM's work is thus different from that which Katherine and Hugh Price Hughes started, but it is still involved with the marginalized and excluded. It depends on professional staff, some 80 in number, who need not be Christian, but who agree with the Mission's aims and values. It works within an increased regulatory environment – visits from the Care Standards Commission, announced or unannounced, concerns for Health and Safety, and new patterns of employment law. Statutory and charity funders now require greater detail on applications and an assessment of measurable outcomes. Such factors affect WLM's room to work, making it consider how much risk can be taken, and ask what contribution the Church can make in a secular field when statutory funding is vital. Can it really be both supportive of vulnerable men and women and also prophetic as a result of its exposure to society's undertow? Clearly, too, there is often acute tension between 'mission' and 'maintenance', the volunteer and the professional, long-term and short-term work, and how support for new initiatives can be found when 'patrons' are in short supply.

One recent development has been establishing a chaplaincy model for each project under a Spirituality in Action project. The idea was regarded with suspicion at its start, but now there is some form of 'Christian presence' for each project. Also the 28-bed student hostel at King's Cross offers the possibility of urban training for a wider group. With Roman Catholic Sisters having their base there, as they exercise a ministry of befriending and helping the area's street sex workers, going out nightly with them, there is surely no danger that the West London Mission will not keep its feet firmly on the ground, as it did at its inception in response to *The Bitter Cry of Outcast London*.[76]

But like so much pioneer work, it is heavily dependent now on local and national government support – with all the complications that can often ensue. Some grants are for limited periods only and it is far from certain they will be renewed, partly as a result of the policies of pump-priming and partly because of financial stringencies when government reviews occur and politicians are worried about voters and their attitudes to escalating costs.

Notes

1 See *Methodist Times*, 27 November 1890, p. 1211, quoted in Christopher Oldstone-Moore, *Hugh Price Hughes: Founder of a New Methodism, Conscience of a New Nonconformity*, Cardiff, University of Wales Press, 1999, p. 214.

2 Hugh Price Hughes, *Methodist Times*, 20 November 1890, p. 1180, quoted in Oldstone-Moore, *Founder*, p. 214.

3 Hugh Price Hughes, quoted in Oldstone-Moore, *Founder*, p. 211.

4 Hugh Price Hughes, quoted in Oldstone-Moore, *Founder*, p. 214.

5 *The Times*, 26 December 1890, p. 7.

6 *The Times*, 26 December 1890, p. 7.

7 Christopher Oldstone-Moore, 'Predicaments of Progressive Methodism', Hugh Price Hughes Lecture, Hinde Street Methodist Church, 30 April 2004, p. 9.

8 Roy Jenkins, *Gladstone*, London, Macmillan Papermac, 1996, p. 572.

9 Jenkins, *Gladstone*, pp. 572–6.

10 Oldstone-Moore, *Founder*, p. 56.

11 Oldstone-Moore, *Founder*, p. 63.

12 Dr Roger Standing, article on Hugh Price Hughes in *The Oxford Dictionary of National Biography*, Oxford, OUP, 2005.

13 Oldstone-Moore, *Founder*, p. 63.

14 Oldstone-Moore, *Founder*, p. 63.

15 Katherine Price Hughes, *The Story of My Life*, Peterborough, Epworth Press, 1945, p. 64.

16 Katherine Price Hughes, *Story*, p. 64.

17 See the *Guardian* G2, 28 February 2006.

18 Katherine Price Hughes, *Story*, p. 64.

19 Katherine Price Hughes, *Story*, p. 67.

20 Katherine Price Hughes, *Story*, p. 67.

21 W. H. Lax, *His Book, the Autobiography of Lax of Poplar*, Peterborough, Epworth Press, 1945, p. 64.

22 Lax, *His Book*, p. 189.

23 Lax, *His Book*, p. 155.

24 Lax, *His Book*, p. 173.

25 Katherine Price Hughes, *Story*, pp. 28–30.

26 Katherine Price Hughes, *Story*, pp. 33–4.

27 Katherine Price Hughes, *Story*, pp. 43–4.

28 Katherine Price Hughes, *Story*, pp. 60–1.

29 Katherine Price Hughes, *Story*, p. 65.

30 Katherine Price Hughes, *Story*, p. 67.

31 Katherine Price Hughes, *Story*, p. 73.

32 Katherine Price Hughes, *Story*, p. 100.

33 Katherine Price Hughes, *Story*, pp. 99–100.

34 London Wesleyan Methodist Mission Report 1898, p. 41, in an article on the West London Mission's work by Sister Margaret.

35 Katherine Price Hughes, *Story*, p. 101.

36 Katherine Price Hughes, *Story*, p. 103.

37 Oldstone-Moore, *Founder*, p. 118.

38 London Wesleyan Methodist Mission Report 1896, p. 19.

39 Oldstone-Moore, *Founder*, p. 169.

40 Oldstone-Moore, *Founder*, p. 168, quoting Katherine Price Hughes, 'Sisterhoods, Anglican and Nonconformist', *Renewal of the Churches*, vol. 1, September 1892, p. 394.

41 Katherine Price Hughes, *Story*, p. 113.

42 Katherine Price Hughes, *Story*, p. 113.

43 Dorothea Price Hughes, *The Life of Hugh Price Hughes*, London, Hodder & Stoughton, 1904, p. vii.

44 Dorothea Price Hughes, *Life*, p. 87.

45 Dorothea Price Hughes, *Life*, p. 138.

46 Dorothea Price Hughes, *Life*, p. 145.

47 Dorothea Price Hughes, *Life*, pp. 365–6.

48 Hugh Price Hughes, 'John Wesley', in *Nineteenth Century*, 29 March 1891, p. 494, cited in Oldstone-Moore, *Founder*, p. 221.

49 Dorothea Price Hughes, *Life*, p. 395.

50 Katherine Price Hughes, *Story*, p. 89.

51 Dorothea Price Hughes, *Life*, p. 556.

52 Dorothea Price Hughes, *Life*, p. 559.

53 Katherine Price Hughes, *Story*, p. 97.

54 Oldstone-Moore, *Founder*, p. 221.

55 *Daily News*, quoted in *Methodist Times*, 20 November 1902.

56 Oldstone-Moore, *Founder*, p. 325.

57 Oldstone-Moore, *Founder*, p. 113.

58 London Mission Report 1914, p. 21.

59 Philip S. Bagwell, *Outcast London, The West London Mission of the*

Methodist Church 1887–1987, Peterborough, Epworth Press, 1987, p. 70.

60 London Wesleyan Methodist Mission Report 1913, pp. 28–9.

61 London Wesleyan Methodist Mission Report 1915, p. 22.

62 Bagwell, *Outcast London*, p. 105, citing West London Mission, 'The Work of the Year Told in Pictures 1928–30', pp. 10–11, and a letter from Mrs Wintringham, 4 March 1986.

63 Bagwell, *Outcast London*, pp. 100–01, citing the West London Social and Redemptive Work, 1930, p. 17.

64 Bagwell, *Outcast London*, pp. 102–03.

65 Bagwell, *Outcast London*, p. 105, citing West London Mission, 'The Challenge of West London', p. 16.

66 Bagwell, *Outcast London*, p. 104.

67 Bagwell, *Outcast London*, p. 115, citing *Kingsway Chronicle*, Spring 1941.

68 Bagwell, *Outcast London*, p. 116.

69 Bagwell, *Outcast London*, p. 118, citing West London Mission, Hungerford Club Council Minutes, 18 December 1946.

70 Bagwell, *Outcast London*, p. 129.

71 Bagwell. *Outcast London*, p.132.

72 Bagwell, *Outcast London*, p. 131.

73 Bagwell, *Outcast London*, p. 132.

74 Bagwell, *Outcast London*, p. 143, quoting Hugh Price Hughes, *Methodist Times*, 19 March 1885.

75 The Revd Dr John Newton, 'West London Mission', 1980, in *The London Experience*, Review of the 119th Year of the London Committee, p. 12.

76 I am indebted to the Revd Geoff Cornell for some of the points made in the previous paragraphs. Material about current work has been taken from 'Walking the Walk, Social Work Services 2003/4', *WLM Social Work Ministry*, April 2003–March 2004. Also from an information sheet accompanying the West London Mission Prayer Diary, March 2005.

3

God Cares Also for Minds
John Scott Lidgett, the Bermondsey Settlement and Methodist Educationalists

In April 1945 President F. D. Roosevelt died. Dr W. E. Sangster, then at the height of his preaching at Westminster Central Hall, met John Scott Lidgett, warden since 1890 of the Bermondsey Settlement. 'This is sad news,' he said. 'I haven't had such a shock since the day Lincoln was assassinated,'[1] Dr Lidgett responded.

Born in Lewisham in August 1854, Lidgett grew up in Blackheath among Methodists, mainly in business, who were 'exemplary in Christian life and devoted to religious activities'.[2] Each morning, after prayers and breakfast, *The Times* was read aloud and he listened keenly to lengthy reports about the progress of the American Civil War,[3] so he understood the significance of Abraham Lincoln's death. At a lunch given in Lidgett's honour in 1949, as he ceased to be warden of the Settlement, he made his hearers equally aware of his longevity – he died in 1953 just before his ninety-ninth birthday – by regaling them with memories of the death of Prince Albert, and the days of Gladstone, Palmerston and Disraeli.[4] Even more striking was the fact that Lidgett's great-grandmother had heard John Wesley preach,[5] one indication that he had been brought up in Methodism's inner circle.[6] Indeed, on becoming president of the Wesleyan Methodist Church in 1908–09, he calculated that he had been personally acquainted with 50 of its 91 presidents since Wesley's own death in 1791.[7]

Dr Lidgett described his grandparents and parents as 'Methodists but not Dissenters'.[8] Moreover, he considered it was largely under his grandparents' influence that his early life and outlook was shaped.[9] His father, he felt, 'inherited to the full all the high qualities of his parents'.[10] But he also appreciated Methodism's Arminian and Evangelical strands, which gave it a passion for the broken and downcast. Most especially, his maternal grandfather, John Scott – the first principal of the Westminster Teacher Training College, whom he considered 'endowed with deep devotion, great dignity of character and remarkable sagacity'[11] –

overshadowed his entire life. He even carried about with him the text of his address given in 1862 on the working class and its entitlement to a good education, along with Scott's paisley dressing-gown and plaid shawl.[12]

In 1868, Lidgett, then aged 14, was so moved by a sermon preached by John Scott that in the following week he asked for Holy Communion at a Covenant service conducted by his grandfather, who died within a matter of days.[13] Two years later Lidgett felt called to the ministry, but he first matriculated and left school, working in a shipping and insurance brokers office. He then attended University College, London, for two years, gaining a first-class degree in logic and philosophy.[14] He had a gap year before his ministerial training, and it was then that he was introduced to the systematic theologian W. B. Pope by his uncle, his guardian since his father's death in 1869.

Pope advised the budding intellectual to study the Scriptures accurately, and in a scholarly way to produce a balanced interpretation, which Lidgett did.[15] He also used Pope's recently published *Compendium of Christian Theology*.[16] For the next six years, Pope became a great formative influence on Scott Lidgett,[17] replacing his grandfather. Pope's understanding of the Fatherhood of God, the way Christ's significance had been interpreted, and the more mystical features of St Paul's Christology, made a deep impact on him.[18] Then, from 1876 to 1890, he tried to live the Fatherhood of God in successive ministries in Tunstall (in the Potteries), Southport, where he came to know W. B. Pope better, Cardiff, Wolverhampton and Cambridge.

Dr Lidgett was also influenced by Mary Kingsley's biography of her husband, Charles, which 'fed the flames' of his social enthusiasms and stimulated 'various forms of social ministry'.[19] In 1881 the life of the Anglican pioneer theologian, F. D. Maurice, was published by his son, which confirmed Lidgett's conclusions about the unity of human life – 'personal and social, spiritual and secular, ecclesiastical and national'.[20] The year 1884 was another watershed year, for he married Emmeline Davies, the daughter of a well-known doctor in Swansea, whom he first noticed at a service he took in Cardiff when 'a strange intimation' had come over him that she was 'a special concern of mine'. Soon an intimate friendship began that led to marriage.[21]

In 1884 a rash of residential Settlements began in London, some Anglican, others Nonconformist and Roman Catholic in background and foundation, starting with Toynbee Hall in Whitechapel and Oxford House in Bethnal Green. Others followed, and by 1934 London alone had 29, with 15 elsewhere, including one in Chicago.[22] Dr Lidgett was well aware of this movement, especially its attempt to meet London's poor by encouraging university students to live alongside them.[23]

In November 1887, Lidgett, now in Cambridge and influenced by Dr W. F. Moulton, formerly at Richmond College and now the first head-master of the Leys School and founder of the Leysian Mission, preached at the school on solidarity with those who suffer, quoting 1 Corinthians (12.26), stressing both the effect that the spiritual, intellectual and physical conditions had on those who were overcrowded in cities and the spiritual loss sustained by those out of contact with its industrial masses.[24] Returning from leading worship in a village service shortly afterwards, he came to the conclusion he had to practise what he preached. 'I stood under a moonlit but stormy sky and vowed to God,' he later recalled, 'that I would renounce all other interests and seek to lead a movement to give practical and permanent expression to the sympathy my sermon had been the means of evoking.'[25]

There was, however, a distinct difference in Dr Lidgett's outlook from others in Methodism as he created the Bermondsey Settlement. If the Methodist Forward Movement, which his friend Dr Moulton sup-ported, was repeating continuously that God cared for bodies as much as souls, Lidgett's conviction was that 'God cares also for minds', as he had shown by his involvement in Cardiff in the creation of its new University College.[26] Yet he never forgot it was the Spirit that inspired and co-ordinated all such activity.

'It seemed to me that I must endeavour to plant a colony somewhat on the lines of Toynbee Hall,' he reflected later, 'in one of the poorest districts of London, to be carried on in a distinctively evangelical spirit,' yet 'with the broadest possible educational and social aims, and free from all merely sectarian or sectional ends'.[27] For such an intellectual, theological and later a political leader, it was a hard decision. 'The remarkable thing was,' he concluded, 'that in serving Bermondsey, God gave me back in fuller measure all I had renounced and enabled me to do theological and educational work, the University classes, the County Councils and the rest – and to carve out all that I had thought I should for ever have to relinquish.'[28]

Emmeline Lidgett was now consulted about her husband's decision, for it implied a radical change from the three-year appointments that their life together had entailed since 1884. 'When I told her of my call to found a settlement in Bermondsey,' he recalled shortly after her death in 1934, 'she accepted my decision, though it meant for her living and bringing up her children [the Lidgetts now had a son and a daughter] in one of the poorest districts of London. She did it, and for more than forty years gave her best to religious and social service, undertaking, with little earthly reward, the onerous and often harassing duties of the domestic management of the Settlement.'[29] Clearly without her support the work would not have been done, though it took its toll on her health. On her death, the District, which Dr Lidgett chaired for 40 years in addition to his other duties, referred to her 'watchful love'.[30]

Dr Lidgett considered a Settlement should be a community of social workers who helped a neighbourhood's well-being through friendship and co-operation.[31] This he did once the Wesleyan Methodist opposition had been overcome, touring Britain for financial help though not garnering enough to make possible the Settlement's immediate completion in Farncombe Street in Dockland. Bermondsey firms were chilly towards the experiment, except for a major leather company, whose head later became Bermondsey's first mayor. Also chilly in their responses were local clergy,[32] but Lidgett persisted, holding his first course in January 1892, after the Settlement's opening by the Lord Mayor in July 1891. 'On the first night the building was thronged by those who sought to enter these classes,' he remembered later, 'for at that time nothing of the kind existed in Bermondsey.'[33]

Eventually the Settlement included a large hall and lecture rooms, a games room and a gym, as well as a library and a sitting-room. Upstairs there was a dining-room, with bed-sitting facilities for 15 to 20 resident men who had their own common room. The Settlement had on display Alfred Aaron Wolmark's *Portrait* of Cissie Esdaile, no doubt to help support the work of the British Jewish Impressionist painter, born into East End poverty whose father was a Jewish migrant from Poland.[34] There was also a caretaker's quarters and a warden's flat, where the Lidgetts lived in somewhat sparse conditions. At one point during his residence Dr Lidgett's daily regime started with a cold bath, two slices of toast, only one with marmalade.[35] He did, though, like smoking cigars. 'There were no curtains in his bedroom and it contained merely an iron bed and a desk,'[36] recalled Harold Finch, who near the end of Dr Lidgett's life ran a nearby youth programme.

The Settlement also included property scattered across the neighbourhood, including a parallel house for female residents. Dr Lidgett was highly successful in attracting women of calibre to help him, and also men like W. F. Lofthouse, who helped one Jewish boy with his Hebrew; John Borland, later musical adviser to the London County Council Education Committee, who ran a Choral Society,[37] and Dr C. W. Kimmins, the one-time London County Council Chief Inspector of Education.[38] Most residents worked part-time, with daytime jobs elsewhere, but by living on-site they helped the Settlement's work and were alerted to the area's social problems.

One lady, Alice Barlow from Edgworth, and her family gave a property, and Mary Simmons, who ran the Women's House from 1893 to 1916, was deeply involved with nursing in the neighbourhood. She pioneered the Beatrice Club for Girls, which ran for 40 years, and was named after Beatrice Dunkin, a woman severely crippled with a spinal condition, who was one of the Settlement's benefactors.[39] Alice Barlow House, as it was called, became the headquarters of a large working Women's Society, founded by Anna Martin, a sister-in-law of Professor James Ward of Cambridge. Becoming a resident worker around 1900, she gathered together waterside mothers whom she enthused with her own interests in civic affairs. Rotherhithe Day Nursery, founded by Lady Newnes, was also run at the House, along with a School for Mothers, numbering some 700 in 1935. It was held in great respect by the borough's medical authority and received a considerable grant from the Council.[40]

Sister Grace Hanna, who had founded a Guild at the West London Mission designed to help disabled people, brought it to Bermondsey in 1894 and in 1898 married Dr Kimmins. Her work was later focused on Heritage Craft Schools at Chailey, which continued into the 1990s.[41] Dr Lidgett chaired its governors for 40 years. One of its residents was Alison Lapper, the mouth and foot painter, a sculpture of whom was recently seen on one of the plinths in Trafalgar Square.[42]

Emmeline Lidgett herself taught French and wood-carving and led women's societies. She was on the management of local schools and organized flower shows to promote ideas for their cultivation in the neighbourhood's small gardens and backyards,[43] while her sister, Winifred Davies, for years ran a Children's Country Holiday Fund and another for women from Bermondsey and Rotherhithe.

Perhaps the most dramatic story in the Settlement's life up to 1939, when World War Two disrupted activities that were never the same again, was that of Ada Brown, who lived in a tenement nearby and ran a Girls' Club for rag sorters, wood choppers and tinsmiths. Its members were rough and tough, but under her influence their personalities changed.[44] In 1900 she married Dr Alfred Salter and became Bermondsey's first woman Mayor,[45] paralleled later by Mrs Drapper JP, one of the Beatrice Club's original members, who became Deptford's Mayor.[46]

Dr Salter, like Bob Mellish, who was also involved with Dr Lidgett's work, both became MPs, but earlier, from 1898 when Salter came from agnosticism to Christianity through discussions with Dr Lidgett, he worked partly as a Settlement resident, before becoming the local doctor. In 1910 he was instrumental in creating the Settlement's Sick Insurance Society, which by 1947 had 9,000 members.[47]

Few university or Methodist residents stayed for three years, but all became aware of the need of social salvation for their fellow citizens. Some had more intimate relations with Dr Lidgett than others, for he 'did not unbutton his heart', as one former resident observed.[48] Like

Lidgett himself, who was not a trained teacher, they learned their skills on the spot as they grappled with classes in French, Latin, Greek and English, or in current affairs, local history and elementary science and maths. The initial pattern remained virtually the same across the decades as a broad spectrum of culture and physical activities for both sexes and all ages was pursued, and welfare agencies gave legal and medical advice, though evangelistic and temperance work associated with Dr Lidgett's role as Circuit Superintendent was pursued through contacts with a number of other local Methodist churches. Indeed, the Settlement had no chapel until the late 1950s, long after Scott Lidgett's departure. For Dr Lidgett, flexibility was enough, as he responded both to individual needs and those of the neighbourhood each year.

'Scott Lidgett has been described as a pioneer,' F. C. Pritchard has written, but 'it might be better to consider him as a particularly able exponent and executant of the rapidly developing spirit of his age. He had too orderly a mind to be a pioneer in the usually accepted sense of the word.'[49] Yet he was the first in Methodism to respond to the Settlement movement, though another priority was for Wesleyan Methodism to encourage education at all levels of society. He therefore used the Bermondsey Settlement as a base from which to influence educational policy in various contexts.

Dr Lidgett's involvement in educational concerns had begun when, aged 15 and 'a strict Sabbatarian', he became a Sunday School teacher and later Sunday School Superintendent. His Blackheath church also decided to set up a day school in East Greenwich, and the Mission premises where he taught on Sundays were selected for this development.[50] Though still at school, he founded and led a Mutual Improvement Class at Blackheath at which he read his first paper – which was on the introduction of the 1870 Education Bill – urging its proponent, Mr Forster, how to proceed. Then, shortly before his sixteenth birthday, Lidgett appealed to his father's friends to contribute to the equipment for the new school. Succeeding in this, he became secretary of the day school, which was eventually taken over by the London School Board. It was 'still standing, embodied in and part of the larger elementary school subsequently built by the Board,'[51] he noted in 1936.

The growth of the Sunday School movement and its impact on urban working-class culture had not always, however, been accompanied by day schools. Certainly many Sunday Schools taught people to read and write, but as late as 1873 advice was proffered that 'only so much secular teaching be given in it on the Sabbath day'. [52] Some feared, too, that literacy might lead to poor people reading political tracts instead of Bible passages. Yet by 1886 churches like Hinde Street were estimating that 23,000 children had received training there and in its various branch schools. Especially in the first 30 years of its life, many admitted to classes were helped to read and write – a fact indicated by a stationer's order for '50 alphabets on boards, 100 spellings Part I and 50 Part II'. [53]

The development of day schools, first authorized by the Wesleyan Methodist Conference,[54] was part of a movement to extend denominational influence. Under the influence of John Scott, it took a major role in this, especially between 1868 and 1870, during Gladstone's first government, before Forster's Bill was enacted. It resulted in Wesleyan Methodists creating schools in many areas of London, including Ealing,[55] Bow, Dalston, Lower and West Norwood (which remained open until 1960), St Pancras, Kentish Town and Homerton, New Cross and Peckham. The other Methodist traditions, which eventually joined with the Wesleyans in 1932 to form the Methodist Church, when Dr Lidgett became its first president, also created schools, but were not so numerous in London. Their energies went into organizing Sunday Schools in London, the United Methodists creating over 20 new churches between 1874 and 1904, and with 5,000 children attending their Sunday Schools.[56]

In 1899 some 8,000 children attended Wesleyan Sunday Schools[57] and in 1918, from Bermondsey, through Peckham to Woolwich, Bromley and Chislehurst, to South Norwood, Croydon and Sutton, there were about 20,000 Sunday School scholars and over 250 teachers.[58] These adults were as significant as the scholars, for they were lay people who had to understand the Bible and Church history if they were to teach satisfactorily.

Besides the Sunday School movement, Dr Lidgett also emphasized the importance of theological training for equipping a more educated Methodist clergy, writing for their benefit a major book called *The Spiritual Principle of the Atonement*.[59] At the same time, he was involved with Methodist secondary schools and teacher training colleges. He engaged with educational policy, too, within the London County Council and the University of London, on whose relevant committees he sat.

The first Methodist attempt at theological education in London was the Hoxton Theological Institution, a former Dissenting Academy rented in September 1834 to train Wesleyan candidates for the ministry. Here they were given insights into the liberal arts, the Bible and theology, worship and sermon construction. Soon a preparatory branch was acquired as the college grew, with a Richmond branch opening in 1843. In addition to theological training from 1869 to 1885, Richmond College trained missionaries. Indeed, Dietrich Bonhoeffer often spoke of the impression left on him by a visit to the college in the 1930s where in the entrance he saw boards with long lists of names 'each followed by the date of ordination and the date of death, often both the same year', an indication to Bonhoeffer that for many decades men from Richmond 'had been rapidly sacrificed one after the other in the fatal climate of the mission station'.[60]

During World War One it also housed Westminster Training College, and in World War Two it became London University's administrative headquarters. During the 1939–45 war, Dr Lidgett intervened to help its negotiations for war damage, using his influence in London University as a senator.[61] Richmond's theological work and link with London University ended, however, as the result of the rationalization of Methodist colleges, closing in 1972 when it was sold. It is now the campus for courses run by an American University.

A Methodist secondary school for ministers' daughters, Queenswood, like Richmond, was also founded in the mid-nineteenth century. Beginning in Clapton in 1893, it moved to Queenswood in Clapham but was closed by the Wesleyan Conference. It reopened later as a limited company, moving in 1925 to Hatfield. From its inception, it offered a balanced liberal education and had its first Cambridge entrance success in 1913. By 1997 it flourished as a boarding and day school for some 400 11–18-year-old girls, with an emphasis on music, science and technology.[62] More long-lived in London has been Farringtons School, founded in 1911 by local Chislehurst residents, including Sir George Hayter Chubb, grandson of the founder of the lock and safe firm. Aiming to provide education for girls on a par with the Leys School in Cambridge, under its first headmistress, Alice Davies, a Methodist with very strong principles, numbers increased rapidly. By the 1920s its continuing growth led to the first of several extensive building programmes. Dr Lidgett was heavily involved with the school and was often called on to give addresses at its Annual Founders Days.[63] Almost 100 years after its foundation, Farringtons can now take some 500 girls, 270 in the senior school itself.

The growth of secondary schools, some created by local Methodists, led Methodist leaders to realize they needed good staff. In 1847, the State itself asked the churches to help train teachers for elementary schools and on 28 February 1849 plans were approved by the Privy Council for a Methodist Teacher Training College to accommodate 100 men and women, and for a satellite 'practising school' of over 1,000.[64] Soon a site was bought for £5,000 from Crown Land on Horseferry Road, then a slum area near Victoria. The first stone was laid in September 1849 and the College opened in 1851, with John Scott, Dr Lidgett's grandfather, as its first principal.[65] It was no easy task to found such an institution, as a subsequent principal – Dr James A. Rigg, who ran Westminster for 35 years – once reminded students, describing how he had heard the College referred to as 'Scott's folly'. [66]

John Scott ran the College for 17 years, with the minimum of written rules, the first Teacher's Certificate examination taking place in December 1852 under a government inspector.[67] Within ten years, the College had settled down with a strong family atmosphere through Scott's influence. One student, Thomas Healing, six years later became assistant to Matthew Arnold, the one-time chief government education inspector, who often consulted Scott on matters of mutual concern. Healing was the first Methodist teacher to receive a government administrative post and a national honour.[68]

Scott's colleagues insisted that students came because they had a vocation to teach.[69] When Scott left the College in 1868, nationwide there were 128 school teachers and 110,000 scholars in Methodist day schools.[70] Under Dr Rigg, when education became increasingly a national and contested issue, there were still many recruits, though the pioneering days were over. Consequently, in 1872 a women's college was established, starting in Battersea.[71] Practising schools for the colleges were also now begun. Wesleyan Methodism trained 230 teachers every two years, though this was never enough.[72] The Battersea site, known as 'Southlands Estate', proved unsatisfactory, so after two years in Dover, 'Southlands', as it was now called, moved in 1930 to a new base overlooking Wimbledon Common. Dr Lidgett preached at its Jubilee two years later.

Meanwhile, at Westminster itself, in 1930 its distinguished scholar-principal Dr H. B. Workman, author of books on the medieval and Reformation period, retired. Everyone here now followed a four-year course comprising a London University degree and professional training. The great improvement in academic standards and closer relations with London University was a fitting culmination of his work. Indeed, besides providing teachers for local schools, Westminster also made significant contributions to the creation and work of the National Union of Teachers. Former students were involved in preparatory meetings, with three of them – James Yoxall, Frederick Mander and Ronald Gould – becoming general-secretaries of the NUT. By 1943 the College had also provided 16 NUT presidents.[73]

While actively involved as governor of schools and of Westminster and Southlands, Dr Lidgett consistently maintained a wide interest in public education. In 1902, for example, the government's Educational Bill planned to abolish School Boards, in which Dr Lidgett believed and on which he had sat, giving control of voluntary and former Board schools to Local Educational Authorities. These authorities were also to provide secondary and higher education and to set up teacher training colleges. Controversy immediately ensued, with the Wesleyan Methodists especially divided. Dr Lidgett, however, a member of the Methodist

Educational Committee, and secretary of the National Free Church Council Education Committee, pledged to support the existence of the School Boards,[74] yet favoured more state education with certain provisos, so had to steer a middle course.

Hugh Price Hughes backed his positive stand, but suddenly – the day after he had preached on Lidgett's recently published book on the Fatherhood of God and only hours after they had both met at a lecture by Paul Sabatier on Francis of Assisi – Hughes died. After half a day quietly alone, Lidgett emerged, realizing on educational and social questions he must now take Hughes's place. The opposition to the Bill by the Free Churches was strident with a country-wide Passive Resistance Movement, whose adherents led by Dr John Clifford refused to pay the rates. But, despite this Free Church, and later Liberal Party, opposition, the Bill became law. Dr Lidgett opposed clauses in it that he judged unjust to Nonconformity, but also sought to keep the Free Church Council from identifying itself closely with Dr Clifford's Movement.[75]

From 1905 to 1928 Dr Lidgett was also active as a London University senator, and while representing the Progressive Party in the London County Council, which for a while he led, he became the London County Council's representative on various schools, colleges and polytechnics. From 1930 to 1932, in recognition of his services to education, he was appointed vice-chancellor of London University. In 1949, aged 95, he even gave the sermon for the new London Institute of Education.[76] Not only had Dr Lidgett earlier helped Richmond College staff become members of London University and be appointed to chairs there, but it was his argument in favour of the Institute that had 'carried the day'. Brandishing his two sticks, he had shouted to the other senators, urging them to establish it.[77]

Clearly, after the 1944 Education Act, which provided state financial help for students from working-class and other backgrounds to attend university for the first time, the post-war world that Dr Lidgett lived to see had an impact on Methodism, as elsewhere. Indeed, Methodists entering Oxbridge increased dramatically in numbers, leading to the creation of John Wesley Societies in British universities. In London itself the University of London Meth Soc, as it was called, was centred at Hinde Street Church in Marylebone, and in the 1950s it regularly attracted over 250 students.

More change came, which Dr Lidgett did not live to see. He might say on Founder's Day, 1952, that 'Bermondsey is in my heart still',[78] but Peter Morley, his assistant, then – from 1949 – his successor, found 'this enormous old-fashioned building used only for an excellent Boys Brigade Company and the Rydal Club'.[79] The building, partly decimated by German bombs, needed drastic renewal and Morley concluded 'never again will we be able to reach the heights of formal education that the Settlement has reached in the past'. 'But,' he added, 'I hope to provide for the people of Bermondsey the best in music, literature and art.'[80]

In 1952 a Methodist congregation was established there that became the dominant body. Despite these best efforts, in 1954 the Settlement became part of the South London Mission.[81] The drain on its funds was too great and plans for a new 'Scott Lidgett Memorial Church and Settlement' fell through.[82] A number of successive wardens tried to develop a new style, but by 1966 – though there were still eight groups for young people and young wives operating, and 21 residents, 16 of whom were taking courses at colleges[83] – the end was near. The following year the Mission felt that the building was outdated and expensive to run and should be sold. Its work would be transferred and incorporated into a new scheme for redeveloping Bermondsey Central Hall. In due course the Settlement itself was demolished and the site used for housing.[84]

Drastic changes also occurred to both Westminster and Southlands. Already by 1951 it was being suggested that Westminster should leave central London for a new and more expansive site, perhaps at Elmstead Woods in Kent. This never materialized, but with increased demands and changes in education nationally in a post-Christian society, clearly Methodism must develop new approaches. By autumn 1953 a move to Oxford was being mooted[85] and by 1959 the College had relocated to North Hinksey, on Oxford's edge, and again became co-educational. Here it expanded, and by 1997 had 2,457 full- or part-time students who were following professional and academic courses, validated by Oxford or the Open University. Later, however, it was adversely affected by a reduction in the number of teacher training students and changes in government funding systems, which led to its merger with Oxford Brookes University in 1999.[86]

A similar development affected Southlands. If in the early 1960s it had been 'very much a Methodist Institution' with predominantly Methodist staff,[87] and 70 per cent of its 300 students from Methodist backgrounds, by the following decade Methodist intake had dropped. But ecumenical links were strengthened when in 1975 it joined a Federation with the Anglican college called Whitelands, and the Roman Catholic Digby Stuart college, who with the secular Froebel Institute formed the Roehampton Institute of Higher Education. By 1989 the Methodist intake had dropped to about 10–20 per cent and the Institute was seeing itself 'as a secular institution',[88] though students of the Institute used the chapel, took part in 'Church Family Week' along the lines pioneered by the Order of Christian Witness, and for years ran a holiday venture for disadvantaged children from Belfast.[89] In 1997, the Southlands site in Wimbledon was sold and the college moved to Roehampton, where 6,500 full-time and part-time students obtained undergraduate and postgraduate degrees, validated by the University of Surrey.[90]

The move was inevitable for the government did not encourage smaller-sized colleges. Yet there was a bonus, for the new Southlands could offer a prospectus 'wider than anything it could have provided on its own'.[91] Despite this seeming secularization of Methodist education, the new venture shows clearly that 'Methodism stands for the highest academic standards',[92] but with the important caveat: that the courses and degrees are to help people serve the wider community, which implies a spiritual aim. 'If that is so,' Dr Greet has observed, 'I am not worried about the Methodist label being defined. How you mention the spiritual aim when a Methodist label is not prominent is a real question, but it was one that was struggled with even at Southlands.'[93]

With the creation of the University of Roehampton in 2004, a further wheel has come full circle from the early days when Scott Lidgett struggled to put training the mind top of his agenda. Yet times no longer seem to require Settlement approaches, Methodist teacher training colleges or, in the main, Methodist schools. But there has been a final twist to Methodist educational priorities with the setting up of supplementary schools in various churches – including recently in Bermondsey Central Hall where a Saturday school offers basic literacy and numeracy skills to help primary school children. 'Each year I am amazed at the talent and ability of our children,' its minister Sheryl Anderson has commented.[94] Such supplementary education has also been the pattern elsewhere, including in Clapham and Stoke Newington.

Perhaps the most complex of these attempts at the grassroots has been the work of the Marsha Phoenix Memorial Trust, which since 1979 has sponsored a residential project in south-east London for homeless girls. Backed with funds from both voluntary and statutory sources, including Lewisham Borough, it has now helped nearly 2,000 girls both to face the emotional troubles caused by the breakdown of family life and to learn skills to enable them to function as adults in a complex society.[95] Its core is the desire to help 'Nobodies' become 'Somebodies', a theme running through all Methodist educational work,[96] even if only recently given that name. But changing city life means different responses, including different language patterns to describe work being done. Indeed, even Dr Lidgett found he had to be flexible in Bermondsey as situations and needs altered over the 59 years he was there.

Notes

1 Quoted in Paul Sangster, *Doctor Sangster*, Peterborough, Epworth Press, 1962, p. 329.

2 J. Scott Lidgett, *My Guided Life*, London, Methuen, 1936, p. 20.

3 Lidgett, *My Guided Life*, p. 20.

4 *Methodist Recorder*, 13 October 1949.

5 Lidgett, *My Guided Life*, p. 8.

6 Lidgett, *My Guided Life*, p. 10.

7 Lidgett, *My Guided Life*, pp. 18–19.

8 Lidgett, *My Guided Life*, p. 21.

9 Lidgett, *My Guided Life*, pp. 17–18.

10 Lidgett, *My Guided Life*, p. 18.

11 Lidgett, *My Guided Life*, p. 8.

12 Alan Turberfield, *John Scott Lidgett, Archbishop of British Methodism?* Peterborough, Epworth Press, 2003, p. 7.

13 Lidgett, *My Guided Life*, pp. 25–6.

14 Turberfield, *Lidgett*, p. 17

15 Turberfield, *Lidgett*, p. 18.

16 Lidgett, *My Guided Life*, pp. 70–1.

17 Lidgett, *My Guided Life*, p. 71.

18 Lidgett, *My Guided Life*, pp. 71–2.

19 Lidgett, *My Guided Life*, p. 73.

20 Lidgett, *My Guided Life*, p. 73.

21 Lidgett, *My Guided Life*, p.58.

22 W. F. Lofthouse, in Rupert E. Davies, ed., *John Scott Lidgett: A Symposium*, Peterborough, Epworth Press, 1957, p. 51.

23 For the Settlements, see K. S. Inglis, *Churches and the Working Classes in Victorian England*, London, Routledge & Kegan Paul, 1963, p. 146.

24 Turberfield, *Lidgett*, p. 29.

25 Lidgett, *My Guided Life*, p. 63.

26 F. C. Pritchard, in Rupert E. Davies, ed., *John Scott Lidgett: A Symposium*, pp. 115–16.

27 Lidgett, *My Guided Life*, p. 63.

28 Pritchard, *A Symposium*, pp. 121–2.

29 Lidgett, *My Guided Life*, pp. 58–9.

30 Minutes of London South West District, meeting at Forest Hill, 16 and 17 May 1934.

31 Lofthouse, *A Symposium*, p. 55.

32 Lidgett, *My Guided Life*, pp. 114–15.

33 Lidgett, *My Guided Life*, p. 118.

34 *British Impressions 1880–1940*, Messum's, The Studio, Lord's Wood, Marlow, Bucks SL7 2QS, 2006, p. 41.

35 Turberfield, *Lidgett*, p. 35.

36 Harold Finch, interview with author, 7 September 2004.

37 Lofthouse, *A Symposium*, p. 62.

38 Lofthouse, *A Symposium*, p. 60.

39 John D. Beasley, *The Bitter Cry Heard and Heeded: The Story of the South London Mission 1889–1989*, SLM, 1990, pp. 123–4.

40 Beasley, *Bitter Cry*, pp. 123–4.

41 Beasley, B*itter Cry*, p. 120.

42 See Marc Alexander, *Paint, Brush, Spirit, The Fascinating Story of the British Mouth and Foot Painting Artists*, 2002, p. 95; available from 9 Inverness Place, London W2 3JG.

43 Lidgett, *My Guided Life*, p. 98.

44 Beasley, *Bitter Cry*, p. 119.

45 Lofthouse, *A Symposium*, p. 59.

46 Beasley, *Bitter Cry*, p. 124.

47 Lofthouse, *A Symposium*, p. 59.

48 Lofthouse, *A Symposium*, p. 62.

49 Pritchard, *A Symposium*, pp. 109–110.

50 Lidgett, *My Guided Life*, p. 56.

51 Lidgett, *My Guided Life*, p. 47.

52 Philip S. Bagwell, *Outcast London, A Christian Response*, Peterborough, Epworth Press, 1987, pp. 89–90, citing Sunday School Committee Minutes, Marylebone Public Library Accession 5920/20. For King's Cross see J. J. Graham, *Chronicles of a Century of Methodism at King's Cross*, Peterborough, Epworth Press, 1923, p. 39.

53 Sunday School Committee Minutes, Marylebone Public Library, Accession 594/20; J. Telford, *Two West End Chapels*, London, 1886, quoted in Bagwell, *Outcast London*, p. 89.

54 Maldwyn Edwards, *Methodism and England*, Peterborough, Epworth Press, 1943.

55 For the day school in Chelsea, see Klaus Huber, *A Ministry of Open Doors, Chelsea Methodist Church 1903–2003*, p. 22, Chelsea Methodist Church, 2003. For Lambeth, see Thomas Tiplady, *Spiritual Adventure, The Story of the Ideal*, United Society for Christian Literature, 1935, p. 11.

56 See *Church Extension in London and Its Suburbs 1874–1904*. A Record of Churches and School erected by the aid of the United Methodist Free Church, London Mission Committee files.

57 London Sunday School figures extracted from Wesley Education Committee Report, 1899, pp. 104–6, by the Revd Dr Henry Rack, letter to author, 25 March 2005.

58 Collated from the London part of the London South East District Synod Minutes up to 31 December 1918.

59 John Scott Lidgett, *The Spiritual Principle of the Atonement*, Peterborough, Epworth Press, 1897, which ran into four editions and was reprinted in 1907, 1914 and 1923.

60 Eberhard Bethge, *Dietrich Bonhoeffer*, London, Collins, 1970, p. 335.

61 Eric S. Waterhouse, *A Symposium*, p. 179.

62 John A. Vickers, ed., *A Dictionary of Methodism in Britain and Ireland*, Peterborough, Epworth Press, 2000, p. 287.

63 Janet Waymark, *Farringtons School 1911–1986*, published by Farringtons School 1986. See especially pp. 23, 25, 27, 43.

64 F. C. Pritchard, *The Story of Westminster College 1851–1951*, Peterborough, Epworth Press, 1951, p. 12.

65 Pritchard, *Story of Westminster College*, p. 13. See also F. C. Pritchard's

chapter on education in Rupert Davies and Gordon Rupp, eds, *A History of the Methodist Church in Great Britain, vol. 3*, Peterborough, Epworth Press, 1965, p. 290.

66 Pritchard, *Story*, p. 15.

67 Pritchard, *Story*, p. 25.

68 Pritchard, *Story*, pp. 28–9.

69 Pritchard, *Story*, p. 42.

70 Pritchard, *Story*, p. 43.

71 Pritchard, *Story*, p. 51.

72 For Southlands' history, see *Methodist Recorder*, 3 November 1932, p. 5.

73 Pritchard, *Story*, p. 66.

74 Pritchard, *A Symposium*, p. 131.

75 Pritchard, *Story*, p. 135.

76 Pritchard, *Story*, p. 155. The sermon was preached on 5 December 1949.

77 F. Ronald Crewes, 'An evaluation of the contribution to education of Rev Dr John Scott Lidgett, with special reference to his work at the Bermondsey Settlement', unpublished MA thesis, held by Southwark Local Studies Library, 211 Borough High St, London SE1 1JA.

78 *Methodist Recorder*, 12 June 1952.

79 The Revd Peter Morley, letter to author, 22 February 2005.

80 Bermondsey Settlement Annual Report, 1949–50, pp. 6–7.

81 Beasley, *Bitter Cry*, p. 127.

82 Beasley, *Bitter Cry*, pp. 128–9.

83 Beasley, *Bitter Cry*, p. 131.

84 Beasley, *Bitter Cry*, p. 132. For a history of the Bermondsey Settlement, see pp. 116–32.

85 Jennifer Bone, *Our Calling to Fulfil, Westminster College and the Changing Face of Teacher Training 1951–2001*, Westminster College Oxford Trust Ltd, 2003, p. 28.

86 Bone, *Our Calling to Fulfil*, pp. 203–12.

87 The Revd James Bates, letter to author, 27 April 2005.

88 Bates, letter to author, 27 April 2005.

89 Bates, letter to author.

90 Vickers, *Dictionary*, p. 328.

91 The Revd Dr Kenneth Greet, interview with author, 11 January 2005.

92 Greet, interview with author.

93 Greet, interview with author.

94 The Revd Sheryl Anderson in South London Mission Annual Report 2003–4, p. 5.

95 See 'The Marsha Phoenix Memorial Trust, Celebrating 25 Years of Service 1979–2005', The Marsha Phoenix Memorial Trust, 90–92 Tressillian Road, Brockley, London SE4 1YD.

96 See Anthony G. Reddie, *Nobodies to Somebodies: A Practical Theology for Education and Liberation*, Peterborough, Epworth Press, 2003.

4

Partners Not Passengers
James (Jimmy) Butterworth, Vic Watson and Clubland

James (Jimmy) Butterworth was born near Oswaldtwistle in Lancashire in 1897, the oldest of five. His life's journey was to be one of struggle, overcoming difficulty and almost endless testing by God. When he was 12 his father died, with his mother having to bring up her family alone. The experience shaped him for 'Clubland's future purpose,' he wrote in 1964. 'She insisted in our poverty on silver not copper in chapel collections, cleanliness in our poor home, paying our way and no debts.'[1]

Jimmy now began work, first in a bleaching factory, then in a cotton mill. His hours were 5 a.m. to 7 p.m., after which he did an evening paper round, sheltering in doorways when the wet papers would not sell. By 17 he was known as 'the boy preacher'. One day, while she was visiting Accrington, he had a perfect view of Queen Mary because crowds left a gap around the bleach-workers and their foul-smelling clothes. As he walked home, Jimmy surprised himself with the thought: 'One day that lovely lady will open my club in London.'[2]

A short time at Cliff College in Yorkshire, where he did not hit it off with its principal, Samuel Chadwick, was followed by a period as a private in the Lancashire Fusiliers, where he stood out because he was only five feet tall. Nevertheless, he was drafted to the Front during World War One, often witnessing the waste of human life. Here he was influenced by the Anglican priest, G. A. Studdert Kennedy, known as 'Woodbine Willie' because of his habit of disbursing cigarettes. Something of a popular poet, he said things 'we could understand,' Jimmy once explained. 'I used to think of him as the parson of all who hadn't any church. I am afraid I hadn't got such faith when this fiery little Irishman was so joyously expressing his.'[3]

When war ended, the pipe-smoking Jimmy went to Didsbury Theological College in Manchester to train for the Methodist ministry. Here his unusual gifts were recognized, he was given a somewhat freer rein than many others, and in 1921 allowed to help a run-down church in Beech Road, Chorlton-cum-Hardy. He began regular visiting in pubs and houses, or anywhere that would receive him, and set up boys' camps alongside existing groups. He also instituted a monthly magazine and a Young Abstainer's League. 'We have aimed solely to establish a fellowship of worshippers of those who are non-church goers and non-chapel goers,' he wrote, 'and seek a congregation to fill our empty mission.'

In 1922 Jimmy was appointed to Walworth Road Methodist Church in south London. This dated from 1813, and for one hundred years had been used for liturgical worship.[4] It was here William Booth had preached his first sermon as an evangelist.[5] 'The thickly populated district, the whirling traffic and the great seething masses of people,' Jimmy confessed, 'are so different from the long and quiet roads of Chorlton.'[6] Though the church was dying, he noticed it still had 'crowds of boys' connected with its youth groups. 'Pray for me that I may witness for Christ and his Church,'[7] he requested.

Living in one room near the Oval, Jimmy felt bewildered and overwhelmed by the 'hundreds of young people in these flats and tenements',[8] in an area of flourishing Sunday markets, saloons, cinemas and dance halls, where pubs and clubs were crowded.[9] However, he soon promoted the church as a centre for love, loyalty, service and brotherhood, and reached out to the 90,000 living within a one-square-mile radius. Urging the congregation to bring friends and neighbours, he gave lectures on Francis Thompson.[10] It could easily have been his heroes Francis of Assisi, Robert Raikes of the Sunday School movement, or John Wesley he talked about. At Christmas he oversaw dinner for 260 poor children and the despatch of 450 parcels. 'We need to get back to Jesus,' he wrote, 'whose birth, life and death witnessed the truth that love is the final solution of every world problem.'[11] Christmas morning 1922 saw the largest congregation in thirty years,[12] for already Jimmy's preaching was riveting.

By June 1923, Jimmy had arranged an August summer camp for 80 boys at Burton in Lonsdale in north Lancashire.[13] But traditional methods, like a Cliff College Mission, made no impact in Walworth, which had few links with any Christian community. Yet, looking back over the summer period, he recognized the previous July 'some boys were there who had never been in church before',[14] many of them 'shoeless and ragged', so he knew he must clothe them, as Reg Turtle, one of his treasurers, remembered later.[15] More significantly, boys' parents had also been present at the camp, often also for the first time.[16] Absent, he noted sorely, were key members of the Church itself.

Jimmy now encouraged boys to write essays about camp experience, publishing the best two in the magazine he edited. By December he was clear about the future. 'We are going to have a Boys' Club all of our very own,' he declared. 'It will cost ever so much money.'[17] Next spring it took off. 'Duties multiply. Demands increase,' he indicated.[18]

In 1922 Jimmy had begun a Friday night Bible Class with six boys, which soon increased in numbers dramatically. Rooms were found under the church, made habitable, and dubbed 'the Dug-Outs'. Soon the young people were divided into houses named after four Methodist theological colleges. Parallel to this a Sunday evening service developed, with boys crowding the gallery opposite the preacher. Sports activities also began, often on a site Jimmy found in New Eltham. A musical operetta *Caractacus* was specially written, involving well over 100 performers in diverse roles.[19] That same year, 20 boys became church members. 'We used the Communion set which Professor Moulton used for the wounded and dying in France,' Jimmy wrote.[20]

There was still no club for girls, for Jimmy was quietly waiting for leaders to emerge. It eventually opened in October 1925, with Lady Lamb presiding.[21] Two years later, both clubs were united. In 1926 there was a further development when Jimmy visited the Revd John Leale in Guernsey, who ran a Boys' Club there, and arranged for 60 Walworth boys to visit that July. Regular Guernsey camps now began until the island was occupied by German troops in 1940. Girls' camps developed separately elsewhere. Some accused Jimmy of being too adventurous, but his sole concern was to take young people from 'Walworth's overcrowded tenements . . . and increasingly sordid surroundings'.[22] Others left Walworth too, but for ever – part of the relentless drift to the suburbs. Jimmy lost 150 members in three years out of a total of 217. 'Clubland,' he wrote, 'is helping to save our Church and is not a negative branch line.'[23] Not everyone took this rosy view. Indeed, stalwarts opposed what he was doing to such an extent he offered to resign.

A breakthrough occurred, however, when the MP Sir Ernest Lamb (later Lord Rochester) promised £20,000 to build proper facilities for the club if local giving was also manifest. Next Sunday, halfway through his sermon, Jimmy heard a noise in the gallery and a little later saw young people kneeling at the Communion rail in confession of faith; others soon followed: 146 recorded their names in the Minister's Bible that evening.

The year 1928 was a significant one as Jimmy negotiated for Clubland to become a Circuit on its own. Finances were now centralized with one yearly appeal, eight causes, and a new magazine, *Clubland Review*, begun. Soon there was a stone-laying ceremony for the new church to replace the old, with Clublanders and others having raised the £5,000 necessary to match Lamb's offer. The previous year a book by

Jimmy had come out, which further publicized his venture.[24] After reading it, one New Zealand minister started a boys' club there. Jimmy might be 'small of stature' as a poem by a club member stated, but he was 'firm of chin'.[25] By 1929, the first clubland church had been opened by London's Lord Mayor; it was designed by Edward Maufe, the creator of Guildford Cathedral.

Jimmy wanted his club to be 'a kind of school or college' for boys and girls, a public school for the underprivileged, as he remembered his own lack of education. At its core was to be a Parliament, meeting on Sunday evenings after worship and also on Tuesday evenings. Club members were elected to all posts, except the head boy, whom Jimmy appointed. 'Ministers' gave reports on departments and each had to face 'Question Time'. Strict procedural rules operated and the Cabinet itself comprised representatives of all club activities. At one point, the Senior Parliament (aged 14–18) unanimously censured Jimmy, asking him 'to refrain from unnecessary notices and jocular comments in the Club Chapel'.[26] As Clubland's activities grew they included groups for art, drama and ballet, and musical appreciation, and there was a band and a gym, with PT and boxing and many sports teams. Topics covered by the Senior Parliament (there was also one for juniors) included 'Is Modern Art Good?', 'Dictatorship and Democracy' and 'Is There a Hell?'

In the 1930s the entire site was redeveloped as the adjoining property was bought and then bulldozed. Club membership rose to 500, some of whom used the dentist's clinic in the former vestry and a doctor's surgery, which soon followed. Visitors arrived from China, South Africa, Ireland, Scotland and northern English towns to see how Clubland functioned. Jimmy's new book, *Clubland*, came out with one *Times Educational Supplement* reviewer saying of its club management chapters that they would be of great value to social workers.

In May 1934 the Duke of Gloucester, nationally involved with the boys' club movement, visited, though Jimmy was never active in this because his stress that there should be talks about sex before boys graduated from junior to senior club, and his espousal of mixed evenings, were not regarded by all as beneficial. In July Jimmy was invited to a Buckingham Palace Garden Party.[27] Despite such acknowledgement, however, the year also brought financial stress, and the chaos that rebuilding brings, and once again Jimmy had to leave Clubland for health reasons.

In 1935, Len Neal, from a rough background, and who worked in Smithfield Market, became Clubland's first lay preacher. Another local boy, Andy Burton, now used his skill in portrait painting to train others. Later, two of his own paintings were hung in the Royal Academy. He and George Steadman, too, were conscientious objectors by 1939, and they reckoned their strong advocacy of the pacifist case before the tribunals was made possible by their experience in Clubland's Parliament.

In 1938 Ambassador Joseph Kennedy brought his sons Edward and Robert to an event for Premiers' and Ambassadors' children, with Edward scrawling his name on the roll and Robert making a brilliant speech, an event Jimmy recalled in the 1960s at a service to commemorate him after Robert's assassination. Sadly, that year builders were called off because of a £10,000 deficit and the project dubbed 'Butterworth's Folly'. But he found 18 famous people, including Henry Wood, Sybil Thorndike and his great friend, Basil Henriques (from the Jewish Boys' Club in the East End), to help raise money.

Already Jimmy had visited the USA (five more visits followed) where he addressed club leaders, which later resulted in the boys clubs' president laying a foundation stone. In 1939, with much press coverage, Queen Mary opened the new Clubland premises costing £100,000, thereby cementing an association with south London that earlier had included a visit to barrow boys in the Cut, and opening what is now the Peckham Settlement. Jimmy called the complex, which was arranged round a quadrangle and garden and included a canteen, lounge workshops, music rooms, baths and changing rooms, the 'Temple of Youth'. His triumph was short-lived, though, for on 10 May 1941, some 20 years' work was destroyed in as many seconds, when Clubland was hit by a German bomb. Queen Mary was quick to offer condolences. 'You must take courage in the thought that the spirit of Clubland remains and will burn more brightly for having passed through the fire,' she wrote.[28]

Only one part of Clubland could now be used. At the height of the fire that raged, boys had risked their lives to extinguish flames, hanging on to a parapet on the roof until a policeman broke the pump's nozzles to compel them to come down.[29] More heartbreak soon came, though, as Clublanders were evacuated and older boys joined the Forces. By 1942, only ten of the 800 members were left, who now sought recruits from the streets and tube shelters. The premises usable were occupied also by bombed-out families. However, Jimmy also obtained three manor houses outside of London to house some of the homeless.

One happy event did occur as war escalated. On 9 May 1942, Clubland's twenty-first birthday was held at Kingsway Hall, and on 27 May – in a secret ceremony – Jimmy married Anna Costain, from Toronto, who was running one of the manor houses. They eventually had two children, John and Mary, who when old enough were introduced to post-war activities. Married at 27, for some 30 years Anna worked alongside Jimmy and was a remarkable hostess for the hundreds of young people, who called her husband 'J. B.', as they flocked to his Temple of Youth.

The Methodist Conference now discussed Clubland, but decided it did not provide a model solution for all youth work problems. There was an attempt to start a club in Preston, but Jimmy disowned it because its leaders refused to accept all of his advice.[30] More positive news came from a former Chorlton member, who had gone to Jamaica and was instrumental in persuading its government to finance a 'Jamaican Clubland', while by the 1950s a successful Clubland had emerged in Georgetown, Guyana, from an initiative begun in 1942 by Deryck Adams, a minister inspired by a visit to Walworth.

In May 1946, Queen Mary visited again, this time to attend a Restoration Service in the ruins and to name two stones, as Jimmy sought 500 donors to give £100 each towards the £50,000 needed for rebuilding. A surprise visit from Governor Dewey led to an invitation to visit the USA again, with a friend paying for the trip and offering hospitality. In California, another friend arranged a visit to Hollywood where Jimmy met Bob Hope when he was invited on to the set of his new film. Hope, originally from south London, was now captivated by 'the little Reverend' as he called Jimmy. Nine months later, in May 1951, he visited London and for two weeks put on a benefit for Clubland at a West End theatre, which raised £11,000.

Bob Hope returned in 1952, this time with Bing Crosby and, aided by the British light entertainer Jack Buchanan, gave another benefit. A third followed in Manchester when Jimmy returned triumphantly to his former stumping ground. Jimmy also gained the support of Laurence Olivier and his then wife, Vivien Leigh, who helped raise funds, but Jimmy again became unwell and was forced to rest after an operation.

Gangs broke into Clubland in the 1950s, causing £1,000 worth of damage, which for two years Jimmy never mentioned, only then commenting on the Teddy-boy phenomenon in the *Methodist Recorder*. Soon the national papers were on his heels and there was further publicity for his work. In May 1954, history repeated itself when six boys appeared on Clubland's forecourt, only to have Jimmy chase them away. When they explained they had nowhere to play, he invited them inside and thus re-established its Junior section, at the same time disbanding the Senior one. By the following March, there were 600 awaiting training.

In 1955, the year that Lord Rank laid a stone for the new church, Jimmy's mother died. Brought up in the mills, one of the highlights of her life had been in 1951 when in Clubland she met the legendary singing star with a mill background, Gracie Fields, who unveiled a restoration stone. Mrs Butterworth had always played an important role in Jimmy's work, visiting him when he was involved in major crises.

Jimmy's fame grew in 1956 when he appeared on the television programme *This is Your Life* with several Clublanders, and his work was written up in the *Reader's Digest*. Now, famous people from the arts, politics, cricket and football visited Clubland, and schools and colleges cemented their relationships. Continually Clublanders put on shows – in the 1960s it was *Oliver* and *My Fair Lady* – and also events, though Sunday evening worship remained at Clubland's heart. Lord Rank now bought the freehold of adjacent property and a floodlit playground was erected on Clubland's roof. A 'Friends of Clubland' began in the USA, with 12 directors from church, political and Hollywood life, and Bob Hope as president.

Parliament was still in operation. Indeed, it had been widely imitated, though in fact the first one was started by an Anglo-Catholic priest in the East End.[31] Jimmy was still as firm in his authority as he was when he turned away Len Neal and Bert Barnes, members of a street gang called the Lamp-post Loungers who delighted in annoying people, when they gatecrashed in the 1930s.[32] He stressed the need for balance in both club and society. 'We know,' he once told Clublanders, 'that it was our revelry in club and reverence in chapel which enabled us to know the Lord of all good life.'[33] Indeed, as worshippers entered, they were met by the words 'Be silent' and 'Be reverent' on the door to set the atmosphere.

The year 1963 was another crisis one as severe depression overcame Jimmy, making him feel that his last 42 years had been futile. He came through it in a slightly unusual way. Back in Lancashire at a cousin's funeral, he recalled a talk they had held when his cousin had drawn attention to Wesley's hymn 'Give me the faith which can remove, and sink a mountain to a plain'.[34] It seemed to breathe the spirit that Jimmy now desired. Then he came across an American doctor's insight into a painter who for 50 years had painted sombre colours, but then used brighter ones. 'The dawn comes suddenly and we face it with hope,' he had suggested.

Jimmy's depression, which now lifted, came because he was tired after a lifetime of hard work. He was now nearly 70, and knew there was little chance to secure for any successor opportunities or leaders, yet was convinced he must set up a resident student hostel. Here there might be new pioneers to ensure continuity, he decided.

On 18 May 1964, Queen Elizabeth the Queen Mother opened the second Clubland. As always, Clublanders had collected money towards costs, over £2,000 in 1961 and £2,500 in 1962. Soon, with the help of Lord Rank, and the Joseph Rank Trust, Jimmy was writing: 'As Clubland began with six boys in one room, so six students begin our first student hostel.'[35]

This new venture delayed the inevitable in the late 1960s – when there was vast housing clearance and the erection of the Aylesbury Estate opposite Clubland. It meant the eventual loss of 300 members and 30 out of 36 officers. Jimmy, of course, knew his work had not failed – there were over 400 weddings to point to and numerous baptisms, and 'no more than a dozen had ended up in police courts'.[36] Still, too, there was support for disabled children and other social work, yet he had to admit there were few left who wanted to be involved.

The year 1972 turned out to be another crucial one with Lord Rank's death; and in June 1972 another change came when a key US supporter died. By now, Jimmy had five grandchildren to enjoy, but he remained defiant that he would stay at Clubland till the end. 'Despite what has been said and published,' he wrote, 'I shall never retire for I have always known that Clubland was God's purpose for my life.'[37] He had recently instituted a monthly Sunday evening event for former Clublanders whom he hoped could also help to secure the future.[38] They honoured Jimmy at his seventy-fifth birthday party, but other people's lives moved on. 'My son has taken over the remnant of the membership,' Jimmy wrote, 'and with his other voluntary workers has already trebled it.'[39] Now only £5,000 was needed to clear all the debts. But Jimmy spoke too soon, for new fire regulations required him to spend much more.[40] In the end, Jimmy did retire to be with his wife in Sussex, but kept returning to Walworth. He died in 1977.

'Christianity, not Churchianity, love in action, deeds not creeds',[41] Jimmy had argued and so had helped thousands, though he had cut himself off from normal Methodist circuit structures and therefore it was difficult to help him as he aged. One former member wrote that such was his influence that 'for fifty years these prayers and readings have inspired Hilda Palm'.[42] She had written these words in her copy of a devotional book that Jimmy had edited in the 1920s.

But had Jimmy been right to concentrate only on adolescents? Some, like Bryan Reed, who had run a successful Church Clubland in Walthamstow, was not convinced by all of Jimmy's arguments. 'Will young people reared in youth centres afterwards settle down in ordinary churches?' he asked.[43] Moreover, was it feasible for others to follow Jimmy, could anyone else attract royalty, stars of the world of film such as Richard Attenborough and his wife Sheila Sims, or the John Mills family, let alone cricketing and sporting heroes? In addition, how many people have the maverick quality that, though it irks some, is often a necessary ingredient in a pioneer? Fred Milson, one-time tutor at Westhill College, Birmingham, was perhaps right when he judged, despite such strictures, that Methodism had developed Jimmy's boys' camp idea, even using his phrase 'partners not passengers'. His respect for human material too, the variety of his programmes, insistence on self-help and in part self-finance, with his desire for quality buildings, 'affected all who came after him . . . whether consciously or not'.[44]

What was Methodism to do with such a legacy? For a year, a care-taker job was undertaken by a senior retired minister, and then in autumn 1977 Vic Watson – who with his wife, Gwenda, had developed a remarkable social ministry in Panama, for which its government had awarded him the country's highest honour – was sent to Clubland. He was promised central funding for three years and insurance cover for the site. It was a daunting task, more difficult than his job at Fernhead Road, Paddington, his previous appointment that had lasted for seven years. Uncannily, Vic came from a Methodist church that had set up the Beech Road Mission, where Jimmy Butterworth learned his skills. Indeed, he had often passed it on his travels.

'Vic Watson had a down-to-earth manner,' Raymond George, his one-time college tutor, wrote, 'and was reliable, popular and easy to get to know.'[45] Vic needed these attributes as he settled in at Clubland with his wife and three teenage children – Andrew, Megan and Phillip – for there was no club, no worship and the hostel was half-empty. 'The prob-lem was,' Vic has said, 'where to start?'[46] Already there were adequate youth facilities in Walworth, so he decided to begin with family worship – all five of them. 'That didn't matter,' he has written, 'we were making a statement.'[47] One problem needed immediate attention: a large brick wall round the site, with four-inch spikes clearly saying: 'Keep out'. These were removed and the wall was made knee-height with space for flowerbeds on the top. A sign over the entrance read 'Methodist Hostel' and 'Methodist Church', which soon attracted a young mother, Esther Badu, from Ghana, who had not known there was a Methodist church locally and needed one for the baptism of her baby.

A baptism was arranged for 11 December 1977. Before this, several other people came into the Watsons' lives, some through the signs and others because Esther and her husband, John, invited them. Now two former Clublanders, who had met and married there, joined, with Kitty Coombes becoming class leader and her husband, Henry, a church steward. Her husband had been one of 'J.B.'s' original six boys. For Kitty's part 'J.B.' had helped 'to set my compass' and had been 'the inspiration' of her life.[48] Another newcomer, Barry Taylor, turned out to be an organist. Soon David and Mary Rees came to run the hostel, with David becoming its warden and Mary being 'mother' to 54 resi-dents. 'Looking back,' Vic has reflected, 'I can only conclude it was God who sent these good people to us.'[49]

On the day of the baptism there were 32 at worship, a figure that had risen to 350 by the time the Watsons retired. They came from many parts of Africa, especially Sierra Leone, Ghana and Nigeria (now the largest group), and the Caribbean. At one point there were people from 21 different countries, including even a few from the UK. Members found a space where they could speak their own language, which led to Fellowships for those from Ghana, Nigeria and Sierra Leone, though as in most congregations there were tensions between groups. Many from the new congregation were living in flats on the Aylesbury Estate which Southwark Council had found hard to let.

Part of the attraction of Walworth Methodist Church, as it was called, more than Clubland – though that name was retained also – was a result of the support that people received when they were going through tough immigration processes. 'Do you remember when you were detained at the airport and given a week to stay?' the choir secretary once asked, 'and Vic drove all the way to Gatwick or Heathrow and you were given full six months as a visitor, then temporary and then permanent stay?'[50]

Vic also often went to the local police station and its cells, standing by people when they were arrested. He found himself liaising with the Housing Department when residents were being evicted. He also made many home visits where he heard about marital problems or financial anxieties. He even had to exorcize properties. By 1994, there were 25 class meetings, each with some 12 members, whose leaders met quarterly with Gwenda. A mid-week fellowship, prayer meeting and Bible study were the hub of this new Clubland, only 1 per cent of whom were white. Vic, ever the community developer, accepted the services of George Jackson, recently retired from the Methodist International House in Bayswater. He looked after the intricate finances and investments, and earlier, when Clubland was under threat of closure, knew he had to help to keep it open.

Vic always sought to make connections between the gospel and society.[51] When, therefore, he learned about the racism that members experienced, he created two units, one for countering prejudice, the other for raising consciousness, which led to the creation of the Methodist Leadership Racism Awareness Training Unit (MELRAW) in 1982. Vic even persuaded Southwark's mayor and councillors to take racism awareness on board, and at one election got prospective candidates to eschew racism publicly, though one local Conservative refused to do so. The borough's deans (Vic represented the Methodist constituency) also produced a document about Equal Opportunities for the Churches.[52]

Vic became heavily involved in citizenship matters, which became more complicated after the British Nationality Act became law on 1 January 1983. He, along with other local church leaders, felt that the government did not want to listen to reasonable arguments and that sometimes, when individuals were clearly under threat, it was important to stand by them. Accordingly, Vic in particular obtained wads of application forms for citizenship and helped people from the congregation or those 'off the streets' to fill them in.[53] He also helped overseas students, especially from Sierra Leone, when their money evaporated as a result of a freefall in their country's economy. Many were from the hostel, along with others from China, Poland, Ghana, Eritrea, Ethiopia, Somalia, Iran, Iraq and El Salvador, some of them seeking political asylum.

The Brixton disturbances of April 1981 brought into sharper focus police–community tensions, and for a year Vic was a member of a group seeking a meeting with senior clergy and police in London. An initial encounter in March 1980 had not led to a hoped-for seminar between them and the Metropolitan Commissioner himself. However, an open letter that Vic wrote in April 1981 *did* lead to sessions at Clubland that took place over five weeks, bringing together young police cadets, church members and other community leaders. Much anger and disagreement was expressed in these sessions, but there was also 'laughter and shared meals and games'.[54] Difficult as it was to evaluate in the long term, these meetings were the first time that many felt that the Church identified with them.[55]

Such efforts were expanded when Vic became involved in the 'Help on Arrest' Scheme, which used volunteers to go to police stations when juveniles were arrested and parents unobtainable. In addition, Walworth Methodists were involved in a 'Victims of Crime Support' venture whereby other volunteers advised, comforted and supported those who had experienced break-ins, muggings and theft.[56] Many other groups also used Clubland, and were given generous rents to help them set up a base, including Southwark Mediation, the UMOJO Dance Group, End Loans to South Africa and the Freddie Mills Club for the Physically and Mentally Handicapped, which had begun in Jimmy Butterworth's time.

It was 'a great trauma'[57] when Vic retired in 1994, for he had been involved from morning till night. As his children commented, he had 'no pretensions, no claims of higher insight or grandeur or arrogance'.[58] Yet behind his hard work lay 'a life of prayer and deep commitment',[59] laced always with a distinctive brand of humour. Like Jimmy, Vic had a unique combination of gifts to draw on. 'Wherever Vic has been,' David Haslam judged, 'people caught glimpses of the Kingdom in the Christian Community he helped to create . . .'[60] By exhibiting what was in essence God's grace mediated to them, Vic and Gwenda also helped others to act generously and unselfishly.

Clubland's building problems did not end, though, because it now housed a dynamic congregation. In its next phase, 1994–2004, a further transformation scheme started under Norman Grigg, who had also pre-viously been minister at Fernhead Road Methodist Church, Padding-ton. A new flat was built on site for a second minister, which Vic knew was vital, and other developments including a hi-tech audio-visual unit operated by local young people. Most of the original fabric was still in place, but radical renovation of the hostel, which was closed for students, was carried out. Half was re-born as a project for those sleep-ing rough with the West London Mission. Still to come were develop-ments in Clubland's Theatre, where Michael Caine first acted, and which made him want a stage career, and where he was chair of the drama group.[61]

Once again a minister and a church found themselves with a large appeal on their hands, this time for £500,000, part of a £1.4 million transformation scheme, to accommodate increasing activities for young people and the 1,500 who use the building weekly. These include a Detain and Support Group, the Big Swing Jazz Group and Arab Cultural Unity.[62] Within the congregation itself, the second minister, Eric Mustapha, has in recent years led a group of African–Caribbean young people who have visited West Africa to become more aware of both their history and their roots.

In May 2004, shortly before leaving for a new job in the Gambia, Norman Grigg was given the Freedom of Southwark Borough for his contribution at a church devoted over decades to social justice and human welfare. He would be the first to admit he was but following in the footsteps of giants.

Notes

1 Jimmy Butterworth, *Clubland Review*, February 1964.

2 Address in Clubland Chapel for Silver Wedding Anniversary, 1968, in Jimmy Butterworth, *Sermons and Addresses, Articles and Speeches*.

3 A Service Book of Prayers and Readings, compiled by the Revd J. Butterworth, Clubland Chapel, Summer Term, June/July/August n.d., circa 1922.

4 Walworth Road Methodist Church 110th Anniversary Brochure.

5 *The Walworth Messenger*, August/September 1926, p. 14, citing Harold Begbie's two-volume *Life of William Booth*.

6 *The Walworth Messenger*, November 1922.

7 *The Walworth Messenger*, November 1922.

8 *The Walworth Messenger*, November 1922.

9 *The Walworth Messenger*, October 1926, p. 2.

10 *The Walworth Messenger*, October 1926, p. 2.

11 *The Walworth Messenger*, December 1922 and January 1923, p. 12.

12 *The Walworth Messenger*, December 1922 and January 1923, p. 23.

13 *The Walworth Messenger*, June 1923, p. 59.

14 *The Walworth Messenger*, September 1925, p. 5.

15 Peter D. Smith, unpublished reflections, analysis and assessments of Club-land and its history, 1965. (No pagination.) Southwark Local Studies Library have the text.

16 *The Walworth Messenger*, September 1925, p. 5.

17 *The Walworth Messenger*, December 1923, p. 7.

18 *The Walworth Messenger*, March 1924, p. 2.

19 *The Walworth Messenger*, May 1925, p. 1.

20 *The Walworth Messenger*, May 1925, p. 9.

21 *Clubland Review*, 1926.

22 *The Walworth Messenger*, August/September 1924, p. 2.

23 *The Walworth Messenger*, May 1926, p. 2.

24 James Butterworth, *Adventures in Boyland*, Peterborough, Epworth Press, 1927.

25 *Clubland Review*, May 1929.

26 Smith, unpublished reflections.

27 *Clubland Review*, August 1934.

28 Quoted by Jimmy Butterworth in Clubland special Brochure, March 1953 on the death of Queen Mary.

29 Jimmy Butterworth in London Mission Report 1959, p. 17.

30 Smith, unpublished reflections.

31 Lady Henriques quoted in Smith, unpublished reflections.

32 Smith, unpublished reflections.

33 Jimmy Butterworth, *Clubland Review*, November 1970.

34 Hymns and Psalms 767.

35 Butterworth, Sermons and Addresses.

36 Butterworth, Sermons and Addresses.

37 January 1974, Clubland New Year Brochure.

38 Clubland Brochure 1922–1972 50 Years' Celebration.

39 Clubland Brochure 1922–1972.

40 Clubland Brochure, January 1974.

41 Butterworth, Silver Wedding Anniversary Addresses.

42 Butterworth, A Service Book of Prayers and Readings.

43 Smith, unpublished reflections.

44 Dr Fred Milson, staff member of Westhill College, Birmingham, in Smith, unpublished reflections.

45 The Revd A. Raymond George, letter in Thanksgiving Testimonial to the Revd Vic Watson MBE, *The Great Bridge Builder*, 1993.

46 The Revd Vic Watson, interview with author, 24 August 2004.

47 Vic Watson, Walworth Methodist Church in Eddie Gibbs, ed., *10 Growing Churches*, London, Marc Europe, the British Church Growth Association 1984, p. 30.

48 Mrs Kitty Coombes, interview with author, 7 March 2005.

49 Watson, in *10 Growing Churches*, pp. 30–1.

50 Thanksgiving Testimonial.

51 Watson, in *10 Growing Churches*, p. 32.

52 See Equal Opportunities Policy for the Churches, a pamphlet produced by

the Commission on Law and Order and Equal Opportunities of the Borough Deans and the Southwark Council's Community Rights Unit.

53 Vic Watson, interview with author.

54 Watson, in *10 Growing Churches*, pp. 38–9.

55 Watson, in *10 Growing Churches*, pp. 38–9.

56 Watson, in *10 Growing Churches*, p. 38.

57 Gwenda Watson, interview with author, 28 August 2004.

58 Andrew, Megan and Phillip Watson, Thanksgiving Testimonial.

59 The Revd Douglas Bartles-Smith, Thanksgiving Testimonial.

60 The Revd David Haslam, Associate Secretary for Racial Justice, Churches Together in Britain and Ireland, Thanksgiving Testimonial.

61 See Michael Freedland, *Michael Caine*, London, Orion, 1999, p. 35; also William Hall, *Arise, Sir Michael*, London, John Blake Publishing Ltd, n.d., p. 31.

62 See *Methodist Recorder*, 20 May 2004, pp. 12–13.

(Much of the material about Jimmy Butterworth can be found at the Southwark Local Studies Library, 211 Borough High Street, London, SE1 1JA.)

Part 2

Social Providers

Introduction by Stuart Jordan

A striking feature of the pioneers described in Part 1 was the wide range of their involvement in contemporary issues. This section, by contrast, is marked by examples of focused responses to very specific needs – for children, the elderly, or those seeking counselling help. It also shows the remarkable extent to which the provisions initiated in London subsequently developed into national ministries.

Each of those whose stories are told not only identified a real unmet need from the experience of their own life and ministry, but was able to design a practical response, then gather enough institutional support and funding to make it happen. The agencies that emerged could have been short-lived experiments, but in fact experienced significant growth, survived their founders, and developed well beyond their original visions. This was due in part to the perennial nature of the needs they were addressing, but also to their ability to stay at the forefront of professional practice, offering quality care in innovative ways in response to the demands of an ever-changing environment.

A number of issues are inevitably associated, however, with the transition from being a local pastoral project to a national agency. A major change occurs when the work grows beyond the energies of the initiators and their devotees, especially when the extent of development requires a more complex structure beyond the capacity of the founder, and the organization takes on a life of its own. As such developments occur, what happens to the organization's original Christian ethos and base, especially when the founders with their initial vision are no longer involved?

Meanwhile, the proper process of professionalization that is necessary quickly moves the work beyond the competence of and voluntary ethos of the Church and creative relationships between the two worlds are not always easy to sustain. Moreover, the search for significant funding needed to sustain growth itself requires a new range of partnerships, often with public bodies and others who have their own agendas, criteria and ways of working that have to be negotiated.

These, and other associated issues, are clearly present in the three major organizations described here. They are also raised on a much more modest scale for many local church projects today which – like the three in this section – seek to embody their instinctive pastoral care in more specific social provision, and then face the complexities of all that might involve.

Yet, as in their early days, the three agencies described in this section demonstrate the creative possibility of combining strong values with quality provision, not least the opportunities provided to influence public policy in areas such as child and family welfare, care for the elderly, and the insights of the social sciences in caring for the whole person. Significantly there are indications here that the spirituality shaping the founders may be being reclaimed in new ways to enhance the work they began.

The national scale of the work described here takes it beyond London but, as with most pioneers, it is the experience, challenge and opportunity of work in a specific context that nurtures the initial vision and sustains the subsequent developments.

5

April Weather . . . Shadow and Shine Alternating
Thomas Bowman Stephenson and the National Children's Home

Walking down Exton Street, formerly Church Street, near Waterloo Station, and the bustling South Bank beyond, it is difficult to imagine what it must have been like when Thomas Bowman Stephenson began his work with children there with two boys and how, from that small beginning, has arisen one of Britain's leading charities dealing with children's many needs, with an annual budget of over £200 million, and a staff exceeding 5,000 spread across the UK.

Thomas had been expecting to go to Leeds after a number of appointments as a Methodist minister in Norwich, Manchester and Bolton, but instead was directed to London when an unexpected vacancy occurred there. 'My parish will be in "New Cut" Lambeth,' he wrote, 'and I shall have to go to chapel every Sunday morning through a street . . . crowded with people engaged in buying and selling, and I shall have to visit members in cellars and garrets in the dense courts of that part of London.'[1]

Born in Red Barn, Newcastle-upon-Tyne, in 1839, the hundredth anniversary of the founding of Methodism,[2] Thomas was the son of a Methodist minister. When young, he lived for three years with an aunt because his mother was in poor health;[3] however, this did not seem to affect him adversely for he grew up to be an adult with both a stability and a forthright confidence. He had, too, a pioneering spirit untroubled by opposition to his unusual methods as Victorian Methodism perceived them. Like many innovators, he had a confidence both in his own convictions and also in his capacity to make them concrete, despite what others might see as insuperable obstacles to overcome.

Educated at different schools, partly because Methodist ministers moved round frequently, Thomas was converted to the Christian faith at a children's Saturday afternoon meeting. Yet 'the experience was like

April weather,' he once admitted, 'shadow and shine alternating, but I never ceased to feel God's ownership of me.'[4] His father moved to Bramley for a year and here, aged 14, he met and fell in love with Ellen Lupton, the daughter of a local cloth manufacturer, who he regarded as possessing a beautiful face and spirit.

While at Wesley College, Sheffield, Thomas took part in a revival and decided to become a Methodist preacher.[5] Later, studying for exams while living in Gateshead, he felt called to the Methodist ministry and in 1858 went to London for a candidates' meeting, staying at Westminster Wesleyan Training College.[6] While there, 12 of them went into a nearby street and tried their hand at open-air evangelism. Thomas stood on a chair and began to sing, whereupon the crowd that had gathered grew rather ugly, with one of them starting to bawl out. 'Never heed him, sir, he sells ceejyars,' said a street urchin in shrill cockney. He was the first of many such boys Thomas was to captivate in the coming years.[7]

Thomas now passed his exam and was accepted as a trainee minister, going to Richmond College. After training, while in Norwich he started a theatre service, as well as signing the pledge to abstain from alcohol.[8] Soon, now in Manchester, he expanded his evangelistic approach, arranging Saturday evening programmes of music and recitation in the schoolroom of a church. The Lancashire cotton troubles began while he was in Manchester, and when shortly afterwards he found himself in Bolton he was thus exposed to poverty and trouble as never before.

He was ordained in 1864 and also married then. His innovative skill was now clearly evident as he argued for a 'union of Christian work', using methods later employed by the Forward Movement with much success.[9] He was also heard to refer to a church worker, Miss Entwhistle, as 'our deaconess', a rare and early use of the word in English Protestantism,[10] though not unheard of in Germany. Thomas was determined to innovate, so he now sponsored popular lectures, magic lantern shows and even explained electrical experiments that he had presented. Often, he held open-air meetings as well.[11]

Thomas loved animals, as well as people, especially children, and at one point looked after a horse, a dog, a goat and turkeys![12] Another unusual characteristic was his wearing of a moustache, a feature infrequent in Methodism then. 'I work very much out of the usual rut,' he once judged. 'There are very few men in Methodism who do.'[13] His wife, and their only child Theodora, who later became a Sister of the Children, were a united family unit, with Thomas rising early to pray and meditate.[14] He had few original theological ideas, but was interested in the Methodist doctrine of entire sanctification.[15] 'The whole people of God are the "clergy" in the true sense of the word,' he maintained,[16] adding he had 'never been afraid of a good roaring prayer meeting of the old-fashioned sort, nor of the practice of kneeling at the penitent form.'[17] At the social level he considered he was 'a Liberal, perhaps a Liberal with a touch of Radicalism about me'.[18]

While Thomas was in Bolton, a Mr Blake, from Harrow, sowed the idea, then only taken up by five Circuits across Britain, of encouraging children to collect for mission abroad.[19] The idea appealed to Thomas, who thought useful service and giving children something to do would keep them out of mischief.[20] It was an idea that, as the Junior Missionary Association (JMA), was to raise millions for the Methodist Missionary Society.

Arriving in London in 1868, Thomas began to work out how to serve in one of the city's most deprived areas, with the Strand just a stone's throw away if you could afford to cross Waterloo Bridge by its toll, which was eventually abolished by the Methodist Lord Mayor of London, Sir William M'Arthur.[21] As Thomas's chapel was immediately opposite Waterloo Station and stood 30 feet from the road, he began open-air services, with his singing becoming a great attraction. Once – on Derby Day – he showed his unconventionality by starting the evening gathering with 'Pretender won the Derby and the suicides have begun'.[22]

When he was in Bolton, Thomas had been considering a foundation for children in need.[23] Now the idea resurfaced as he saw local conditions in the 'New Cut' where children 'were ragged, shoeless, filthy, their faces pinched with hunger and premature wretchedness staring out of their too bright eyes'. 'I have begun to feel that my time had come,' he wrote.[24]

Two young men, Francis Horner from Dublin, just beginning a London business career, and Alfred Mager, who worked in a bank, had already held religious services in a 'Thieves' Kitchen' at the Mint in Southwark, which they intended to buy and convert into a model lodging house. They asked Thomas to support an appeal to Methodism. For his part, Thomas visited Mager and told him about the homeless and friendless boys he had met near Waterloo and his idea of a training home where they could be taught to live in a Christian and industrious way. The three of them met and agreed to Thomas's idea. 'The lines of a life-boat were laid down that evening,' Francis Horner wrote subsequently.[25]

The time for action was propitious. Already Charles Dickens had stirred the public conscience through books like *Oliver Twist*, *Bleak House* and *Hard Times*. Then Lord Shaftesbury's work for chimney boys and children working in factories and mines had become well known. In 1869, Dr Barnardo, a teacher in the Ragged School movement, had begun his life's work, and about a year earlier a lady had given the Baptist preacher C. H. Spurgeon £20,000 for an orphanage.[26]

Then in 1870, Forster's Education Act had become law, giving every child a right to education at a time when one and a half million children were not attending schools – or at least good ones.[27]

London's outcast children were the most pitiable, as Francis Horner had discovered. Stephenson too was horrified when one Christmas in the snow near London Bridge, a policeman showed what conditions were like by turning on his 'bulls eyes' and 'out swarmed shoeless, ragged and miserable children in profusion who were sheltering under the bridge'.[28] By the middle of 1869, Thomas and his new friends had rented 8 Church Street, Waterloo Road, and were ready to receive the first two boys of some 100,000 estimated to be in acute need.[29] At its rear a stable became the dining room and a loft became the dormitory. The house was named the 'Children's Home'.[30]

During the first year, 20 boys were crammed in, who spilled into the next-door cottage that had been taken over that September. One had three brothers. 'His mother was a cinder-sifter, known everywhere as "Long Annie". Her four children were half-brothers, all illegitimate. In her fits of passion she would seize a poker, candlestick or broom handle, with which she would belabour her children without mercy,'[31] one writer has explained. Soon after the discovery of street children under the Thames' bridges, or in the City itself, there were referrals by parents or individual well-wishers. Now a 'Council of Action and Aid' was established, with prominent Methodist leaders like Sir Francis Lycett, John Chubb and Sir William M'Arthur on it.[32] The Home's object was 'To rescue children who, through the death or vice or extreme poverty of their parents are in danger of getting into criminal ways.'[33]

Thomas was designated Honorary Director and there was also a Honorary Medical Attendant. Mr and Mrs Austin, for a small salary, were appointed Home 'Father' and 'Mother', and were informed they should consider themselves 'heads of a family'. They were not allowed to inflict serious punishment 'without consulting the Director'.[34] Family prayers were twice daily; each boy owned his own Bible, and had to make his own bed and clean his own boots. They were expected to help in the Home with housework, cooking and waiting at table. Food was basic: cocoa, a large sack of potatoes, all donated, as was a large water butt.

Thomas set the style, but he was influenced to establish 'the family' principle by the Rauhes Haus near Hamburg in Germany, work he had learned of while in Bolton. It was an approach that lasted 100 years, though with modifications. 'If a boy passed the medical examination,' Thomas wrote, 'he is next photographed before bidding farewell to the rags of his roving life – and thus his clothes are burned or otherwise disposed of.'[35] He ran no easy schedule – the day started, for example, at 6.00 a.m. and ended at 9.00 p.m. after the 'duty and privilege' of praising God. All was geared to moral improvement, work and physical fitness so, though the regime was personal in that Christian names were always used, idle or disobedient boys were made to sit on the 'Bad Boys' Chair' and watch the rest at work.[36]

Wages were given for work done, which included chopping firewood, taken round on a donkey, donated by well-wishers, and sold locally. Money earned was put into a Penny Bank, but boys were expected to pay for clothes. Thus Thomas hoped 'habits of thrift and industry will be cultivated'.[37] Sometimes he was pleased to discover boys had begun to regret past actions and 'sought advice as to restitution and reformation'.[38]

In 1870 the Children's Home received its first large donation – of £100 – which was set aside for the extension of the property; but the demand was such that when Thomas was invited to Bethnal Green Circuit, where in Bonner Road there were adjacent houses available, in 1871 he moved there, renting to begin with, and then buying the property.[39]

At the opening on 4 October 1871, Dr Barnardo himself spoke. Already there were 37 boys and six girls in residence.[40] In the same year the Methodist Conference itself recognized 'the establishment of the Children's Home and commends the undertaking to the support of the Christian public, with the understanding that of the Committee of Management at least one half shall be members of the Education Committee, that the report of the proceedings of this Committee be made, from time to time, to the General Education Committee and the Conference'.[41] Thus a link with Methodism was set up, with the Home's principal always being a Methodist minister, a policy that lasted until 1990, when Tom White, President of the Association of Directors of Social Services and Director of Coventry Social Services, became the first lay chief executive, as the post was now described. The Children's Home, which had undergone several name changes, from National Children's Home, then with Orphanage added, now became NCH Action for Children as work with children became community-based rather than in institutions. It later reverted to the initials NCH.

In 1873 Thomas Stephenson was set apart as principal and saw the Children's Home grow with each decade. A farm was given to him in Edgworth in Lancashire in 1872 and a new work began in Hamilton in Ontario in 1873, which lasted until 1935 with many helped to emigrate and seek new life because it was felt there were better opportunities for work in Canada. The farm at Edgworth was significant for it enabled Thomas to take young people away from the city and give them a chance to succeed in a less damaging environment.[42] New work also

began at Milton, near Gravesend, which then transferred to Farnborough in Hampshire. In addition, in 1880 a branch of the Children's
Home was established in the Isle of Man and an orphanage opened in
1882 near Birmingham named after Princess Alice, with Queen Victoria's
consent. Alverstoke was started in 1887.

Very early on, Dr Stephenson, as he became, found difficulties in
employing suitable staff, so provided training programmes for them. He
was still focused on religion, of course, with Morning Prayer suitably
adapted for children. He also wrote them a service book to use, printed
in the Home's own workshops.[43] There were also short orders of worship for Sunday morning and evening and an outline for weekdays; also
orders for baptism and those leaving for Canada.

Thomas's musical gifts found outlets in the choir and later the band,
which toured northern England in 1878, when 20 boys, aged between
14 and 16, raised £400 for the Children's Home.[44] The Bonner Road
chapel was opened in May 1877 when W. E. Forster, the Minister of
Education, took the chair and spoke of the 'substantial work' the Home
was doing.[45] Boys and girls were judged as excellent, good, moderate or
bad, with most in the first two categories.[46] Locally, Dr Stephenson
reached out when he started a Ragged School for poor children. There
were, too, open air meetings and a Temperance Sunday, always a great
event, though when he started his work such gatherings were disallowed
on Wesleyan premises until 1874.[47] Thomas kept a book in those
early days where he wrote the names, stories, progress and moral and
spiritual condition of every child in the Home.[48]

Gradually Thomas's work developed as he aimed to help staff to learn
on the job by combining study with practical experiences. He always
retained more women than men, but one, A. E. Gregory, succeeded by
becoming a Methodist minister, and then in 1900, for 12 years, became
Dr Stephenson's successor as principal. Perhaps it was inevitable that
men went to other work, but the Home was able to employ many
remarkable women like Mother McDougall, as she was known, from a
respected Manchester family, who started her work in 1876. Two years
later a group of young women, former orphans and foundlings, were
accepted by the Children's Home for a training course comprising Bible
Study and child care. At its conclusion they were deemed 'Sisters of the
Children' and by 1892 they were working full-time. 'It is a huge mistake
to suppose that anybody who can wash a child's face or sew a button on
a child's dress is fit for such work as ours,' Thomas once declared.[49]

Thomas also studied the Kaiserswerth am Rhein scheme whereby
deaconesses were trained for mission work.[50] It encouraged him in the
training offered to the Sisters of the Children, but also in the creation of
the 'Sisters of the People'. These would visit the poor and sick in their

homes and have a knowledge of nursing and midwifery. Later, in 1898, Willard House was set up as a training centre with Sister Ruth Northcott in charge. 'We must have a sense of justice,' she judged, 'or we shall do harm; a steadiness of will to maintain order and authority, and a definite idea of the value of time, leading to punctuality, and of money, leading to thrift. In a word, we must be full "of the spirit of love, of power, of joy and a sound mind", and have a body fit to put it into practice.'[51]

By now, Thomas had discovered not only delinquent children, but those who were physically damaged, inspired in part by schemes in France and Germany. Hope House, for example, was set up in London in the 1890s for epileptic girls, the boys being housed in Gravesend.[52] He also presided over adoptions – 25 of which had been dealt with in this way in 1891.[53] The 1890s, however, were not easy for Dr Stephenson, with his wife dying in 1890, who latterly had lived the life of an invalid.[54] She had not liked her husband's frequent absences from home, nor London, overmuch. Nevertheless, she had taken into their home the first girls and ran a weekly religious meeting for them at the Home itself.[55] Eventually Thomas married Sister Ella Macpherson from the Isle of Man branch, where she worked, one of 47 Sisters of the Children and 20 Sisters of the People then working in Britain.[56] It became her task to help him as more work came his way and he needed time off, sometimes abroad, because of the strain it imposed on him.

Clearly, handling both the Home and work developing across Britain was too much for one person and in 1889, when he was 60, Thomas and his wife went to live in Stroud Green in north London. Next year, with Hugh Price Hughes in the chair, at the Home's AGM he asked permission to retire on medical grounds. He then left London for Ilkley, where he founded the Wesley Deaconess Order and was its first warden until 1907. It was the culmination of work over several decades and an idea that he had first cradled in his mind during his time in Bolton.

While Thomas was at Ilkley, Arthur Gregory presided over further expansion – a Home for disabled children in Chipping Norton (1903); two more newly built Homes, one in 1903 in Frodsham, the other in 1907 at Bramhope. More followed, including the Harpenden Sanatorium in 1910, destined to play a key role in the Home's life in the ensuing decades. By 1909, the Homes had received 7,924 children, of whom 2,008 were still resident, including 20 in Canada. In addition, 477 were in foster homes.[57] The average length of stay was four or five years.[58]

Ironically, Arthur Gregory's death occurred on 21 June 1912, a month before Thomas Stephenson's. As he declined, Thomas's last few years left him housebound, but were lit up by visits from former residents, some now ministers, teachers or missionaries.[59] With him at the end, besides his wife, was a young woman, Florence, who as a seven-year-old orphan had come into the Home's care, then trained as a nurse at a London teaching hospital. Dr Stephenson was buried at Ilford, in a plot set apart for those who had died at the Children's Home.[60] It was the end of an era in many ways, for other pioneers ceased to be personally active then, Barnardo in 1905, Waugh of the NSPCC in 1908, and Rudolph of Waifs and Strays in 1919, though he did not die until 1933.[61]

Dr Stephenson had combined warm-heartedness and practical skills that served the institution he created well. Moreover, he was recognized as a real friend by children, someone to whom they could turn when in trouble. Little could he have foreseen how each decade after his death his work would continue to grow, with more than a dozen new Homes established between 1913 and 1924, under W. Hodson Smith, principal from 1912 to 1933. The base was now moved to City Road, then in 1925 to Highbury, where it has remained, the centre of its practical work shifting to Harpenden.

The choirs, one from London, the other from Birmingham, still raised funds, as did the Boys' Band from Farnborough, but in the 1930s they were abandoned as interrupting the boys' education. Many children, made fatherless by World War One, came into care in the 1920s,[62] with Hodson Smith's successor, John H. Litten (1933–50), acting swiftly in the 1930s to set up a training college at Highbury. During this time, many changes occurred at the political level that affected the way the Home worked – the first Children's Act (1908) setting up the probation service, juvenile courts, and liberal reforms in the treatment of delinquency leading inexorably to the 1933 Children and Young Person's Act.[63] The Adoption Act of 1926[64] led to an increase of adoptions, and this also affected the Home.

By the 1930s, there were 350 serving Sisters, who now sat for qualifications offered by the Froebel Institute. There was also a qualification for nursery nurses available.[65] New ideas flourished too; babies were housed in well-run residential nurseries; and under-fives were provided with nursery schools as the number of children in a family group was steadily reduced and staff ratios raised. Dietary scales were revised, and women trained in mental health were employed to give special attention to groups of disturbed and maladjusted children. Some Homes were devoted to children of significant ability, and special arrangements made to place them in local grammar schools.[66] The medical secretary of the Home from 1910 to 1941 even spoke of 'the rights of the child'.[67] It was not until 1939, however, that the Adoption of Children (Regulation) Act registered adoption societies like the Children's Home, regulated their conduct, and gave local authorities supervision of children aged under nine placed through a third party in what in effect was an adoption,[68] a move for which the Children's Home had been campaigning.[69]

From 1936, 'A Child Welfare Certificate' was given to trained and ordained Sisters, which took into account satisfactory service after training and continued reading, study and other relevant experience and training.[70] From 1936 to 1948, 320 were trained at Highbury itself, with nearly 30 per cent receiving the award.[71] During World War Two the college and office moved to Harpenden, but soon returned to Highbury and forged ahead despite the conflict. The principal set up a Commission of Reconstruction for all ages, which was to consider plans for mixed-sex groups and nursery schools for the under-fives. John Litten was highly regarded as modern childcare policies emerged, serving on two important national groups – the Curtis Committee and the Central Training Council. He set up a second training college, in Birmingham, and both it and Highbury were recognized by the Home Office in 1949, which made possible more grants from public bodies. Moreover, students could now qualify for the Home Office Certificate in Residential Child Care.[72]

Another Children's Act was passed in 1948, which led to improvements in the standards of public care, with the result that the numbers of children in voluntary care declined. At the time of the Curtis Report on the Care of Children (1946), there were 33,000 overall; by the time the Seebohm Report on the Social Services (1971) came out, there were 11,500.[73] The ensuing years saw government and local authority support grow. Under John W. Waterhouse (1950–69) the number of Homes still grew, though some, like Aubert Park, which was opened in 1934 in Highbury, closed because its hostel had become unsuitable. By 1960 all training was concentrated in Stephenson Hall in Highbury, as the number of married couples offering service had increased and available single women decreased.[74] Moreover, the number of childcare workers who were not Sisters also grew. One trainee came from Japan and went to the institute to learn about new approaches to childcare.[75]

The Curtis Report had favoured (in order): adoption; fostering; residential care. If children lived in residential homes, preferably there should be eight children and certainly not more than twelve.[76] The original Children's Home could well regard itself in the vanguard here for it has been estimated it saw 800 adoptions in its first 100 years.[77] Indeed, it had been one of the first agencies to pay adoption allowances.[78]

In 1969 the NCH was 100 and a plaque was erected in Exton Street to commemorate the anniversary of the founding. In 1964–5 it had raised £1 million; later it was nearly £2 million, with money coming from government and local authorities with whom NCH had entered into a partnership. That year, another Children and Young People's Act was passed, one of a number at the time, including a recommendation that approved schools, detention centres, remand Homes and assessment centres should be merged into a new type of community Home.[79]

In the agitation for change, Highbury staff had been active for the four years leading up to the 1969 Act, consulting with Children's Departments, other voluntary agencies and the regional inspectorate of the Home Office, to ensure an effective contribution from voluntary agencies in discussions and decision-making.[80] The key policy that emerged altered drastically how NCH operated. 'Action by society to deal with children in trouble,' the Home Office report stated, 'should be designated where possible to support the child in the family, encouraging and helping parents to fulfil their responsibilities and preserving the child's link with his local community.'[81]

The Children's Act led to new Children's Departments and more jobs for women, which meant more men working in the Homes.[82] Within 25 years agencies were drastically altered with dozens of new laws impinging directly, or indirectly, on how they operated. This change occurred when John Waterhouse's successor, Dr Gordon Barritt, was principal, as with growing rapidity homes were closed and sold and community-based family work emerged. By 1994 few Homes were left; instead there were in the UK alone 215 projects (NCH also had work in Jamaica, St Vincent and Zimbabwe). The philosophical arguments, begun in Dr Barritt's time, are now more prominent than ever. The key question, as he has indicated, is: 'How much to co-operate with local authorities and so lose independence?'[83] Of course, the germ of the policy had been there in the 1950s, when social workers had been employed to assist families and follow up young people when they left the Home both for work and new residence;[84] but the new developments were on a much larger scale.

The growing professionalization of care has meant those formerly employed with skills, but untrained, lose precedence over people with qualifications, which may lead to a loss of workers with flair. But local authorities, who in 2002–03 gave £128.6 million for services given out of a total of £150.7 million now call the tune. With only £2.7 million from individual supporters and £2 million from investments,[85] agencies like NCH cannot afford to stray far from government guidelines. It has to be admitted, too, that even before Dr Barritt's years, the £5 million from voluntary giving was dwarfed by the £12 million from local authorities, the largest amount then given to any voluntary agency.[86]

How did the move to community-based work affect London initiatives? In the 1970s it involved the joint sponsoring of a children's worker to organize pre-school playgroups and school holiday projects at Railton Road Youth and Community Centre,[87] while in the 1990s the Imani Project for families living with domestic violence was set up jointly with Battersea Central Mission. Another, at Ealing, originally a nursery, added care for children suffering from non-accidental injury, with a unit for severely disabled people and residential respite care to relieve parents from the stress of continuous caring.[88]

Meanwhile, Family Centres at Deptford and Lambeth provided places where daily care for children could be combined with work with parents, thereby strengthening family life. It was a type of Centre capable of many variants – as at Barking, where a NCH staff member worked with families in co-operation with a Methodist church and the local authority.[89] Earlier, in 1927, the Young Leaguer's Union Hospital had served as a day nursery until 1968, then becoming a day nursery on the ground floor, with family flats on the first and second. The Legard Family Support Centre there[90] helped socially isolated mothers, often those in debt and overwhelmed by the pressures on them, by the 1990s becoming the Support Service. It is yet another example of work done in co-operation with the local authority.

Issues with which NCH grappled from the 1980s were very different from earlier decades and included telephone counselling for abused children, known now as NCH Careline, begun in London and then becoming a national provision. Co-operation with Guy's Hospital on a new research project involving what families thought of services for sexual abuse, issued in 1989 in a six-year £4 million scheme to provide Britain with a network of child sexual abuse centres, was also a new initiative.[91] But, whereas in 1979 there were still 39 homes nationally and eight residential schools with but four family centres, by 1994 there were 215 projects, residential care reduced and specialist, with half NCH's £50 million budget spent on family and community centres.[92]

In London alone, in addition to the Imani Centre, there was 'Surviving Together', a project based at St Leonard's Hospital in Hackney for families experiencing child sexual abuse, with centres at Bayswater, Shepherd's Bush, Harlesden, Stamford Hill, Islington, Camberwell and Hackney, where there was also a young carers scheme, Stepney, Wimbledon, Hampstead, Stratford, Morden, Kingston and Twickenham, the base for a Women's Information and Resource Centre. In addition, there was the Monroe Family Centre in Camden from 1989 in co-operation with the Child and Family Department of the Tavistock Clinic and the ILEA, offering psychotherapy, groupwork and family therapy for families with children under five. By 1994 there were some 40 projects in London, with stress on children's health, family mediation (the Eye to Eye scheme in Camberwell for example) and family support. After 1997, NCH co-operated with the Labour government's Sure

Start initiative. In addition, NCH's residential centre for disability at Warren Park, near Kingston, with its special focus on respite care, continues to be prominent.

NCH has long had a high-profile campaigning role as its research brief, launched at a fringe meeting during the 2004 Labour Party Conference, indicates. In this it draws attention to the great number of children whose parents separate without giving an explanation to them of what is happening, with only 5 per cent of children having the situation explained to them or a chance to ask questions.[93] Also in 2004, NCH changed its relation with Methodism. Till then it had been formally and legally accountable to the annual Methodist Conference. From that year, it was agreed Conference would receive NCH's Report and that a new pattern of partnership was necessary and appropriate. While it remained the official children's charity of British Methodism, which was to appoint its trustees, with the aim of securing 50 per cent representation, in future the link would be with its pastoral director, a NCH employee who was also to be accountable to the Methodist Conference.

The core of its work, however, remained as at its beginning: a passion for justice and care. It is easy to be overwhelmed by NCH's size, with over 6,000 staff[94] and a budget of over £200 million; yet each of its 500 and more projects, involving 140,000 people, is about caring for unique individuals. The question that now has to be faced is how vulnerable is a project-oriented organization that relies so heavily on institutional funding in a political context that can become startlingly fluid due to economic pressures?

NCH chief executive Clare Tickell is especially aware of the 'time-lapse' between identifying a need and obtaining funding contracts from health and local authorities. Only by NCH maintaining full independence, she has indicated, 'could NCH meet its aim of helping the most vulnerable children and young people'.[95]

Notes

1 William Bradfield, *The Life of Thomas Bowman Stephenson BA, LLD, DD*, London, Charles H. Kelly, 1913, p. 67.

2 Bradfield, *Life*, p. 19.

3 Bradfield, *Life*, p. 21.

4 Bradfield, *Life*, p. 23.

5 Bradfield, *Life*, p. 24.

6 Bradfield, *Life*, p. 33.

7 Bradfield, *Life*, pp. 34–5.

8 Bradfield, *Life*, p. 44.

9 Bradfield, *Life*, p. 53.

10 Bradfield, *Life*, p. 51.

11 Bradfield, *Life*, p. 54.

12 Bradfield, *Life*, p. 60.

13 Bradfield, *Life*, p. 72.

14 Bradfield, *Life*, p. 62.

15 Bradfield, *Life*, p. 62.

16 Bradfield, *Life*, p. 63.

17 Bradfield, *Life*, p. 64.

18 Bradfield, *Life*, p. 65.

19 Cyril Davey, *A Man for All Children*, National Children's Home 1969, Peterborough, Epworth Press, 1968.

20 Bradfield, *Life*, p. 28.

21 Bradfield, *Life*, p. 75.

22 Bradfield, *Life*, p. 76.

23 Bradfield, *Life*, p. 78.

24 Bradfield, *Life*, p. 78.

25 Bradfield, *Life*, pp. 81–2.

26 Bradfield, *Life*, p. 82.

27 Bradfield, *Life*, p. 82.

28 Bradfield, *Life*, p. 83.

29 Bradfield, *Life*, p. 88.

30 Gordon Barritt, *Thomas Bowman Stephenson*, Peterborough, Foundery Press, 1996, p. 10. The booklet is no. 14 in the series 'People Called Methodists' and is available from the Methodist Publishing House.

31 Barritt, *Stephenson*, p. 10.

32 Davey, *A Man for All Children*, p. 44.

33 Bradfield, *Life*, p. 85.

34 Bradfield, *Life*, p. 91.

35 Bradfield, *Life*, p. 98.

36 Bradfield, *Life*, p. 100.

37 Bradfield, *Life*, p. 89.

38 Bradfield, *Life*, p. 100.

39 Bradfield, *Life*, p. 151.

40 Bradfield, *Life*, p. 112.

41 Bradfield, *Life*, pp. 125–6.

42 The Revd Dr Gordon Barritt, interview with author, 13 October 2004.

43 Davey, *A Man for All Children*, p. 85.

44 Davey, *A Man for All Children*, p. 85.

45 Bradfield, *Life*, p. 205.

46 Bradfield, *Life*, p. 216.

47 Davey, *A Man for All Children*, p. 89.

48 Davey, *A Man for All Children*, p. 91.

49 Quoted in NCH Action for Children brochure 1996.

50 Barritt, *Stephenson*, pp. 17–18.

51 Quoted by Barritt, *Stephenson*, pp. 17–18.

52 Alan Jacka, *The Story of the Children's Homes*, NCH, 1969, p. 21.

53 Pat Turner and Jeremy Elliott, *Adoption – Reviewing the Record*, NCH, 1992, p. 50, quoted in Terry Philpot, *NCH Action for Children: The Story of Britain's Foremost Children's Charity*, London, Lion, 1994, p. 50.

54 Bradfield, *Life*, p. 239.

55 Bradfield, *Life*, p. 279.

56 Jacka, *Story*, p. 23.

57 Jacka, *Story*, p. 27.

58 Jacka, *Story*, p. 28.

59 Davey, *A Man for All Children*, p. 127.

60 Bradfield, *Life*, p. 449.

61 Roy Parker, *Away from Home: A History of Child Care*, Barnardo's, 1990, cited in Philpot, *NCH Action for Children*, pp. 66–7.

62 Jacka, *Story*, p. 32.

63 Jacka, *Story*, p. 26.

64 Jacka, *Story*, p. 35.

65 Jacka, *Story*, p. 37.

66 Jacka, *Story*, p. 38.

67 Jacka, *Story*, p. 38.

68 Philpot, *NCH Action for Children*, p. 65, quoting Ivy Pinchbeck and Margaret Hewitt, *Children in English Society, Vol 2, From the 18th Century to the Children's Act of 1948*, London, Routledge and Kegan Paul, 1973.

69 Philpot, *NCH Action for Children*, p. 65.

70 Jacka, *Story*, p. 41.

71 Jacka, *Story*, p. 42.

72 Jacka, *Story*, p. 4.

73 Eileen Younghusband, *Social Work in Britain 1950–75: A Follow-Up Study Volume*, London, George Allen and Unwin, 1979, quoted in Jacka, *Story*, p. 87.

74 Jacka, *Story*, p. 49.

75 The Revd Dr Gordon Barritt, interview with author.

76 Philpot, *NCH Action for Children*, p. 86.

77 Pat Taylor and Jeremy Elliott, quoted in Philpot, *NCH Action for Children*, p. 87.

78 Philpot, *NCH Action for Children*, p. 9.

79 Philpot, *NCH Action for Children*, p. 90.

80 Philpot, *NCH Action for Children*, p. 90.

81 Philpot, *NCH Action for Children*, p. 90, quoting Home Office, Children in Trouble, HMSO, 1968.

82 Philpot, *NCH Action for Children*, p. 92.

83 Barritt, interview with author.

84 Barritt, interview with author.

85 NCH Annual Review 2002–03.

86 Philpot, *NCH Action for Children*, p.154.

87 NCH Year Book 'Community', 1971, p. 13.

88 The Revd Dr Gordon Barritt, memorandum prepared for author, 31 April 2005.

89 *A Good Day's Work*, NCH Report 1970–1.

90 *A Good Day's Work*, p. 17.

91 *A Good Day's Work*, p. 162.

92 *A Good Day's Work*, p. 172.

93 See NCH website www.nch.org.uk/stuckinthemiddle.

94 Gordon Eddington, *Methodist Recorder*, 8 July 2004, p. 10.

95 Clare Tickell, in conversation with Andrew Fagg, *Methodist Recorder*, 27 October 2005, p. 9.

6

A Divine Imperative
Walter Hall, Hilda Bartlett Lang and Methodist Homes

'Dear Mr Rank,' Walter Hall wrote, 'I enclose a statement concerning Bowran House, also an Architect's plan and a letter for adapting it to the purpose of a Home for elderly Methodist people.' It was early 1935 when, in his own meticulous and firm handwriting, he sent a letter to explain that if Bowran House were retained for Methodism (before Methodist Union in 1932 it was a deaconess hostel owned by the United Methodists) it could be bought for £2,500. 'I am writing to enquire whether you could see your way to purchase it at this price for Methodism,' he continued,[1] describing the house in Battersea which, with extensions, he judged could take ten or so staff and residents.

He also wrote to the Revd C. Ensor Walters, with whom Joseph Rank met regularly to allocate charitable giving, explaining tactfully he had no right to assume he could accept responsibility, but he hoped, if appropriate, he would 'say a commendatory word'. 'I have felt a need for such a home for several years,' Walter explained, 'and have resisted the idea that I had to do something, because of other pressing duties. Latterly, however, the urge has become imperative, and I have had to explore the possibilities of the situation if only to relieve a burdened conscience . . . I have simply and honestly tried to respond throughout to what I believed to be a divine imperative,'[2] he concluded, an indication of his spirit that his one-time secretary, Barbara Phillips, has described as one of 'quiet confidence, untiring life-style and deep faith . . .'[3] His appeal to Mr Rank received no positive response.

Born in Nottingham in 1876 and educated there, Walter Hall had become a United Methodist Church minister in 1906, after college working for two years in Jamaica. Back in the UK, he had several jobs before coming to London as a minister in Streatham and Tottenham. Meg Hall, who lived in the same Tottenham street, recalls 'his lovely smile, his gentleness and the way the whole family looked after Mrs Hall'.[4] Such a person was bound to want to act to help those who feared life in the workhouse, which was not abolished until 1947. Their wards, poorly lit by windows high up, sometimes had beds less than two feet apart, with no lockers, privacy or room for personal belongings. Common rooms were filled with people slumped in chairs, often controlled by restrictive rules.[5]

On the surface, a cool and efficient man, well able to cope with being a Superintendent minister and chair a District (in those days the jobs were combined), Walter had a deep sense of justice and anger against systems that oppressed people. So when out visiting one day (he travelled by public transport or walked) he met a 65-year-old lady, looking ten years older through under-nourishment, who told him she must leave her home because 'there's no money for the rent', he was filled with compassion. 'Please, Mr Hall,' she pleaded, 'don't let them take me to the Union,' a name often used to describe the workhouse.

Walter Hall was not the first to found a Home for the elderly, for as the Methodist Conference looked into the matter in the 1940s it found there were a number of individual Homes, besides those run by Roman Catholic religious orders and specific charities. But when in 1937 he called friends together he was determined, even though they told him they were unclear how to proceed and too busy to give support. It was another rebuff, and he needed all the support of his invalid wife, which she gladly gave, despite her deafness and life in a wheelchair.

Joseph Rank died in 1943, but had set up a charity to disburse his considerable funds. Called the Joseph Rank Benevolent Trust, it had been run since 1940 by the Revd Fred Bartlett Lang, a minister in Greenwich, where he and his wife, Hilda, created a group for people with physical disabilities and she also ran a Guide Troop. It had been at a Methodist Conference in Plymouth that a friend had introduced Hilda to a quiet good-looking young minister and left them talking. 'What did you think of him?' the friend asked Hilda Rank. 'I wasn't going to tell her what I thought,' Hilda commented later, 'but I married him.'[6]

Hilda was the daughter closest to Joseph Rank, a relationship cemented when she married a minister. Regarded as 'this wild child' by her teachers when a boarder at Wintersdorf School in Southport, like her father, she knew what she wanted and how to get it.[7] One of the first women to drive a car, she was also one of the first to break the male solidarity of the Wesleyan Conference. Moreover, she had a habit of sticking with problems, as her treasurership of a group helping the National Children's Home indicates: she was treasurer for 55 years.[8]

Shy and self-effacing, yet punctilious in her conduct of affairs, Hilda was a woman used to servants and staff to help her. In the early 1940s, she had begun to collect money for a Home for the elderly, with Bognor Regis in mind, because she and her husband were now living there. She had already heard of Walter Hall's aim, so was not surprised when, at the 1943 Methodist Conference in Birmingham, the Committee, which through his persistence had been appointed the previous year, reported 'a widespread need' for a Home and that 'there had been a number of bequests, including one of £3,000', if a home were established, though conditions were attached to the gift.[9]

The Report, on the last day, so insignificant it seemed, hoped even the poor could 'maintain themselves' in Methodist Homes, with perhaps help from Supplementary Pensions. Such places, for between 20 to 50, with maximum privacy and economic independence, combined with common meals and fellowship, seemed the way forward. The Committee therefore recommended a Home for widows and spinsters, and other Homes if possible, through local initiatives, open to Methodists and others. Publicity should be given to the idea and funds sought. Such Homes would come under an Executive Committee appointed by the Conference and would be for those over 60. The new group was to be called the Methodist Homes for the Aged (MHA).

Several ministers, besides Walter Hall, who was to convene the group, were appointed to carry the recommendations forward, along with 15 lay people, including Lord Rochester and Sir George Martin. The treasurership was left vacant. The Conference was unenthusiastic, but Dr Scott Lidgett intervened and it was agreed to ask for a further report in 1944.[10] Arriving home in Selsdon, where Walter and his wife now lived, he beamed with happiness, sensing that his ten-year struggle to make a dream a reality was now being accomplished – though to start with he had only envisaged Homes for elderly church workers.

Like many pioneers, he was really effective when he attracted others to work with him, like the Revd Charles Hulbert, who said: 'Why don't you ask Mrs Lang to be treasurer?' Sir George Martin, a well-known Yorkshire layman concerned with public health issues, a member of Leeds City Council in 1926, and later Lord Mayor and High Sheriff of Yorkshire,[11] had the same idea. One day when he and Hilda were talking, she said, 'Of course you'll be chairman'. 'Provided you'll be treasurer', Sir George replied.[12] As treasurer, Hilda took great interest 'in visiting the sites once they were completed and occupied by residents', her daughter Jean has explained. 'She got to know many of the Matrons and residents especially in homes in the area where she lived.'[13]

In 1943 a Committee member reported a house called Ryelands in Wallington, Surrey, was for sale for £3,000 – £300 less if used as a Home for the elderly. Adapting it would cost another £500. If they were to purchase it, a bank overdraft was necessary as there was only £1,337 in their account. By January 1944, a bank loan negotiated, Ryelands was purchased. Such was the interest that 80 applications were received, many from widows and spinsters, a figure that rose to 130 by the Conference Committee's AGM. Soon the first matron was appointed for a six-month trial at £1 weekly. At that critical meeting, however, Hilda was bold, advocating a target of £50,000 for a strong Central Fund 'from which new homes could be purchased, adapted or furnished'.[14] Walter now had to persuade the Conference, meeting in Leeds, about the £50,000 suggestion, but also said, 'I have changed my mind.' This was because he had in his pocket a challenge offer of £15,000 to match the first £15,000 if the Fund's goal was £60,000. What he did not reveal was that the letter was from Hilda from the Rank Trust run by her husband, the Revd Fred Bartlett Lang. The stunned Conference agreed to Walter's request.

Now retired from his north London appointment and still with an invalid wife to support, Walter worked with his part-time secretary, Barbara Phillips, whom he once called 'the daughter I never had', from an office in his Selsdon home. Clearly, the new body was up and running so that, by May 1945, Hilda was able to report to the Conference Committee an excess of income over expenditure and a capital fund of just above £3,000. Walter's report to the Methodist Conference itself included the opening of Ryelands, with two more Homes on the way. The Ministry of Health itself was regarding the enterprise with 'increasing sympathy', he told delegates, as he asked for a generous response to the £60,000 appeal.[15]

Both Walter and Hilda were now well in harness, with Sir George Martin as chair of the Conference Committee itself. Walter became a crucial figure in handling problems at Ryelands, as well as being national convenor. While Hilda chaired the Ladies' sub-Committee of the Homes, he also chaired a group to arrange for a constitution and the supervision of the voluntary management committees that ran the Homes, sometimes in a paternalistic manner in the early years. Hilda went through accounts in great detail and was quick to discover overspending.[16] Covenanted gifts were increasing, partly as a result of the distribution of 45,000 brochures and the journalists who were writing about the problems of ageing, so she realized the overdraft could be halved.

New Homes were opened in 1946 in Harrogate and Tankerton in Kent, both the result of local initiatives. By 1950 there were eight, including one in Liverpool and one in Bath. Midway through 1952 two more Homes were opened, which now had 165 residents between them. Hilda's hoped-for Home in Bognor Regis had opened in 1948, the year the Labour government, its plans for the welfare state now formulated, insisted that older people be accommodated in 'small houses rather than large institutions'.[17] Public bodies, like the National Old People's

Welfare Council of which Walter was a member, also began to give Methodist Homes positive appraisals. There were, naturally, other types of Homes, but what seemed distinctive about Methodist Homes for the Aged (MHA) was its stress on privacy – a room of your own, with basin and, later, a toilet – fellowship with others through shared experiences, and confidentiality about finances.[18] Moreover, each resident could bring possessions (but not a bed) and rules were minimal, though in its first ten years the residents of Ryelands had conflicts regarding the way the matron ran it. In 1951 this led to her departure, but a successor was soon appointed at £156 annually, 'more in line with similar appointments with other organizations'.[19]

In 1948, when he was 72, Walter surrendered his national role and was followed by another minister, Willam Stoate. But he stayed a key figure and often handled Ryelands's difficulties, though it was chaired by successive local clergy. He mediated too between local and national situations when the 1947 Conference decided to raise residents' contributions because of pension rises, an important matter because half the £3,000 annual running costs were met by residents' money. A most difficult incident occurred in 1949 when the Methodist Conference refused to buy the property adjoining Ryelands because there was a restrictive covenant on it. The issue was later resolved and Ryelands was able to expand. But by now some residents were frail and the question had to be faced: who was responsible for deciding they must enter a Nursing Home? It was suggested as national policy that the person named as the resident's 'best friend' should undertake this when the document agreeing to this role was signed. Walter himself did not always agree with decisions, however, and once opposed the transfer of a resident, but he was overruled, though her room was left vacant for a possible return.

A further development occurred by 1960: the erection of more purpose-built properties. The first had been at Woking in 1952, with Hall Grange in Shirley, near Croydon, among others, in 1958. This was intended to have special care of the sick, part of its premises being designed for this purpose, but as a result of recruiting difficulties this aspect of the work was almost entirely discontinued.[20]

How were Methodist Homes faring by 1980 when there were 35 residential ones? In the case of the Meadow, in Muswell Hill, provision was much improved from Homes that had not been purpose-built. It had *en suite* facilities and non-slip floors, a television in each room, menus prepared in consultation with residents, and lounges and rooms designed in groups of six to fit round bays. Moreover, there were good views over north London and it was part of the Chester House estate, which included a hostel for young people in their first London job.

By this time, it was apparent that more people in the UK were living to greater ages. Clearly there was a limit to what local groups, however well motivated, or even Trusts, could do. Problems, especially the need for greater income, were occurring that Walter Hall, who had died aged 90 in July 1966, 'a practical idealist whose faith and social concern resulted in a courageous and successful attempt to face one of the great needs of our century', as his obituary indicated,[21] could not have envisaged. One way to generate this income was through legacies. The wife of Reginald Spray, national administrator from 1957 to 1975, was asked by Sir George Martin to arrange for letters to be sent to all solicitors in Britain suggesting they inform clients about MHA when drawing up wills. Mrs Spray, as a volunteer, typed 23,000 top copy letters. 'With commitment like that', David Wigley has commented, 'you can move mountains.'[22] From then onwards, MHA received legacies, sometimes substantial ones, for its work. Moreover, several large donors, like Westons, also emerged, thereby putting finances on a substantial footing.

The 1970s proved a particular time of upheaval for MHA when the Revd R. J. Connell ended his time as general-secretary (he finished in 1975) and was succeeded by Brian Callin, who began a necessary process of modernization. Sir George Martin, too, now in his nineties (he died aged 92 in 1976), ceased to be chairman in 1975. Hilda herself, who had lived 'by the spirit that problems that seemed difficult should be tackled at once', as a friend observed, and 'those she was warned were impossible of solution might take a little longer',[23] was also realistic enough to end her stint. For both of them it had been a moment of quiet satisfaction when Sir Keith Joseph had opened their thirtieth Home in 30 years at Poole in Dorset.

In 1971 Mary Trembath had become joint treasurer with Hilda,[24] a task they shared till 1975 when Mary's husband, Humphrey, a relative of Hilda's, took over from her. Derek Lyons, a layman with immense business and administrative and business experience, like the treasurers and Hilda herself, from Reigate Methodism, had been pitchforked into MHA in the early 1970s when Mary Trembath asked 'Would you like to sit in on a meeting to see what MHA is all about?'[25] Soon he found himself on the national committee and from 1984 to 1992 was its chair when Jack Miller, a former Methodist vice-president and George Martin's successor, gave up.

By 1977, however, fewer Homes were being opened, though MHA's income had risen from £170,000 to nearly £900,000. Problems were becoming more complex, too, with several disastrous fires stirring local authorities into vigorous action.[26] Moreover, new trends favoured more sheltered housing and there was a greater need to update existing properties. Soon, too, there were growing problems, which involved consultation with health and social work agencies as life spans continued to increase, partly through better medical care and nutrition.

Hilda Bartlett Lang had one more task to perform – to allow her name to be used for 'Target 90', built round her birthday, as Mary Trembath suggested a new appeal for three blocks of flats in Midsomer Norton in Somerset, the group's first sheltered housing project. The challenge was to raise £90,000 to be matched by a further £90,000 from the Rank Trust. With many small donations and one large one, the flats were bought and opened in 1978. So MHA moved in yet another direction as its income topped £1 million.[27] By 1981 another record was broken when legacies alone produced more than £1 million.[28]

In 1977 the MHA Housing Association was established, making it possible to receive capital grants and loans from the Housing Corporation, a quango that the Department of the Environment had created earlier to relieve Britain's housing crisis, especially in the larger cities. It offered 100 per cent loans and grants and its monitoring procedures were not too severe. Under this umbrella it became possible to help churches with sites too large for them, like Broomwood Methodist Church in Battersea, to develop them. Thus half their building became MHA property and 12 one-bedroom flats were built, in co-operation with the local authority. Such support, however, meant that the local authority was now able to nominate residents to Ash Court from any background when the flats were opened in 1984.

MHA diversified and settled in Derby, having cut the umbilical cord with London, where it had been since its beginning. It was now influenced, as were all such organizations, by 'Home Life', a code of practice for residential care published by the Centre for Policy on Ageing[29]and by the Registered Homes Act, which required both registration and monitoring by the statutory authority, including some unannounced visits.

Snags now developed with Housing Corporation policy, whereby some applicants were denied access to sheltered housing schemes if they owned a house, others being judged in greater need. In addition, a former pattern, whereby a minister was asked to support applications, was dropped. Indeed, it was forbidden to ask an applicant for sheltered housing questions about religious inclinations as now only half of them were selected by MHA itself.[30] Equal opportunities policies meant public funding must be even-handed, yet implementation of this was by no means straightforward. An attempt by MHA to build sheltered housing in the London Borough of Southwark, for example, came to a halt when its Council insisted that to receive funds housing must be available according to Southwark's ethnic mix. Leaving aside cultural sensitivities in an older generation only slowly coming to terms with multicultural Britain, clearly it was impossible for MHA to guarantee this in advance, especially when older people in some cultures were still adequately supported at home by their extended family network. 'Translating noble concerns into realities is not easy,' David Wigley has observed.[31]

Other matters, too, gained higher profile, especially gender and disability issues. This meant best standard practice for access to care or housing also had implications for recruitment and training of staff and the award of contracts.[32] There was, too, the hurdle of regular monitoring. The 1993 Charities Act provided another challenge as the Charity Commissioners became more detailed in demands and scrutiny. This led to increasing professionalism, both among employed staff, the governing group (the trustees) and relations with management (staff roles).[33] Gone indeed were the days when Homes could be run by local voluntary committees.

Moreover, the 1990 NHS and Community Care Act, together with the 1993 full introduction of Care in the Community, had delegated responsibility for assessing need and arranging care to local authorities. Now people were to be helped to live at home with help from domiciliary services. This changed the pattern of care provision and had a major impact on MHA. It meant they had to secure contracts with over 100 different local authorities and that people coming into residential care tended to be older. 'Before 1982 Methodist Homes had residents who sometimes needed care,' David Wigley has reflected. 'After that they needed care because they were older and had mental confusion.'[34] Hence traditional categories, sheltered housing, residential or nursing care, needed modification.[35] In addition, increased specifications from local authorities, Westminster or Brussels meant new controls for lowering risks.[36]

To meet some of these new challenges, in 1989 MHA opened special care homes for dementia and those needing other nursing. Two years earlier it had begun Live-at-Home Schemes, whereby a local and often ecumenical group helped people to stay in their own homes. This led to the creation of local management groups and access to car drivers for help with shopping visits and sometimes holidays. By 2000, over 50 such schemes across England had been established which supported over 5,000. Only one, however, exists in London – in Northwood. Started in 1998 with representatives from many churches and the local synagogue, it is a community venture involving some 50 volunteers in a befriending scheme, including one-to-one friendship, social gatherings and outings. Most members are over 80 and two are over 100. The scheme sometimes acts as a go-between in housing problems, and involves sixth formers in home visiting, though a few elderly people are nervous of the Muslim headdress worn by some of the girls. Many volunteers themselves are retired, as in the scheme in Reigate and Redhill, just beyond the London Borough of Croydon. Like both these strongly middle-class areas, there is support from the local council and a pool of labour on which to draw, not always evident in inner London boroughs where population trends are less stable.[37]

Despite these changing patterns, at Ryelands it has been possible to re-model the site, adding a dementia care unit for 15.[38] In Pimlico, near Victoria, 13 flats for sale have been built on church property and since 1997 another dementia wing added at Muswell Hill. Keith Albans, MHA's Director of Chaplaincy and Spirituality, assists staff, residents and friends to interpret dementia in theological terms. 'Holy Saturday shows us God in the emptiness and God taking the emptiness unto himself,' he has written. 'To be held at a point where looking back brings no comfort and looking forward brings no hope is an experience which the first disciples have in common with those who watch a loved one overtaken by dementia. But our testimony,' he adds, 'is that where visitors and staff persevere through their own discomfort to give dignity and individuality to even the most frail of people, then God does not simply meet us in emptiness but transforms it. Easter Day does follow Holy Saturday, not cancelling it out but revealing its true meaning.'[39]

With its sixtieth anniversary well behind it, its fiftieth care home opened in Coventry, and the average age of residents being nearly 90, compared with the first ones at Ryelands, who were in their sixties, MHA finds it even more important to develop a spirituality of ageing, work pioneered by Albert Jewell and Geoffrey Harris in the 1990s, and for a few years focused in a centre in Leeds, which it sponsored. Homes do, of course, have chaplains, but there is surely a need for national groups like MHA to go on raising the issue, along with others, of the tendency in the UK, as elsewhere, to exalt youth above age. Using the credibility it has gained with government and local authorities, MHA can continue the agenda of the Millennium Debate of the Age, even if politicians are reluctant fully to face the facts as a result of short-term interests and the need for substantial lateral thinking. As Dr Donald English said in his sermon at the fiftieth anniversary of Ryelands: 'MHA is sending a message about our view of the elderly as the third age on the way to the fourth, not on the way out, and we're sending a message about our commitment to give everything we can to the care of the vulnerable.'[40]

A second issue is how to cope with ageing in the context of a multi-racial society. For just as funding has become more diverse, so have the potential residents of Homes, though the complexities of this are not always sufficiently realized. A start has been made outside London whereby the Methodist Housing Association, the Kirklees Black Elders' Association and local services have co-operated over residential care. With half of the residents coming from the African–Caribbean community, Methodist Homes was designated the provider of management and housing support, specialist agencies with an understanding of Caribbean culture, providing catering and care staff.[41]

A third issue concerns numbers. In no way can residential care providers meet the needs of Britain's ageing population, now over a million and projected to be four million by around 2050. No matter how many homes are built, most people will have to live and die at home, with ancillary and hospital support. Who will cater for the numerous policies such a fact implies when already social services and the health service are over-stretched? Surely Methodism, out of long experience, is well qualified with others to suggest ways to create new forms of paid service in the community as traditional bonds weaken. Maybe this is a theme that churches in London, and beyond, should take up with vigour.

Above all, as policy initiatives come and go, and different groups seek to handle diverse support systems and funding, a situation so different from what Walter Hall and Hilda Bartlett experienced, the final words must be with those who receive care. David Wigley, for example, has reminded people of his meeting with a Chinese Muslim woman who came to stay in a Methodist Home because of its reputation. Happy there for some years, finally she went back to Beijing to her family.[42] In a different vein, in 1994 *Cinderella* was performed at Ryelands four times in full costume, with residents and staff playing the parts, written for them by a resident, and produced by another from her wheelchair. At 92, the writer seemed the soul of the party, determined to live life to the end.[43]

Perhaps even more striking was Ethel Wheeler, who celebrated her one-hundredth birthday at Hall Grange (named after Walter Hall) and who went to church as usual. Having lost all, except what she stood up in, during World War Two, and rescued from the basement of her bombed home, she yet continued to help at the Westminster Central Hall, having retired in 1939. Even at 100 she took no medication, did her own laundry and shopping, and seemed to other residents to possess a serenity that encouraged all who met her, even as they struggled for such an outlook.[44]

Ruth Gledhill, writing about the Centre for the Policy of Ageing report 'Religion, Spirituality and Older People' had as her caption in *The Times* 'Faith helps the aged to stay healthy'.[45] Maybe Ethel Wheeler had found just that.

Notes

1 The Revd Walter Hall, letter to Joseph Rank, London Committee files, from the 1930s.

2 Walter Hall, letter to the Revd C. Ensor Walters, 22 February 1935, London Mission files.

3 Barbara Phillips, letter to author, 22 September 2004.

4 Meg Hall, wife of the Revd Bernard Hall, interview with author, 24 November 2004.

5 Cyril Davey, *Home from Home, The Story of Methodist Homes*, Methodist Homes for the Aged, n.d., pp. 19–20.

6 Davey, *Home from Home*, p. 37.

7 Davey, *Home from Home*, p. 37.

8 *Methodist Recorder*, 1 March 1984.

9 Methodist Conference, Representative Session 1943, Eventide Homes.

10 Methodist Conference, Representative Session 1943, Eventide Homes.

11 Obituary, *Methodist Recorder*, 28 October 1976, p. 11.

12 Davey, *Home from Home*, p. 32.

13 Mrs Jean Moon, letter to author, 19 October 2004.

14 Methodist Homes for the Aged AGM, 25 May 1944.

15 Minutes of the Methodist Conference, 1945.

16 Mrs Jean Moon, letter to author, 19 October 2004.

17 Cyril Davey, *Home for Good, Methodist Homes for the Aged, 1943–1983*, MHA, 1983, p. 4.

18 Davey, *Home for Good*, p. 5.

19 'Ryelands' First Minute Book, Committee Meeting, 19 October 1954.

20 Davey, *Home from Home*, p. 91.

21 Minutes of the Methodist Conference 1967, pp. 178–9.

22 Extract from a lecture to the United Methodist Health and Welfare Ministries Ageing Section, Miami, USA, 18 March 1981.

23 *Methodist Recorder*, obituary, 19 March 1984, p. 4.

24 *Methodist Recorder Supplement*, 26 October 1972.

25 Derek Lyons, interview with author, 22 October 2004.

26 Davey, *Home for Good*, p. 14.

27 Davey, *Home for Good*, p. 17. (The actual figure was £1,182,933.)

28 Davey, *Home for Good*, p. 20.

29 David Wigley, *The Person not the Problem*, MHA, 1997, p. 24.

30 Wigley, *The Person not the Problem*, p. 26.

31 David Wigley, interview with author, 22 September 2004.

32 Wigley, *The Person not the Problem*, p. 39.

33 Wigley, *The Person not the Problem*, p. 28.

34 Wigley, interview.

35 Wigley, *The Person not the Problem*, p. 39.

36 Wigley, *The Person not the Problem*, p. 30.

37 Interview with Northwood Live at Home Organizer, 10 November 2004.

38 See MHA, *Heart and Soul*, Easter 2000, p. 6.

39 The Revd Keith Albans, 'Heart and Soul', Easter 2000, pp. 16–17.

40 The Revd Dr Donald English, Sermon at 'Ryelands' Anniversary, 18 June 1995.

41 MHA, *Heart and Soul*, Autumn 2004, p. 18.
42 Wigley, *The Person not the Problem*, p. 27.
43 Wigley, *The Person not the Problem*, pp. 54–5.
44 Davey, *Home for Good*, p. 30.
45 *The Times*, 16 July 1999.

7

Life Abundant
William Kyle and the Westminster Pastoral Foundation

William Kyle, known always as Bill, for it was impossible to call this 'extremely human' minister with 'exceptional talents'[1] otherwise, was born in Birmingham, Alabama, of British parents. They had emigrated there in the 1920s to find work, which his father did by becoming a rivet boy in the local steelworks. They were poor, yet Bill remembered his Deep South experience with unabated affection, especially his own involvement in a local evangelical mission, which welcomed his family – his sister, Pauline, was born in 1930 – when they felt far from home.

In 1935, however, after his grandfather's death, Bill and his family returned to Plymouth. He now lost his southern 'drawl' and also some of his childhood memories because of the move, only recovering them when he underwent analysis in the 1960s as a necessary part of his psychotherapy training.[2] From 1941, Bill was a marine engineer in Devonport dockyard and this gave him a first-hand experience of a well-run organization.[3] He also joined a Mission, similar to that in Alabama, but through membership of a fellowship group was drawn into Methodism. Soon he was training to be a lay preacher and exhibiting leadership skills he knew he possessed from his work with the Boy Scout Movement.

Bill's theology was then straightforward. He was particularly clear that he must respond to 'what the Lord wanted him to do', a view shared by Benita Kyle, as she became, whom he met through a Methodist youth camp in Swanage in 1952, by which time Bill was training to be a Methodist minister at Richmond Theological College in Surrey, after a pre-collegiate year in Cornwall. Benita, from a Welsh Baptist background, had a father whose career was like Bill's because, from a humble start on a Welsh hill farm, he rose to be director of a successful company.[4]

Like Bill, Benita was a student, reading social studies at Bedford College. As they talked, Bill became convinced that her training for social work was more relevant than his, for already he was critical of the lack of grounding in pastoral work that potential ministers received. He was aware, too, of the special contribution women could make. They talked much about their respective visions. 'We dreamed our dreams,' Benita has recalled. 'They were the same – fortunately.'[5]

Both attended lectures by the Revd David Mace, the one-time Methodist minister who founded the Marriage Guidance Council, now called Relate. These had a major impact on them. Bill was ordained in 1954, the year they married. After 12 months in Norfolk, he was then sent to country chapels. 'Even in those days Bill's heart and mind seemed to be turning to the care of people in emotional distress,' a former colleague has remembered.[6]

In 1957 Bill joined the Highgate Circuit, thereafter remaining in London. He was responsible for two churches, one in Kentish Town. Here in September 1960 he became a mediator between the United Tenants' Association and the St Pancras Borough Council who were in dispute over rents. It was alleged that the riots involved Communist Party members.[7] From 1957 to 1963 Bill and Benita were counsellors at the London branch of the Marriage Guidance Council. Bill was also honing his skills through membership of the Family Discussion Bureau of the Tavistock Institute (1961–3) and Clergy Case Discussion Groups (1963–4).

In 1960 Bill founded the Highgate Counselling Centre, which still exists.[8] Convinced the Church had a unique role to play in helping people to wholeness, he wrote: 'What we have to give is love, warmth, persistence . . . a quality of counselling that is different. Otherwise we should be just a pale shadow of the social services.'[9] He was always quoting John's Gospel where Jesus is depicted as saying his purpose was for people to have 'life, and have it abundantly'.[10]

Rooms in his church were made available for the voluntary counsellors Bill recruited, who were given a comprehensive course of lectures on the sociology and background of both young people and adults, the social services, legal affairs and aspects of psychiatry. Numbers were limited to 16. Counsellors joined a fortnightly case discussion group led by professionals. Solicitors, accountants, surveyors and an architect, and various social workers, were also on hand to offer help. Church members provided the nucleus of an advisory committee on to which experienced advisers were co-opted.[11]

'The inauguration of the Highgate Counselling Centre in the 1960s was, with hindsight,' Denis Duncan, one of Bill's earliest and closest colleagues, has reflected, 'of greater importance than perhaps even he realised for it was in fact to herald the coming of pastoral counselling in England.'[12] Already Bill's capacity to attract people of calibre was evident when Dr Henrietta Meyer, a Jungian psychotherapist, and a refugee from Germany, became a consultant.[13] Later Dr Alexander Duddington, a member of the Russian Orthodox Church, was the consultant psychiatrist for the Westminster Pastoral Foundation (WPF) for many years.

Bill was not, however, the only pioneer in religion and psychiatry. Indeed he had been encouraged by the Revd Dr Leslie Weatherhead, one of three British Methodist ministers – the other two were Lord Soper of Kingsway (as he became) and the Revd Dr Edwin Sangster at Westminster Central Hall – who were drawing large congregations in central London in the 1950s. Dr Weatherhead, with his Clinic at the City Temple, stressed psychology and healing in his writings from *The Mastery of Sex Through Psychology and Religion*[14] to *Psychology, Religion and Healing*.[15] Indeed, he wrote over 60 books to help lay people find both a contemporary faith and peace of mind for emotional afflictions.

Bill called Leslie Weatherhead 'the greatest human being I have known', and at his death in 1976, when his Clinic became part of WPF, recalled how he had 'conferred a rich depth of friendship on a younger colleague'.[16] For his part, Leslie wrote of Bill's Highgate work: 'I have watched this adventure from its first beginning to its present development and so highly do I think of it I shall prophesy that it may well mark a turning point in the history of the Churches.'[17]

While at Highgate, Bill began his own psychotherapy. By 1964, when he was appointed to Sanderstead Methodist Church for five years, he drafted a memorandum to the Methodist Home Mission Department proposing to its head, Dr Leslie Davison, a 'London Methodist Centre or foundation of Pastoral Care'.[18] Subsequent plans for the Westminster Pastoral Foundation stemmed from this paper. Now, because someone of Dr Davison's stature accepted them, Bill began to negotiate a visit to the USA for further training, which would lead to a qualification in pastoral counselling.

He did so when other movements were beginning, including the Institute for Religion and Medicine and the Samaritans, founded by the Anglican priest Chad Varah. Perhaps the most significant of these was the attempt to marry theology and psychodynamic theory by Dr Frank Lake, who created the Clinical Theology Association. In addition, the writings of 'gurus' like Carl Rogers in the USA and Paul Tournier in Switzerland were much in vogue.

Bill saw the primary needs, however, somewhat differently from these people, wanting a 'synthesis between social casework and pastoral counselling', because in each congregation there were people 'whose emotional problems were beyond the resources of the normal ministry'.[19] He undergirded this Christian component in counselling with the suggestion that 'services such as the Laying on of Hands could be conducted under careful supervision'.[20] Ideally, premises would be purpose-built, including a church, a canteen, counselling and lecture rooms. Trustees would be needed to find resources and administer such a Foundation.[21]

Bill's desire to obtain a Certificate in Pastoral Counselling from the American Foundation of Religion and Psychiatry (later Religion and Health), taking his family with him to the USA, was not easy to organize. Even though his church was supportive, some were not persuaded. Bill, however, advertised and found a replacement from the USA for a year. He also sought funds from Norman Vincent Peale and a wealthy businessman called W. Clement Stone, among others. Stone paid for Bill and his family – by now there were three daughters aged five, seven and nine – to travel to New York on the *Queen Elizabeth*. He also paid Bill's training fees.

Bill took on part-time charge of two churches in New Jersey. His day began at 6.00 a.m. to enable him to travel to New York for his training course. Benita, who had been working as a part-time psychiatric social worker and college lecturer for the Croydon Mental Health Department, at first had been cautious about Bill's seemingly grandiose plans. Yet, as she shared his keenness to see them realized, she overruled her initial reservations. 'My contribution,' she has remarked, 'was in Bill's growth and commitment.'[22]

Bill did one other thing before leaving for the USA. He approached Lord Rank, then heavily involved in the refurbishment of Westminster Central Hall, and convinced him that London needed a counselling centre. 'I'll build you a unit in the part I'm developing,' he promised. Asked what his needs were, Bill replied: 'Counselling rooms and a lecture room.' 'I just pulled it out of the air,' he later confided in Benita.[23]

While Bill was in New York studying, Benita visited members of two congregations, acting pastorally where necessary, and learned about social work in the USA.[24] It turned out to be a 'magical year' for everyone as from June 1967 till August 1968 Bill rediscovered his roots. For his last two months, he began his study at Andover Newton Theological Seminary in Boston, which led to a Doctorate in Pastoral Counselling based on the creation of the WPF. He also had a clinical appointment in a hospital, but by now his mind was more preoccupied with the new Westminster Centre.

Back in London, Bill had a final year in Sanderstead. He was also given a room in the Central Hall and had a part-time secretary. 'I hope God knows what is going to happen,' he said wryly, 'because I don't.'[25] When he had told Dr Weatherhead of his plans in the USA, he had reacted: 'You won't come back.' 'Yes, I will,' Bill had responded[26] and was now there to prove it, with the opening on 27 May 1970 of his Foundation, sub-titled 'A National Counselling Service', with premises, a few professional staff and clients. Its numbers soon increased. There was also a series of lectures on various themes in what was advertised as 'The University of Life'. By autumn 1971 Bill was asking supporters to 'help us; work with us; pray for us', adding 'as Lord Rank remarked at a recent meeting, the church has much to make up for in our ministry to the mental and spiritual needs of people'.[27]

By the following year, Bill, part entrepreneur, part pioneer, with formidable capacity to gain the support and affection of those in responsible positions, had persuaded the Rt Hon Selwyn Lloyd, MP, the Methodist Speaker of the House of Commons, to write an Anniversary Appeal, which was sent to the president of the Institute of Religion and Health, among others. By 1974 Bill had secured a grant from the Voluntary Service Unit of the Home Office of £20,000, which led to the appointment of a former trainee, David Black, to 'supervise' the counselling services that were now springing up through church contacts outside London, and who looked to WPF for guidance. These were the first 'affiliate' centres, as they are known.[28] In 1978, when WPF was nearly ten years old, it was seeing more than 1,500 clients yearly,[29] a massive increase from the initial 12 full-time trainees in 1972. The American Foundation was impressed at WPF's evident success, which it felt was due in part to Bill's courage.[30] For Bill, the future could only be positive. 'There's money out there,' he would say. 'I believe in what we're doing. So why shouldn't we get it?'[31]

Bill, the engineer, realized besides attracting competent analysts and counsellors, many of them Jungians, he needed an experienced Council of Management, especially when seeking government support. Initially Lord Rank provided £3,000 for each of three years and, when WPF had a track record, Sir Bernard Cocks, Clerk to the House of Commons, who chaired the Council, helped it gain access to government funding. Successive Speakers, all Methodists – Selwyn Lloyd, Horace King, and George Thomas – became presidents, followed by Bernard Weatherhill, who stayed on when Betty Boothroyd did not wish to undertake the role. Lord Alderdice, Speaker of the Northern Ireland Assembly, followed him.

After Peggy Kelsey, Bill's secretary, the first person to join him was Beryl Mason from his Sanderstead congregation. Before her marriage, she had been a secretary in the Commonwealth Relations Office and in due course became Head of a WPF Department. Over three decades, until 1992, her input under three directors brought administrative stability and continuity.[32] She was one of several talented women whom

Bill attracted whose contributions he valued. Increasingly, women held senior posts and in 2002 Lesley Murdin and Val Porter succeeded Tim Woolmer, who had been WPF's first non-clerical director. An educationalist, qualified group analyst and strategic thinker, he was of great use when the Foundation had funding difficulties in the 1990s climate. Difficult decisions had to be made that involved closing one specialist department, while retaining its expertise elsewhere. This decision helped WPF to survive financially as it learned to become more self-supporting.

Bill was especially glad to have Benita on the staff almost from the start, using her professional skills in psychological assessment. 'We were a double act with different roles,' she has remarked.[33] It was clear also that because their marriage was built on shared interests, Bill had a home security, with Benita more sensitive to music and the arts, though Bill grew to appreciate music too. Sometimes, Benita has remembered, after a difficult day, he would listen to classical music 'and that restored him'.[34] He evolved theologically too, always being open to new and radical thinking and was influenced by books like *Honest to God* and *The Myth of God Incarnate*.[35]

Bill often maintained 'the most important thing is for this show to go on'. If it meant he must adapt he would, provided that what emerged 'conforms to our ethos'.[36] The British–American mixture in him – he often ended encounters with 'take care', then put an arm round the person he was leaving – combined with a streak of ruthless determination to succeed, did, however, cause some ambivalence in the reactions of others to him. 'He could be very manipulative and seductive,' David Black has written, and 'his insistence on doing things "personally" gave rise to a lot of difficulty when he had to deal with a large and quite often sophisticated staff' – an aspect that colleagues noticed when they tried, not always successfully, to conceal anger and irritation because they felt Bill had acted in a dictatorial way, without due consultation.[37]

Yet the prayer Bill wrote for WPF shows his understanding of what it meant to be human. 'The world which is our home,' he suggested, 'is a place of light and dark, sunshine and shadow, laughter and crying, gaiety and drabness, a cradle of innocence, a mountain of glory, a hill of anguish, a cross of agony, a tomb of death and a garden of life.' He asked people to 'deal with each moment – to see meaning in grief as well as in ecstasy – to find a deeper sympathy and tolerance through suffering' and 'to enshrine an eternity of joy in a brief encounter'.[38]

But what did Bill Kyle mean by 'counselling'? Today used frequently – even in news bulletins after major disasters in relation to the victims – in the 1970s it found formal expression in the Association of Pastoral Care and Counselling (APCC), which Bill chaired. For him, the word was rooted in the Christian tradition and implied support for the emotional needs of congregations he served that were not being met. As Denis Duncan, who from January 1972 was for 11 years WPF's associate director and first training director, has written, Bill 'always insisted that the binding element in his counselling organisations was the spiritual dimension'.[39] From the start there were two dimensions as Bill encouraged multi-faith participation, which included a Jewish ingredient. Significantly, at WPF's Twenty-first Anniversary Service in Westminster Abbey in May 1991, Rabbi Hugo Gryn gave the address. Initially Bill also wanted to provide in-service training for clergy. However, the demand by lay people for further training and professional qualifications in counselling and psychotherapy overtook the main initial thrust of the Foundation, which soon became highly sophisticated. It also became clear that support from the institutional Churches was minimal and that increasingly WPF must rely on grants and support from referrals and others sources.[40]

There were, too, conflicts involving employees. 'My impression was of considerable liking but professional mistrust among staff,' David Black has commented,[41] adding 'this could hardly be otherwise.[42] Psychotherapy is a profession which engages the passionate concern of its practitioners, emotions are involved both of a parental kind, towards students and clients, and of infantile kind, towards one's own trainers and one's own training therapist.'[43]

Whatever Bill's hopes for WPF's future, they were dashed in 1977 when Central Hall authorities dropped a bombshell. They needed the premises for office space for the Methodist headquarters staff also working in the building, they maintained, and set July as the date for WPF's departure. Underlying the situation, it emerged, was an irreconcilable disagreement between Dr Maurice Barnett, the Central Hall's superintendent, and Bill, whose theologies had grown distinctly apart. 'Drs Kyle and Barnett had differing views of what ministry ought to be,' Dr Greet has observed, 'and neither was able to accommodate the other.'[44] There seemed, too, some duplicity, for it became clear that Methodist authorities had not 'directed' developments as indicated in an earlier letter to Bill. Bill felt betrayed, but with Lord Rank's death in 1972 there was no final way of confirming details of his agreements with the Central Hall. However, in March 1977 a new path was opening up, when Sister Gabriel, a member of the Sisters of the Assumption in Kensington Square, who had been on a WPF course, told her Superior of Bill's need for new premises, who suggested they took the space recently vacated by their teacher training college, which had closed. By September 1978, its entire work had been transferred to Kensington.

Stimulated by an address from Benita, the Croydon Council of Churches created one of the first Counselling Centres along WPF lines, which still operates. Another such venture was in East London. 'I was involved in East Ham to extend Bill Kyle's ministry of Pastoral Counselling there,' Rowland Joiner has written. 'I had been trained as a counsellor by the Marriage Guidance Council. When a new minister arrived at Barking Central Hall with an interest in counselling, we managed to open the Barking Counselling Centre with the assistance of Bill.'[45] Other centres emerged elsewhere, so by 1990, 18 were affiliated, some with satellite groups attached to them.

The Foundation was hardly settled in Kensington when another crisis hit it with the death of its founder. Bill seemed to have an inkling of this when he told Beryl Mason that he did not think he would see old age.[46] Indeed, he had just put in place co-ordinators to oversee the counselling service, affiliates, the administration and the training. The four people involved had been meeting with him regularly to share insights and pool needs.[47] The Revd Edwin Robertson too, a Baptist minister who had been involved with WPF from its early days and who latterly gave courses in ontology, felt Bill was consciously 'setting his lands in order'. He was particularly impressed with Bill's acceptance even 'that it was the right time'.[48]

At 3 a.m. on 16 January 1980, Bill suffered a cerebral haemorrhage and never fully regained consciousness. By 5.30 p.m. on 28 March he had died. He was 54.[49] Benita received some 1,000 letters, such was the shock and grief experienced. Some felt the pressures Bill had been enduring – especially a growing desire for more adequate professionalization and accreditation, with procedures in place to keep up with ongoing developments – had contributed to his death, but of course it was never possible to know for sure.

Now the four co-ordinators had to manage WPF maturely with little time for their own grief because the Foundation's tenth anniversary was scheduled for 21 May at which Benita was to preach, and there were to be major speeches by Sir George Young, then Under-Secretary at the DHSS, and Dr Edward Thornton, Professor of Psychology and Religion at a Baptist Seminary in Kentucky, who had worked with Bill in 1978. 'The future is yours who are gathered here tonight,' he concluded his address. 'The era of the sons and daughters has begun.'[50] It was a helpful remark for people like Bill's brother-in-law, Mervyn Phillips, who chaired the Council of Management.[51]

As WPF developed, a pyramidical training structure emerged, each stage building on the last, but involving fewer students. At entry level there were some 300 in skills training, which could be helpful for everyday work situations. Students completing this, or its equivalent, could apply for training as counsellors, either full-time or on day-release, which took a further number of years. These entered therapy at least weekly, gaining a Diploma and Counsellor-Membership of the then-named Institute of Psychotherapy and Counselling, the professional body of graduates from WPF training.

A small number of counsellors applied for further training in psychotherapy, involving two years or more, part-time personal therapy three times weekly, and seeing clients twice-weekly. They then became psychotherapy members of the Institute. Concurrently, qualifications were offered for specialized training in group therapy, family therapy and supervision.[52] In addition, a Certificate of Competence in Counselling was awarded in the Affiliate network.[53]

When its twenty-first anniversary was due, WPF was clearly held in high professional esteem by those in the health service, consultants and GPs, the social services, and managers in the business world who were responsible for staff welfare.[54] Much of the period had been presided over by Canon Derek Blows, who had known Bill when he was chaplain at Warlingham Park Psychiatric Hospital and Bill was part-time Free Church chaplain. Derek, formerly director of Pastoral Care and Counselling in the Southwark Diocese of the Church of England, had trained as an analyst with the Society of Analytical Psychology. Well able to reflect on basic questions and assumptions, he now saw clearly that the opening up of WPF to lay people, and ultimately not requiring any disclosure of religious convictions, had taken the Foundation beyond Bill's original intentions.

Derek understood, too, that the 'pastoral-clinical' debate, which had raged in the WPF for some years, was founded on a misapprehension, because the word pastoral related 'strictly to a liturgical community and in a community context'. Since this was not the way that WPF counsellors saw clients, they were not therefore doing pastoral counselling, he concluded.[55] Moreover, because initially training had been full-time, clergy and others had not easily been able to attend.[56] Thus the boundaries needed clarification in many different areas. This led to the departure of some staff not working within an agreed methodology, either Jungian or Freudian, a policy implemented with the help of a panel of therapy advisers. Derek Blows also introduced two Freudian psychoanalysts, whose contribution helped to broaden the analytical base of WPF training beyond the Jungian, which hitherto had become predominant. He did, though, seek to retain the commitment that no one would be refused help through the inability to afford fees, though this was now modified, with clients being asked to contribute as they could. He also ensured a seminar on ontology was available in which students were encouraged to explore belief systems and how they affected their understanding. This was extended into a trainee's final year and was compulsory.[57]

Derek's leadership was strongly delegatory. Attention was paid not only to types of analytic help on offer, but also management structure, especially how to disentangle the different functions of managers and professional counsellors. Derek co-operated well with Benita, who was still responsible for assessment. She remained loyal to her husband's vision and 'what he stood for',[58] as a member of the Council of Management giving talks about WPF's work. It cannot have been easy for Derek or Benita, but their relationship became mutually appreciative and supportive.[59]

Though her role changed, Benita felt Derek handled her 11 years with him well, 'custodian' though she was of the early years, though some questioned how best to remember the past creatively. Yet as Derek Blows has intimated, Benita stood for the human face of WPF, which could be lost in its clinical and professional approach. For her part, though Benita disagreed over some methods of evaluation,[60] she recognized that her husband, had he lived, would need to 'let go' if WPF were to grow. She understood too its inevitable secularization, for the Foundation relied on public funding that would only continue if, once trainees began to work, they joined the health and social service arenas.

Derek's stress on boundaries meant other approaches – Transactional Analysis, Gestalt, Psycho-synthesis, Behavioural Therapy, Hypnotherapy, for example – could be confusing for trainees. Thus if affiliates wanted to practise them, they had to disaffiliate. But this emphasis on psychodynamic theory and practice did not preclude workshops, in 2004–05, on eating disorders, sexual identity, working with the abused partner, and effective group work.

At the structural level, one new initiative was Counselling in Companies, created by Derek and a colleague; this became a separate unit within WPF. It made available help for stressed employees and generated income for the Foundation's core work, which in 2003 alone meant 1,100 used its psychotherapy services, involving 140 counsellors and over 20,000 hours of counselling, either with individuals or groups.

Like many professional caring groups, WPF tries to balance its funding sources – earned income, statutory funding, grants and donations – which helps it to maintain stability if one source declines. It also seeks to hold six months' operating costs in reserve for fulfilling contractual commitments, obligations to clients, and responsibilities to employees. Such a complex operation is naturally stabilized by the commitment of paid and voluntary staff, who have seen, through the vision of one man, the creation of one of the largest organizations for affordable counselling and therapy in Britain.

Despite its growth, however, WPF has remained firmly rooted in the south and south-west of England, as have the affiliates and the 600 or so

Stepney Central Hall, built on the site of Stepney Temple, the former Seaman's Mission Chapel in Commercial Road, E1. © Geoffrey Ridgway. (See pages 21 and 26.)

Southfields Central Hall, Wandsworth, drawn a few days before its demolition. Used by permission of Hilda Marsh. (See pages 120 and 123.)

The Revd Thomas Bowman Stephenson with three of his companions at the start of the National Children's Home, founded as The Children's Home in 1869. (See page 80.)

The Rt Hon. John Smith, MP, Leader of the Labour Party, presenting the outgoing Chairman of the Christian Socialist Movement, Peter Dawe, with a gift after Mr Smith's R. H. Tawney Lecture at Bloomsbury Baptist Church, WC1, March 1993. (See page 183.)

The headquarters of the Revd Thomas Jackson's Working Lads' Institute in Whitechapel in the 1920s. (See page 19.)

The Revd Thomas Jackson.

The Revd Thomas Tiplady and Mr Len Bradbrook at the Sunday Evening Children's Service in the Spencer Hall, Lambeth Mission, early 1930s. (See pages 22–3.)

Hilda Porter, MBE, with residents of
Methodist International House, Paddington, W2,
in the 1950s. (See pages 133–5.)

Hilda Porter explains
hospitality arrangements to
a student who has just arrived.

Students in one year at Methodist International House, set up by the
Lambeth Mission in 1968. (See pages 138–9.)

Pauline Webb and David Haslam (far right) at
an anti-apartheid protest outside South Africa
House, Trafalgar Square, to demand justice
for Cedric Mayson, a Methodist minister held
without trial in South Africa. Early 1980s.
(See pages 189 ff.)

Lord Soper at Hyde
Park, mid-1990s.
© Lilly Massicott.

A Petition of Distress from the Cities presented to the
Queen on 21 April 1993 by Baroness Richardson,
Methodist Conference President, and the Revd Dr
John Vincent and Tony Holden. (See pages 6–7.)

Clublanders welcome Hollywood actor Bob Hope, 5 May 1951. (See page 65.)

The Revd Vic Watson at the Tenth Anniversary Thanksgiving Service for the Ghana Fellowship at Clubland, 11 July 1999. (See page 69.)

Clubland, Georgetown, Guyana, 1952. Courtesy of the Revd Deryck U. Adams. (See page 160.)

Sybil Phoenix, MBE, a former Georgetown Clubland member, with HRH The Prince of Wales, during his first visit to Moonshot Youth Club. © South London Press. (See page 205.)

Westminster Central Hall with the flags of the nations displayed for the first meeting of the United Nations' General Assembly, January 1946.

Prime Minister Clement Attlee addressing the General Assembly of the United Nations in the Great Hall of Westminster Central Hall, 11 January 1946.

The Secretary-General of the United Nations, Dr Boutros Boutros-Ghali addresses the audience at an evening of commemoration on 10 January 1996, the fiftieth anniversary of the founding of the United Nations.

Photos used by courtesy of Archivist, Westminster Central Hall.
(See pages 127–8.)

The Revd Reg Bedford with guest celebrities Cleo Laine and Johnny Dankworth in the London Weekend event in the Royal Albert Hall, 1959. © E. N. Smith. (See page 144.)

Methodists from across Britain in Trafalgar Square during the 1982 London Weekend. © Tim Humphrey. (See page 145.)

Guy Chester at Chester House with the Muswell Hill Youth Club hosting Weelsby Road, Grimsby, Youth Club during London Weekend 1958. Guy Chester is front row in the centre. © E. N. Smith. Courtesy of MAYC. (See page 140.)

The Revd Graham Kent, minister of Railton Road Methodist Church at the time of the Brixton riots, 1981, outside the church which was one of the Ten Youth and Community Centres inspired by Terry Walton of London MAYC. (See page 168.)

The Dean of St Paul's, the Very Revd Alan Webster, welcoming visitors to the 1979 opening of London Entertains on the steps of St Paul's. (See page 211.)

Cypriot Dancers at London Entertains lunchtime opening in the 1980s.

JULY 22-23

جشن لندن. Festival de Londres የሉንዶን በሷል ፐፕንቱ ጋርደን

लंदन में मनोरंजन Celebran con Londres لندن تسلیے

Ceád Míle Fáilte লন্ডন উ সবে ডাকে Londyn zabawia

倫敦文娛總滙 Londres recebe זינדאָ מ ין דרן ת

Eku Odun o! ロンドンはあなたを歓迎します London yawafurahisha

Londra si diverte ΤΟ ΛΟΝΔΙΝΟ ΣΑΣ ΔΙΛΣΚΕΔΑΖΒΙ London szórakoztat

LONDON ENTERTAINS

A festival of many cultures at covered sites in and around
COVENT GARDEN PIAZZA W.C.2

Chinese musicians, Black drama groups, African drumming. Irish, Spanish, Central and Eastern European dancing. Caribbean, Indian, Irish and Latin American folk music Pearly Kings and Queens. Clowns. Mediterranean and Middle Eastern dramatic poetry and Choirs

FOOD ARTS & CRAFTS FROM MANY NATIONALITIES

JUBILEE MARKET

11am till dusk

Programmes available on the day

Nearest tube, Leicester Sq., Embankment

For further information write to The Organiser, 3/35 Buckingham Gate, London S.W.1

The first London Entertains poster, 1978. (See page 211.)

trained members of the Institute, now called the Association of WPF Graduates. Perhaps this is because of economic or cultural reasons, with a more supportive family system still in place in the north of England and less money available for the rigorous training necessary. Some argue it is the distance from London that inhibits growth, yet an attempt to establish a significant presence in Leeds, with surrounding satellites, despite dynamic leadership from Paul Keeble, a former Baptist minister, developed only in a partial way.[61]

WPF has a further potential tension to manage. With the decline of Christian belief in Western societies, and the shrinking of the churches as significant forces in society, many have turned to psychotherapy to find meaning. Such people do not necessarily come from faith communities. Yet with the growing multicultural nature of WPF's staff, and the arrival of Muslims seeking training (if currently only small in number), could faith matters become centre stage again? Together with more affordable short-term courses, which are in great demand, and a more diverse approach to different groups, like the over-60s and the under-25s, WPF may find a new pattern emerging.

What is clear is that WPF has, as Tim Woolmer has explained, 'burst out beyond the banks of the churches, beyond the concept of the pastoral, to enter a field of what was called "depth psychology" and gradually settle down as counselling and psychotherapy, more particularly of the psycho-dynamic variety'.[62] It is this approach that gives WPF its distinctive identity.

Notes

1 Beryl Mason, interview with author, 5 January 2005.
2 David Black, *A Place of Exploration, The Story of Westminster Pastoral Foundation 1969–1990*, WPF, 1991, p. 8.
3 Black, *Place*, p. 9.
4 Black, *Place*, p. 9.
5 Benita Kyle, interview with author, 18 October 2004.
6 The Revd Colin Rowe, letter to author, 25 October 2004.
7 *Kentish Town Mercury*, October 1960.
8 See W. Kyle, *Healing Through Counselling*, Peterborough, Epworth Press, 1964.
9 William Kyle, *Methodist Recorder*, 7 March 1963.
10 John 10.10.
11 London Mission Report 1964, p. 27.
12 The Revd Denis Duncan, *The Road Taken*, Ecclesia Services, 1997, p. 94.
13 Duncan, *The Road Taken*, p. 95.
14 London, SCM Press, 1931.
15 London, Hodder & Stoughton 1951, revised 1955.

16 *WPF Quarterly*, spring 1976.
17 The Revd Dr Leslie Weatherhead, Foreword to Kyle, *Healing Through Counselling*.
18 Black, *Place*, p. 6.
19 Black, *Place*, p. 6.
20 Black, *Place*, p. 6.
21 Black, *Place*, p. 7.
22 Benita Kyle, interview.
23 Benita Kyle, interview.
24 Benita Kyle, interview.
25 Benita Kyle, interview.
26 Benita Kyle, interview.
27 WPF Archives, Book 1 1969–80, summer 1971 Newsletter.
28 Black, *Place*, p. 30.
29 WPF Archive, Book 1.
30 Director of Training, American Foundation, in Benita Kyle, personal files.
31 Benita Kyle, interview.
32 Black, *Place*, p. 20.
33 Benita Kyle, interview, 8 June 2005.
34 Benita Kyle, interview, 18 October 2005.
35 Benita Kyle, interview, 8 June 2005.
36 Benita Kyle, interview, 18 October 2004.
37 Black, *Place*, pp. 7–8, 55–6.
38 *WPF Quarterly*, no. 13, spring 1980, p. 23.
39 Denis Duncan, *The Road Taken*, p. 97.
40 See WPF Archive, Book 1.
41 Denis Duncan, *The Road Taken*, p. 99, quoting Black, *Place*, p. 58.
42 Black, *Place*, p. 58.
43 Denis Duncan, *The Road Taken*, pp. 98–9, quoting Black, *Place*, p. 40.
44 The Revd Dr Kenneth Greet, interview with author, 11 November 2004.
45 The Revd Rowland Joiner, letter to author, November 2004.
46 Beryl Mason, interview.
47 Black, *Place*, p. 59.
48 Black, *Place*, p. 59.
49 Black, *Place*, p. 60.
50 *WPF Quarterly*, p. 10.
51 *WPF Quarterly*, pp. 3–4.
52 Black, *Place*, p. 88.
53 Black, *Place*, p. 89.
54 WPF Archive, Book 1.
55 Canon Derek Blows, interview with author, 30 November 2004.
56 Black, *Place*, p. 94.
57 Black, *Place*, p. 95.
58 Blows, interview with author.
59 Canon Derek Blows, letter with attached note, 7 April 2005.
60 Benita Kyle, interview, 18 October 2004.
61 Blows, interview with author.
62 Chris Roles and Tim Woolmer, Introduction to Strategic Conclusions, *WPF Strategic Review 1990s*.

Part 3

Community Builders

Introduction by Stuart Jordan

Each of the ventures described in Part 2 were responses to the issues of a particular time, and some have proven more adaptable than others to changing circumstances. The extent of their far-reaching impact on the many people they involved and influenced, however, is doubtless much more important than the survival of the original visions.

Whereas Part 2 focused on perennial social issues and the creation of long-term national agencies, this section records attempts to engage the Church with ever-shifting communities.

Joseph Rank used his personal resources and influence to encourage the building of Central Halls, which provided extensive facilities for the new forms of work and worship. They embodied a grandiose vision of the Church's significance in the community, though one that, with hindsight at least, often outstripped the evidence. Despite the business acumen that built retail units – and hence future income – into the model, the demise of the halls shows how inflexible they proved to be as buildings unless, as with the rare exception of Westminster Central Hall, they were able to translate their size and central location into major assets.

Buildings were also central to Hilda Porter's desire to provide residential accommodation for overseas students – though the Bayswater Methodist International House was far from purpose-built! The international community created there, as in the other hostels, offered a powerful lived experience for its residents with potentially far-reaching repercussions. In time, the ethos of the work inevitably changed, however, not least as a result of public policies on overseas students' fees and of subsequent developments in the nature of higher education institutions. Despite the improved facilities now on offer, student community itself is much harder to build, even in residential settings.

The annual Methodist Association of Youth Club (MAYC) Weekend impacted not only on its participants, but also on many local London churches which opened their halls to provide accommodation for groups of teenagers – and, momentarily, on central London itself, as the teenagers' green and yellow scarves swirled along its streets. At a local level, youth work proved increasingly difficult to sustain as youth culture began to fragment, formal youth service provision decreased, and the churches themselves found it more and more difficult to involve young people in its core activities. Meanwhile, the experience of fragmentation and alienation was even more evident for all age-groups on London's estates, where the need for community building – and the challenges to the churches – has always been at its greatest.

Within that wider context, the Ten Centre youth and community project was an ambitious attempt to offer a new model. Its very scale required a major investment in premises, staffing, training and hence statutory partnerships: all of which created complexities. For a variety of reasons, few of the original centres have managed to sustain significant youth and community work into the twenty-first century. Where it has been possible, it has been assisted by the adoption of community development values and collaborative models (working *with* rather than *for* others). Certainly that was a major contribution of AVEC, an agency that has mediated the insights of secular disciplines and fostered skills in action-reflection that have facilitated many practitioners in their own ministries as community-builders.

8

As Unchurchlike as Possible
Joseph Rank and Central Halls

Joseph Rank, the multi-millionaire miller from Hull, was born in 1854. His mother died when he was four and his father remarried. As a young boy, he was put to work in the mill and given menial tasks such as mending bags and sweeping floors and then 'grinding, packing and the dressing of old millstones'.[1] When in 1874 his father also died, leaving his property to two uncles, both of whom had married his sisters, Joseph Rank felt abandoned. Such was his determination to succeed, however, he was loaned a mill and began working it alone, grinding the wheat, collecting the flour in sacks, then canvassing for orders and delivering them himself. Within 30 years he owned his own business, which became the largest personal investment in flour milling in the world.[2]

By 1880 Joseph Rank had married Emily Voase, a local farmer's daughter he had met while buying grain.[3] They were to have three sons, James, Arthur and Roland, and four daughters. A happy marriage was important for Joseph, and when his wife died in 1916, two years later he married her sister, Annie,[4] who was to pre-decease him by only three years. 'We must both be thankful,' he once wrote to Ensor Walters, when they were working together on the London Committee in the 1930s, 'that we have good wives to look after us, this is helpful in many ways.'[5]

Increasingly the Ranks became interested in Christianity, reading the Bible together, and holding family prayers. They worshipped in their parish church until a vicar's sermon on pre-destination revolted them and they began attending the local Methodist chapel. At one particular service, Rank was converted during the singing of a Sankey hymn. From then until his death in 1943, religion was an overriding passion, but of a straightforward kind that would brook no complexity. Indeed his ire was raised when in the 1930s the Methodist Sacramental Fellowship was being formed and he let rip in a letter to Ensor Walters, maintaining 'No minister holding alliance with this new movement should be allowed to remain a member of the Methodist Conference.'[6]

At the height of his fame as one of Britain's richest people Joseph was offered a title, but he refused – saying, 'I'm Joe Rank and everybody knows me as I am',[7] an indication of his lack of pomposity and his individuality, soon to be expressed in his commitment to the movement for Central Halls, part of Wesleyan Methodism's attempt to reach the unchurched urban masses.

The Rank family moved to London in 1904, settling in Tooting. On his first Sunday, Joseph walked over Tooting Common and offered assistance in the Sunday School at Upper Tooting. Told there was no vacancy, he said he would teach the naughtiest boys, which he soon did, making his class one of the best.[8] One Sunday morning he overheard a communist orator at Tooting Broadway, which was then a mini Speaker's Corner, mocking Christianity and espousing materialism. Rank knew instinctively the Upper Tooting services, with their modified Anglican liturgy (which his friend there, Sir Henry Holloway, loved), would never reach working people as the orator could. So Rank decided on the spot that a Central Hall must be built at Tooting Broadway to attract people who otherwise might be over-influenced by political agitators.[9]

Once he was determined, there was no stopping him. He soon mobilized, even from his own family, a group to establish the Hall. Here Christ would be offered in a building without pew rents and no overawing aspect like liturgical worship. It was a time when the Music Hall was still drawing large crowds because of its conviviality and the Central Hall movement 'followed from the Music Hall experience,' Peter Graves has explained. 'Now the equivalent would be TV ministries.'[10] Here people could sing popular hymns and songs, often with catchy tunes; hear preachers who were part actors, part prophets, and evangelists as well; and be in a friendly atmosphere. They were, as a later Secretary of the London Mission Committee, Dr Irvonwy Morgan, has said, 'open air meetings with the roof on'.

'Central Halls,' David Driver has written, 'were built to look as unchurchlike as possible, both from the outside and from within.'[11] 'They quickly developed,' George Sails has added, 'a programme of religion and rescue work. It tried to help the masses in their poverty, disease and unemployment, and those converted to resist the temptation to return to their former ways of life.'[12] For some, it totally encompassed their lives. 'I love every stick and stone of the Central Hall,' said one adherent at Barking. 'I went there when I was a child, all my evenings were spent there when I was in my teens, all my interests outside the home were there, I found my husband there, all my friends are there.'[13]

It is easy to see why Joseph Rank, a practical man who liked results, seized on the Central Hall phenomenon and backed it with his wealth, especially when Methodist work, which had begun in Tooting in 1885, by 1910 became focused on its new Hall, for which he had given most of the £33,000 needed to build it.[14] As he sat down after his first speech as its treasurer, he turned to Simpson Johnson, his minister from Hull, and said: 'But for this man this hall might never have been built; for it was he who led me out of darkness into light.'[15] Soon he saw the returns he expected as hundreds worshipped there regularly on Sunday evenings, most of them working men and their families.[16] Besides a choir of 120, there was also a Brass Band for Saturday afternoon films at 1*d.* a time. In 1911 Katherine Price Hughes addressed the Women's Hour, which at one point had 700 members. A crèche, a drapery club, second-hand clothes store, savings bank and a coal club were also created. The Sunday afternoon Brotherhood attracted some 1,000 men, entertained by an orchestra and edified by famous speakers.

At its height, Central Hall laity visited 10,000 homes and there was a thriving Wesley Guild, as in many other London congregations, which helped them grow in their faith. Philanthropic activity included annual Boxing Day dinners for 1,000 poor children, and during World War One, there was one hall that had a soup kitchen and another an air raid shelter. Even the Band of Hope, which aimed for total abstinence from alcohol, was successful, while special visitors like Gipsy Smith and William Booth's daughter, Catherine, known as La Maréchale, heightened overall commitments.[17]

Joseph Rank now became Superintendent of a large Sunday School, gathering round him teachers as single-minded as himself. Even when he went to live in Tadworth, he drove to Tooting each Sunday, stayed after morning Sunday School in the vestry and ate a frugal meal, then – before its afternoon session – visited absent pupils in their homes.[18] They, like his work colleagues, knew Rank could be trusted, though they smiled at his thrift, once even refusing to buy a morning paper because its price had just increased![19] His Sunday School class especially liked the visit he arranged to his Silvertown milling complex in East London's dockland.[20]

With Joseph Rank's support, the London Mission Committee helped to build Central Halls in Archway, Barking, Becontree, Bethnal Green, Bromley, Dagenham, Deptford, East and West Ham, Greenwich, Hackney, Islington, Lower Edmonton, Plumstead, St Helier, Stratford, Stepney, Uxbridge, West Drayton and Yiewsley – though Bermondsey and Westminster Central Halls were earlier. The King's Hall in Southall and Springfield Hall in the Wandsworth Road, established by Sir Henry Holloway, were Central Halls in all but name. So was the most famous one, Kingsway Hall, opened in 1912. Donald Soper, however, who had run the Islington Central Hall, took a somewhat different approach at

Kingsway, especially in worship, which for him always focused on the regular celebration of the Eucharist. Between 1919 and 1939, when many of these developments occurred, the London Committee, convened by Ensor Walters, sanctioned nearly £2 million on extension and reconstruction sites, which included 17 Central Halls and numerous other buildings. Between 1930 and 1939, Joseph Rank gave £330,000 towards this amount.[21] By 1942, however, he had given up involvement in his benevolent funds, and put them into the hands of trustees, who were to run a Joseph Rank Benevolent Trust.

Joseph Rank regularly gave £50,000 from his Special Gifts Account, as he and Ensor Walters met either at his office or at the Central Hall, Westminster to apportion it. He always insisted on anonymity. 'I would like to emphasize that one of the reasons for dealing with the money in this way,' he reiterated, 'is to prevent as far as possible my name appearing in connection with any of the schemes.'[22] Sometimes they would visit projects, and often Rank would match £1 raised with £1 from his funds. He could, however, be very rigid on his visits. As Jimmy Butterworth made plans to build Clubland, Rank visited him and offered £30,000 if he would build a Central Hall. Butterworth declined, but Rank suggested he sleep on the offer. A short while later he returned, the cheque in his hands. Again Butterworth declined and Rank went away. Butterworth went away, too, and cried. Had he done the right thing, he asked himself? Some years later, when Clubland was ruined by a German bomb, Rank made another visit, saying the Holy Spirit had sent him. 'It takes the Holy Spirit a long time to get through to you,' Butterworth quipped.[23]

Deaconess Gwendolen Marsh remembers another incident concerning money for a Central Hall in Southfields when local Methodists wanted something different. Because of Rank's offer, however, in 1924 they built a Central Hall that cost £40,000, with 1,000 seats, as Rank had stipulated.[24] Like its counterpart in Tooting, Rank felt justified when it was soon full and remained that way until 1939.

It was, of course, a period with no television and few cars for outings, yet people still sought companionship. Central Hall Saturday night events met this need. 'Elsie and Doris Waters always drew a crowd,' Gwendolen's sister, Hilda, has reminisced. 'So did Arthur Askey who arrived on his bike.' After his Southfields slot, he would cycle to Tooting, do a similar act after the interval, then cycle back to Southfields for a second appearance 'towards the close of the concert'.[25]

As at Tooting, the Sunday School was over 1,000 and its Superintendent knew every pupil by name. On Saturdays children would queue for two films and *Pathé News*, organized by A. E. Binks, the minister. Binks was used to preaching to over 1,000 regularly, his sermons helping the congregation to grow spiritually. Despite this success, however, by 1939 membership began to decline, as in many other Central Halls. During World War Two, Southfields was requisitioned as a Rest Centre, sheltering 600 blitzed from their homes, who brought with them their dogs, cats and birds. In the evenings, young people took food and drinks to people in over 100 air raid shelters, from Wimbledon to Barnes Common.[26] Similar shelters existed in the basement of Westminster Central Hall, where Dr Sangster organized cinema presentations, and at Kingsway Hall where breakfast canteen facilities were available for those in the all-night shelters in the nearby tube.

Tooting was partly damaged by the bombs and Greenwich had to be re-built. Barking Central Hall was totally destroyed, but not before it had been used to house European refugees. A direct hit ruined Stepney Central Hall, and Deptford Central Hall, which had earlier pioneered significant work with disability, fared no better. Here many were buried and killed beneath its ruins after another direct hit. Bermondsey Central Hall, however, which was reinforced and housed 800 daily, survived the worst air raids.[27]

Joseph Rank was not immune to the pains of the London experience of the blitz and also knew that his mills in Hull were destroyed in an air raid, making a special visit to the city to view the wreckage.[28] But he knew his life was ending so, when told in 1941 that war damage to Methodist property in London was estimated at £1.5 million, he replied: 'It will be a matter for the Trustees of my Benevolent Fund,'[29] and by the next June had ceased to be involved in disbursing monies. As he looked back he could recall the evening he chaired the initial meeting in the King's Hall, Southall, the only building that Methodism – with Rank's help – opened during World War One. He could recall, too, the opening meeting at Archway in February 1932, and presiding over the London Mission Rally, introducing Lax of Poplar, Ira Goldhawk from Kingsway Hall and Isaac Foot, then Parliamentary Secretary for Mines.

Rank knew the work that he and C. Ensor Walters had done from 1919 till Walters's death in 1938 had been significant, though Walters was very different from Joseph Rank, as Bernard Shaw, who worked with him on the St Pancras Vestry, has written: 'When he let himself go the effect was startling,' Shaw remembered. 'His word was like a fire,'[30] adding, 'He has reached the earthly top without ever having condescended to climb a single step, by sheer gravitation of a noble spirit.'[31] Such was the impact on Shaw after reading the autobiography of the Labour MP Jack Lawson that he considered Methodism changed people for good. 'I very much doubt whether Shavianism would have been equally successful,' he quipped.[32]

With Joseph Rank's conviction that God had helped him to make money to use in God's service,[33] and Ensor Walters's care for 'the London nipper', one of whom, with only one arm, had stopped him in his tracks when he asked him to tie his bootlace as he rushed along,[34] they were a formidable partnership. Without doubt Rank was a convinced capitalist, espousing the law of the survival of the fittest when it came to business,[35] even admitting to colleagues he had been divinely guided towards a profit-making decision.[36] Yet he found 'as much real joy in handing out as I have ever found in raking in'.[37] For his part, Ensor Walters, 'Mr Great-Heart', as he was dubbed, 'with a good earpiece as well', as a Cockney friend once said,[38] agreed with Rank that the job of evangelism was important but knew also 'you must first minister to the body'.[39]

As they journeyed together, Ensor Walters found Rank was not as rigid as some supposed, which became evident when he disagreed with the proposal to demolish an entire building in Battersea in the process of acquisition and replace it with a Central Hall. Again, a minister at Harlesden was told that Rank preferred refurbishment rather than his architect's plan for a Central Hall there.[40] Joseph Rank would have disliked what happened to Central Halls after 1945, as did his son, J. Arthur Rank, when he became chairman of his father's Trust; but times change and, above all, Joseph Rank was a realist.

'After 1945 the day of the Central Hall was over,' Kenneth Greet has judged. 'Latterly Methodism has been left with huge and expensive properties which no longer fit the bill.'[41] 'The primary factor was dwindling congregations and rising costs,' Dr Brian Beck, who grew up Tooting Central Hall, has added, 'but theology entered into it. There was growing dissatisfaction with the ecclesiology involved, lack of liturgical depth and the sense of passivity and dependency generated in the worshippers. The period post-1945 has seen Methodist recovery of the sense of the church.'[42]

Tooting Central Hall came to recognize that the Welfare State made much former social work redundant, and the day of the great preacher was over. In 1966, therefore, it was sold to Marks and Spencer's and demolished. A new church was built on a nearby site where a different congregation emerged, replenished with men and women from the Caribbean, who had begun to live in the area from the late 1950s. They have produced a bustling, multiracial society with diverse ministries. A similar change occurred at Southfields, though it held its own until 1960. Donald McNeil, who at Upper Tooting had received such a response from the congregation after a sermon on humanitarian issues, set up the Fund for Human Need when, shortly afterwards, he became minister at Southfields. Over the ensuing years, the Fund gave grants to refugees and asylum seekers, foreign students in Panama, Addis Ababa and to Boy's Town, Kingston, Jamaica.

Youth work at Southfields was also adapted post-1945, and summer holiday play schemes and Christmas Day dinners for the lonely were sponsored. A branch of Amnesty International was formed, now known as the Merton Group. One minister was chaplain to a young offenders' detention centre which led to some congregational involvement there. Later, homeless people used some of the many rooms that peppered Southfields Central Hall who came there via a Trust for those sleeping rough. But the inevitable was never far away and in the 1980s the Hall was pulled down, much of the site sold, and a more modest church erected to serve the needs of a severely truncated congregation.

Joseph Rank's other interest, King's Hall, Southall, with its strong social passion – raising money for a children's hospital ward near Anlu in China in the 1920s; in the 1930s supporting miners from Wales coming to London to present a petition to the Prime Minister; decades later, via MAYC, raising £1,200 towards the cost of a hospital in the Ivory Coast[43] – changed when in the 1950s the area's social mix altered. Now people from India and Pakistan came to work first in the Southall rubber works, and then at Heathrow, and Christians of all traditions found themselves no longer a majority. Instead, Southall became a focus for Sikhs from across Britain who built their own Gudwaras and a Hindu Temple emerged on the site of a former Anglican church hall.

Today, the Methodist church finds itself with similar numbers to when it began in Southall in 1832. However, alongside its multiracial congregation, a Hindi-Urdu-speaking one has emerged, served at times by presbyters from the Church of Pakistan. On key festivals and occasions, these two groups meet up – but they are not easy to manage because of divergences in cultural responses. It is a far cry from Joseph Rank and his straightforward sense of mission and interpretation of the role of Christ in history.

Rank would be equally surprised at developments in Hackney and at Archway. In the 1960s, the Rank Trust thought Hackney Central Hall was a 'white elephant' and declined to fund its redevelopment. Latterly, however, after complex negotiations with Hackney Council, it has been sold, and an alternative site obtained in Mare Street for a new church with a growing multicultural congregation.

Archway, too, has had to undergo a death and resurrection experience, though it has been more stable financially because of the shops from which it draws a regular income. Once as successful under Charles Hulbert as Southall itself had been under his leadership, its post-war decline was only arrested by the arrival in 1968 of John Beech, who had worked in Ghana, a fact that attracted many Ghanaian members. Since then, Archway's congregation has been consolidated, though its main hall has been sold and another smaller one adapted for social use. More recently, a worship centre has been opened upstairs and the whole building made more disabled-friendly.

John Beech established youth projects at Archway, funded by Islington Council, which were jointly sponsored by churches and schools. Local police and parents were relieved as they saw the seasonal juvenile crime rate recede.[44] He also set up an after-school playgroup with the local Roman Catholics and invited a Pentecostal group to use the premises regularly. 'At Archway,' he commented, 'we cannot live by theological abstractions, and doctrinaire standards of success and failure would reduce us to neurosis in months. We simply attempt to respond intuitively and lovingly to each situation.'[45]

Archway Central Hall, the last to be built, has survived. So, too, has Bermondsey, the first to be erected in London. The year 1966 was the pivotal date in its history for it then underwent a complete makeover. What an earlier minister, Henry Meakin, had called 'a new departure in Methodist aggressive work in London',[46] was over. No doubt S. F. Collier, who had opened the first Central Hall in Manchester in 1886[47] and who with Hugh Price Hughes was present at Bermondsey's opening,[48] would have been sad to see the 2,000-seater Hall demolished, but times had changed drastically. Indeed, all that remained was a memory of the sacrifice of elderly women from the sweat shops, whose weekly farthings had bought the pulpit chair and the young factory girls whose similar gifts purchased the pulpit Bible.[49] Gone, too, were the crowded Saturday Nights for the People, but church members had the satisfaction of knowing in 1931 that so successful was their Child Welfare and Maternity section that Megan Lloyd George, youngest daughter of the former Prime Minister, had opened their Annexe.[50] They knew, also, thousands had been helped through free breakfasts and Christmas dinners, and horizons expanded through the Sisterhoods and Brotherhoods. So well-known was one minister, Roderick Kedward, that Bermondsey's streets were lined waiting for his cortège after the packed funeral service in the Hall, and 'men, women and little children wept unashamedly'.[51]

One post-war minister, Joseph Jones, caught the 1960s mood when he indicated there were still many 'old and lonely people and hundreds of teenagers' growing up in the area 'in an atmosphere of reconstruction and rehabilitation', as soaring blocks of flats replaced former bad housing, and as a bonus there were now more open spaces.[52] Since 1960, the Central Hall has provided 5,000 midday meals and distributed over 10,000 garments annually. But with only 147 members when the Hall was pulled down, its foyer was sufficient to become a chapel for worship and preaching. In its place, 20 flats for senior citizens and students were built and opened in January 1968 by the Bermondsey-born singer and actor Tommy Steele. Meanwhile, open air witness continued in East Street Market at a pitch shared with communist orators and members of the peace movement.

By 1984, a very active doctor's surgery hired some of the new rooms; another was used by the Royal Society for the Mentally Handicapped.[53] Yet still by 1988, food was distributed worth £10,000, including butter and beef from the EEC as well as the Hall's own food parcels.[54] In the late 1980s, another floor was built above the flats as the number of elderly residents declined and students from several countries took their places. With the growth of container traffic, Bermondsey life changed dramatically, too, and the local council, using a policy of letting property only to Bermondsey-born residents, found there were not enough, so invited applications from others. Thus, increasingly, West Africans and others moved into the area and the Central Hall found new life and energy.

During its centenary year, the 1960s chapel became an after-school playgroup and a former hall and dining area was refurbished for worship as the congregation, 250-strong in 2005, grew. Another room was refurbished, named after Scott Lidgett, and opened daily as a Pop-In for elderly people, and used also by a large branch of Alcoholics Anonymous. The MP Simon Hughes also has a constituency office at the Central Hall. Though Christmas food parcels are still needed, but not in large numbers, and the Scout Troop remains as a reminder of the Hall's long past, the focus of ministry has altered. It has changed too in the South London Mission itself, of which the Central Hall is the head, as the churches linked with it – Manor and Peckham – have sought new identities around their predominantly African-Carribean membership. The Peckham Church also includes a French-speaking Methodist congregation which meets there on Sunday afternoons.[55]

One Central Hall stands out uniquely. Opened in 1912 in place of the Royal Westminster Aquarium and Winter Gardens, which closed in 1903, Westminster Central Hall was bought for £300,000 with money raised by the Twentieth Century Fund for new work in Wesleyan Methodism. Parts were never finished through lack of money and there was no sinking fund, so there have been recurring financial troubles. More recently, however, lettings from major national enquiries have contributed to the availability of funds needed for a refurbishment scheme in excess of £6 million.[56]

Since 1912, the work of the Central Hall has had three dimensions. Until the 1990s, it was the headquarters of Methodism, the three main strands of which had come together in 1932.[57] It also housed a congregation that met in its Great Hall, and distinguished preachers – most notably Dr Dinsdale Young and Dr Edwin Sangster – drew large crowds. It fell to the latter on his first Sunday as minister to inform the congregation on 3 September 1939 that Britain was at war with Germany. Over the years, the congregation has waxed and waned, drawn to the city centre church for diverse reasons. Now over 300-strong, its lively multiracial life can be accommodated either in the renewed Great Hall or in the smaller chapel recently established in an area vacated by the Midland Bank who had been tenants since 1912.

The third strand of the Hall's life has been the diverse groups that have hired its facilities. The Great Hall itself was reopened in 2005 in time to host the Royal British Legion sixtieth anniversary concert commemorating the end of World War Two, attended by Queen Elizabeth and ambassadors from countries involved.[58] It followed on from her 2003 visit for the signing of the Anglican–Methodist Covenant, an event concluded in Westminster Abbey opposite.

As a very young girl, the Queen and her sister had attended Robert Mayer's Saturday concerts, which ran for many years in the Great Hall. Those concerts were part of the Hall's strong musical tradition which has included recordings by Isobel Baillie, the pianist Solomon,[59] the first European performance of Stravinsky's Ebony Concerto and also *Joseph and the Amazing Technicolor Dream Coat*,[60] one of whose composers, Andrew Lloyd Webber, is the son of a former Central Hall organist. Many leading politicians and activists have attended meetings or spoken there – from Lloyd George, Jo Grimond and Charles Kennedy, George Lansbury to Tony Blair, Harold Macmillan, Margaret Thatcher and Edward Heath, who regularly held his Christmas concert in the Great Hall. In July 1945 Clement Attlee went from Buckingham Palace on becoming Prime Minister to the Labour Party Victory Rally there.[61] In March, just before Hitler's demise, Winston Churchill addressed a Party Conference assuring Conservatives that 'Victory is certain, victory is certain.'[62]

On 10 November 1955 the Campaign Against Capital Punishment, initiated by Arthur Koestler, was launched in the Great Hall,[63] and on 17 February 1958 J. B. Priestley, Bertrand Russell and Canon John Collins, among others, launched the Campaign for Nuclear Disarmament.[64] In 1979 Fenner Brockway and Philip Noel-Baker held a convention for 2,500 prior to launching the World Disarmament Movement in the House of Commons. Speakers included Cardinal Hume and Donald Soper.[65] Sometimes significant press conferences have been staged, like one by Trevor Huddleston in 1956, shortly after his book, *Naught for Your Comfort*, was published.[66] Even more journalists, 400 in fact, turned up for the 1956 press gathering that concluded Marshal

Bulganin and Nikita Khrushchev's British visit. More recently, Mikhail Gorbachev has come twice – most recently in 1996 to launch his *Memoirs*.[67]

Celebrations have also occurred – for Indian Independence on 26 January 1950, and in 1968 to recall 1918, when the first 30 women gained the vote. It was attended by Prime Minister Harold Wilson, Margaret Thatcher, Shirley Williams, Edith Summerskill and Sybil Morrison, one of the original hunger-striker suffragettes, among others.[68] Why do people come for such events? Perhaps it is because the Central Hall lies in the parliamentary precinct and is seen, as Tony Benn once observed, as 'our Town Hall', but also because a group needs a higher profile, or a place that is 'neutral'.

Two of the most moving events confirming this happened in 1961 and 1988. In 1961 Martin Luther King was the key figure at a Christian Action gathering on racism. His poetic cadences, reiteration of phrases, passion for social justice and hope for humanity, shone that night,[69] yet despite his prescience he could not foresee that evening in March 1969 when his widow would stand there, with his two eldest children and Canon Collins, to launch the Martin Luther King Memorial Foundation, which opposed racism in Britain. In 1988, at the 'Remember for the Future' gathering, prior to an Oxford Conference on the theme, Elie Wiesel, Nobel Prize winner and holocaust survivor, addressed 1,600 from the Jewish community. Remembering the past gave the future 'a new lease of life, and humanity a new possibility of dignity,' he explained, proclaiming that never again would Jews tolerate oppression.[70]

Such events are small compared with the First United Nations General Assembly from 10 January to 14 February 1946. Few African nations were present as many were under colonial rule, but Muslim countries were well represented. 'The beautiful flowing robes and headgear of the keffiya and agal of the Saudi delegates harmonised with the delicate setting of the occasion,' one journalist wrote.[71] India, not yet independent, was present, though Gandhi, who had spoken at a temperance meeting in a small hall in 1931,[72] was not a delegate. At the Assembly were the Russian Andreis – Gromyko and Vyshinsky; and Eleanor Roosevelt and Adlai Stevenson from the USA, along with a young Peruvian delegate destined to become UN Secretary-General, Perez de Cuellar.

In 1946 all current UN structures were created – the Security Council itself, the International Court of Justice, the Economic and Social Council and the first Secretary-General appointed. 'A chapter in the history of the world has been written,' said Senator Tom Connally.[73] Some 50 years later, the then Secretary-General returned to attend celebrations and uncover a plaque above the one unveiled by Prime

Minister Attlee and Dr Sangster on 28 May 1946. In February 2006, the Central Hall hosted the sixtieth anniversary celebration of the General Assembly's first meeting, organized by the United Nations Association. At it, Secretary-General Kofi Annan addressed an audience of 1,500, including Britain's Foreign Secretary and many diplomats based in London, focusing on the successes and disappointments of the Autumn 2005 United Nations summit.[74]

Many other UN matters have been debated or remembered in the Great Hall, with Southern Africa and peace issues being high profile. Social workers, teachers, probation officers, police and railway men and women, home helps, miners, solicitors and health professionals of many hues, have also gathered to wrestle with diverse themes, sometimes lobbying Parliament. Two key ones have been equal pay for women and the problems of pensioners. Prominent among groups have been trade unionists, including Ernest Bevin, once his Transport and General Workers' Union was formed, who even had an office in the Central Hall before Transport House was built.[75]

Fast forward to post-millennium gatherings when the Central Hall played host to four significant events – the first Holocaust Day commemoration; 'Standing in Solidarity', a gathering after September 11th 2001 at which members of the world faith communities in London committed themselves to work together more closely; as they did again in 2005 when an analogous event after the 7 July bombings in Central London occurred. In 2004, the Dalai Lama lectured on world peace in the Great Hall, an event attended by the Prince of Wales.[76]

Joseph Rank could not have envisaged such gatherings when he attended meetings and chaired events there. Subsequent developments at Westminster Central Hall, however, represent Methodism's concern for the whole of society, secular, Christian, and other world faiths. Perhaps those who argue that it prevents the Church from becoming sectarian are right?

Notes

1 Joseph Rank, in R. G. Burnett, 'The Master Millers', reprinted from *Milling*, 2 September 1922, cited in Michael Wakelin, *J. Arthur Rank, The Man behind the Gong*, London, Lion, 1996, p. 16.

2 Wakelin, *J. Arthur Rank*, p. 17.

3 Wakelin, *J. Arthur Rank*, p. 17.

4 Wakelin, *J. Arthur Rank*, p. 17.

5 London Mission Files, Correspondence with Joseph Rank, 1920–43.

6 Joseph Rank to the Revd C. Ensor Walters, 25 June 1936, London Mission Files – Rank.

7 Wakelin, *J. Arthur Rank*, p. 93.

8 R. G. Burnett, *Through the Mill: The Life of Joseph Rank*, Peterborough, Epworth Press, 1945, p. 147.

9 Burnett, *Through the Mill*, p. 148.

10 The Revd Dr Peter Graves, interview with author, 13 August 2004.

11 The Revd David Driver, 'A distinctive spirituality in mission to the city', in *The Role of the City Centre Church*, Home Mission Division, June 1983, p. 13.

12 The Revd George Sails, *At the Centre*, the Story of Methodism's Central Missions, Home Mission Department, 1970, p. 11.

13 London Mission Report 1959, p. 38.

14 Burnett, *Through the Mill*, p. 50.

15 Burnett, *Through the Mill*, p. 151.

16 Burnett, *Through the Mill*, p. 150.

17 Tooting Central Hall, *Sixty Glorious Years*, 1910–1970, pp. 4–7.

18 Tooting Central Hall, *Sixty Glorious Years*, p. 4.

19 Burnett, *Through the Mill*, pp. 142–3.

20 Burnett, *Through the Mill*, p. 154.

21 London Mission Files – Rank.

22 Joseph Rank, letter to the Revd C. Ensor Walters, 8 January 1931, London Mission Files – Rank.

23 The Revd Dr George Lovell to the author, 7 June 2005, recounting the story of the Revd James Butterworth as told to him.

24 See Burnett, *Through the Mill*, p. 156. Deaconess Gwendolen Marsh was interviewed by the author on 7 September 2004.

25 Hilda Marsh, interview with author, 7 September 2004.

26 Hilda Marsh, interview.

27 W. J. Smart, London, 'Its tragedy and triumph', A Wartime London Mission Report, p. 14.

28 Wakelin, *J. Arthur Rank*, p. 29.

29 Joseph Rank, letter to the Revd Robinson Whittaker, London Mission Secretary, 27 October 1941, London Mission Files – Rank.

30 E. M. Walters, *C. Ensor Walters and the London He Loves*, Peterborough, Epworth Press, 1937, p. 12.

31 George Bernard Shaw, 'Memories of Early Years', 17 February 1937, E. Ensor Walters, p. 12.

32 Letter to the Revd C. Ensor Walters, London Mission Files – Rank.

33 Burnett, *Through the Mill*, p. 27.

34 Walters, *C. Ensor Walters*, p. 30.

35 Wakelin, *J. Arthur Rank*, p. 24, citing 'The Master Millers', reprinted from *Milling*, 2 September 1922.

36 Wakelin, *J. Arthur Rank*, p. 25.

37 Wakelin, *J. Arthur Rank*, p. 27.

38 Walters, *C. Ensor Walters*, p. 118.

39 Walters, *C. Ensor Walters*, p. 81.

40 London Mission Files – Rank.

41 The Revd Dr Kenneth Greet, interview with author, 11 September 2004.

42 The Revd Dr Brian Beck, letter to author, 6 August 2004.

43 Kenneth Hulbert, *Passion for Souls: The Story of Charles H. Hulbert, Methodist Missioner*, Peterborough, Epworth Press, 1959, pp. 2–3.

44 The Revd John Beech, 'London Contrasts', *110th London Mission Report*, p. 5.

45 Beech, 'London Contrasts', p. 8.

46 John D. Beasley, *The Bitter Cry Heard and Heeded: The Story of the South London Mission 1889–1989*, London, South London Mission, 1990, p. 22.

47 See George Jackson, *Collier of Manchester*, London, Hodder & Stoughton, 1923, pp. 45–6.

48 *South London Press*, 29 September 1900, cited in Beasley, *Bitter Cry*, p. 32.

49 Beasley, *Bitter Cry*.

50 See Walter Spencer, *The Glory in the Garret*, Peterborough, Epworth Press, 1932, cited in Beasley, *Bitter Cry*, p. 63.

51 Beasley, *Bitter Cry*, p. 68.

52 Beasley, *Bitter Cry*, p. 87.

53 Beasley, *Bitter Cry*, p. 98.

54 Beasley, *Bitter Cry*, p. 109.

55 See South London Mission, Annual Report 2003–4, p. 7.

56 *Methodist Recorder*, 20 January 2005, p. 4.

57 The three uniting traditions were the Primitive, United and Wesleyan Methodists.

58 *Methodist Recorder*, 16 June 2005, p. 1.

59 The National Sound Archives at the British Library have a list of nearly 200 items from the recordings at the Central Hall, Westminster, from which these details have been obtained.

60 First performed in the Great Hall in 1968.

61 See *The Times*, 27 July 1945, p. 4.

62 Kenneth Hulbert, *To Serve the Present Age*, Westminster Central Hall 1991, Bi-centenary Commemoration, p. 26.

63 See David Cesarani, *Arthur Koestler, The Homeless Mind*, London, Heinemann, 1998, p. 437.

64 See Bertrand Russell, *The Autobiography of Bertrand Russell, Vol 3. 1944–1967*, London, Allen and Unwin, 1969, p. 103. Also John Collins, *Faith under Fire*, London, Leslie Frewin, 1966, p. 108.

65 Fenner Brockway, *98 Not Out*, London, Quartet Books, 1986, p. 69.

66 *The Times*, 17 April 1956, p. 6.

67 *The Times*, 30 October 1996, p. 15.

68 See Mary Stott, *Before I Go*, London, Virago, 1985, p. 21.

69 See Collins Papers, Lambeth Palace Library, 3297, pp. 130ff.

70 *Jewish Chronicle*, 22 July 1988, p. 10.

71 *The Times*, 11 January 1946.

72 Kenneth Hulbert, interview with author, 22 October 1997. Mr Hulbert was present at the 1931 occasion.

73 For details of the First Assembly of the United Nations General Assembly, see Official Records, verbatim report, 10 January–14 February, Plenary Meeting of the General Assembly, Central Hall, Westminster, London.

74 *Methodist Recorder*, 9 February 2006, p. 3.

75 Alan Bullock, *The Life and Times of Ernest Bevin: Trade Union Leader, 1881–1940*, vol. 1, London, Heinemann, 1960, p. 198.

76 28 May 2004, during the Dalai Lama's visit to Britain.

9

The Richest Woman In the World
Hilda Porter and Methodist International House

Hilda Porter, who was born in April 1892, came from Barnsley in Yorkshire. The daughter of a managing director of a textile firm, she grew up with a younger brother and sister and was educated at a Quaker school. In 1914 she gave up her plan to study medicine to become sales representative for her father's business when it was rare to find women in such positions. Her blunt stubbornness and determination to succeed, brooking no opposition, enabled her to be successful in her job and learn about administration as well, a skill that later served her well.[1]

From her devout Methodist family she absorbed stories about missionaries and found events associated with China in the nineteenth century exciting. More significantly, she came from a church associated with Hudson Taylor's family and thus learned about the China Inland Mission, which he had founded. After hearing the story of two people, children of CIM missionaries, who fled 3,000 miles overland to Shanghai, and whose daughter, Vera, had then died, Hilda prayed: 'Lord Jesus, if you want me to go to China instead of Vera Green, I'll go.'[2]

The Methodist Missionary Society (MMS), however, to whom eventually she offered her services, decided she would go to India and sent her to Kingsmead College in Birmingham to train. Soon Hilda was ecstatic – plans had changed and she would go to China – and soon.[3] One of the first two women to receive a year's course for non-medical missionaries at Livingstone College in Leyton, Hilda eventually arrived in China in 1923, where she had a year's language training in Suzhou, an area rife with banditry.

Her colleague in China, the Revd H. B. Rattenbury, who had already spotted Hilda's unique gifts, remarked: 'If the bandits ever get hold of Hilda Porter, they'll deserve what they get!'[4] She was intrepid, visiting distant places to teach the Christian faith, taking medicines with her. Soon she was well-known in Suzhou itself, seen as remarkable because she lived alone and in a two-floor house![5] Hilda's time in China was barely eight years, however, because the upheavals in the country in the late 1920s meant all missionaries were sent home. By 1934 she had become Home Affairs Women's Secretary for the Missionary Society, working with H. B. Rattenbury again. After World War Two, during which Hilda had been an assistant air-raid warden at Rivercourt Methodist Church in Hammersmith, Hilda and H. B. Rattenbury re-visited China, travelling across 13 out of 18 Provinces. On her return, she criss-crossed Britain, speaking about her visit and also about the increasing numbers of overseas students coming to Britain for study and the racial prejudice they were experiencing.

China always remained part of Hilda's consciousness for she was involved in an accident during her China visit when a man sleeping above her during a boat journey fell and his elbow caught her front tooth, which then had to be crowned.[6] While in China Hilda had met the intrepid missionary Gladys Aylward, whose story was made into a film with Ingrid Bergman playing Gladys. Hilda and Gladys roared with laughter at the moments that were pure Hollywood fabrication as they watched the *Inn of the Sixth Happiness* together.[7]

While working with the MMS at its headquarters in Marylebone Road in London, Hilda lived in a nearby flat. She soon discovered students from abroad living nearby, some in an old fire-watching station and others in derelict warehouses or dwellings, whose rents were exor-bitant. She also discovered they had inadequate knowledge about the facilities available to them. Aware that many were the products of the worldwide missionary movement, which had invested money and per-sonnel in education abroad, she found herself putting up students in her flat to the annoyance of her immediate neighbours.

By now, the MMS General Committee was discussing the possibility of a full-time job for someone who would oversee student care, and at one meeting Hilda was passed a note that read: 'Have you ever thought of doing this?' That night she spent hours praying – Hilda's life was laced with prayer – trying to decide if this was God's will, as well as hers![8] The answer was 'Yes'.

Soon Hilda was convinced that a hostel for students was needed as more and more came to see her with housing and other difficulties. In mock desperation, the MMS treasurer said to Hilda: 'Go and get your hotel',[9] knowing the Society would give a loan to buy property that she deemed suitable. One day, having ruled out several, she was with her Nigerian friend, Grace Okon, who was in London to study medicine, when they came across a hotel for sale in Inverness Terrace, Bayswater. It was an area of gentility, but as the middle classes moved out in the late 1950s, it was to become a red-light district. Hilda haggled over the price and bought it for £27,000 – half the asking price. The freehold was secured subsequently.[10]

So numbers 2, 4, 6, Inverness Terrace became the first Methodist International House (MIH), with an Annexe later at numbers 48 and 50. There were, however, objections. Some said it was immoral to put men and women from different backgrounds under one roof; others said that it was an impractical ideal to think goodwill could be generated by putting young students from diverse countries together with the aim of helping them to learn how to live in peace.

Nevertheless, Hilda forged ahead. Friends from Yorkshire and elsewhere moved in with buckets, mops, paint and scrubbing brushes and painted and sewed until order emerged from the chaos. The students also mucked in. Meanwhile, Hilda begged furniture from everyone she knew. There were soon far too many applicants for the 140 beds on offer in single, double and four-bedded rooms.

The House was opened on 10 August 1950, by Princess Alice, Duchess of Gloucester, who often attended events in the early days and remained patron until her death in 2004, aged 102. One of the first residents, Margaret Prothero, has explained that MIH was 'a very much down-at-heel Bayswater Hotel',[11] where the cook had to struggle with a gas cooker and an old-fashioned sink 'in a tiny room about eight feet square'.[12] But for her, as for Grace Okon and a student from China,[13] the experience was formative. 'It seemed quite natural to go creeping downstairs with Oke [Dr Okoronko Ofa], a doctor from Nigeria, about midnight to make Nescafé in the Students' Utility Room,' she recalled. 'But had I been told a fortnight earlier that I should be doing that I would have been astonished.'[14] Later she was to help international houses in Nottingham, Birmingham and finally Hull.

At the start, two-thirds of the students were male,[15] with men and women on different floors. 'Sleeping with the opposite sex is strictly forbidden,' said a later MIH brochure given to each student on arrival, but students spent hours together in discussion in front of the gas fires in their rooms. Soon, too, they appointed a House Committee. There was no curfew, but they had to be in by 10 p.m. Another student, now Mary Ludlow, has remembered how the House Chaplain, whom Hilda supported when he canvassed for student lodging elsewhere on her behalf, arranged to let her in after her Graduation Ball, arriving in his pyjamas at the front door when she knocked, looking distinctly sheepish.[16]

'We all shared in the progress of the house,' Margaret Prothero has written. 'Any news of a legacy was announced at breakfast or if a letter to Methodist manufacturers had resulted in goods supplied at cost price.'[17] Students sat round two large tables for meals, which gave maximum interaction as slowly the houses were adapted, and in the third a rest room for African–Caribbean nurses was created. Hilda now became a negotiator between music students, who often practised six hours a day on their instruments, and Bayswater residents, who complained of the noise. 'I doubt if anybody could get the better of Miss Porter when she felt she was in the right,' Margaret Prothero has commented. In that first period, MIH students were a mini-United Nations, yet even so some kept together with colleagues from the same country. Nevertheless, an attempt was made to help them come to understand those from another culture by putting people of different backgrounds in the shared rooms with their consent – a policy that was not always successful.

Originally there was a morning prayer meeting for 15 minutes which then became weekly, taken either by students or staff. There was also Bible study and Sunday morning worship, led by a local minister. Communion was monthly. Students also went to central London churches, sometimes led by Hilda in procession. Yet though she was authoritarian, students respected, even loved, 'Auntie Hilda', as she was known. One elderly African headmaster, studying at the Institute of Education, was treated the same as the younger residents. 'He used to laugh about it,' Mary Ludlow has remembered.[18]

Life at MIH was not always serious, and there were parties at the start and end of term. The Christmas party was special, and for 48 years it included a concert with contributions from music students and sketches and dances from various of the countries represented. Then followed carol singing for some 70, between the ages of 18 and 40, singing in unison, often in their own language.[19] Sometimes residents who married would return after the wedding to celebrate. The baptism of children of previous students was also an occasion for celebration. A further development was when the child of a former resident was brought to the House by a parent.[20]

Though Hilda was known across the world for her strict code, she was always available to deal with student problems. Once she stayed in hospital with a Ghanaian girl dying of cancer and came home crying. She also stayed with a student recovering from a major heart operation.[21] Hilda once called a taxi at 2 a.m. to visit a married couple because, after much prayer, she had felt that their marriage was in trouble.[22] They all talked through the night. Later, the couple claimed Hilda's surprise visit had saved the marriage.[23]

Residents studied many subjects including law, business management and accountancy and there were numerous music students.[24] Frances Smart, who began work in 1951 in Bayswater, working with several wardens until her retirement in the early 1990s, has estimated that between 1951 and 1991 a figure approaching 1,000 a year came through the hostel, including both short-term and long-stay residents. Most were Christians from various traditions, but there were Muslims from Nigeria, who sometimes attended chapel services, especially at Christmas. They liked the hostel because no smoking or alcohol was allowed. One student even said that he liked it because it was near Hyde Park, where he could easily buy his Arab newspapers.

There were Hindu and Buddhist residents also. One Hindu wrote thanking MIH for 'your silent prayer, the warmth of which I could feel during the short but most difficult part of my life',[25] and a professor from Japan commented: 'As a Buddhist I always appreciate the Christian spirit and atmosphere of the House . . . This does not mean other religious belief was barred . . . '[26] None of the work of course could have developed without strong support from London Methodism and beyond, which supported Hilda's work by providing homes and inviting students to visit. Eventually a London Metropolitan Committee was created, with representatives from the Districts and the Rank Trust, to raise money and clear what remained of the initial loan and the cost of the Annexe. Volunteers helped with extra-hostel work and the meeting of students at mainline railway stations and airports – as had been the custom from MIH's start, and indeed from earlier. As the work grew inevitably it became necessary to hand over much of it, including the fostering in homes of children whose parents were studying intensively, to a new group, the Conference Committee for the Care of Overseas Students (CCCOS). This was a development that Hilda found hard to accept. Indeed, Frances Smart considers 'she nearly had her heart broken when the work split from MIH'.[27]

As Chris Hughes Smith, one-time General Secretary of the Division of Education and Youth, which eventually took over the work of CCCOS, noticed, MIH shows the Methodist capacity for replication. Thus some Methodist Districts imitated Hilda Porter's idea, hostels being established in Newcastle (1953); Liverpool (1954); Birmingham (1955); Manchester (1956); Bristol (1957). Later there were more – in Hull (1961), partly inspired by Fred Pratt Green, the hymn-writer, and his enthusiasm; Penarth (1965), opened by Princess Margaret, and Southampton (1967–8). These were followed by hostels in York and Leeds.

Not all fared equally well and each had its unique problems to such an extent that in the 1980s the Methodist Conference judged no further hostels should be sponsored. The Newcastle House, closed in 1972, was followed by an Overseas Students Centre, where counselling, hospitality and English tuition was available. Hull, though still running, as are the hostels in Birmingham, Bristol and Manchester, found difficulty in filling its places as universities provided accommodation themselves, and health and safety restrictions made extra financial and physical demands. It did at one point even find alleviation when Leeds students, on courses at a Hull hospital, stayed for periods. Two asylum seekers, paid for by a local church, were also residents. 'We also took some for a short time when the Council had to accommodate a large number,' Margaret Prothero has written. 'I am sure Hilda Porter would have done so, too.'[28] Muslim students were present in Hull in the early 1980s and, Ramadan being strictly observed, staff at Hull made provision for their requirements, an emphasis other hostels found necessary as more students came to Britain from the Middle East and South East Asia.

What did students do when they went home? Originally they tended to be the new élite as, one by one, independence was granted from colonial powers, though some also came to study dressmaking or secretarial work. Thus one student became Chief Justice of Kenya and another became Trinidad's Finance Minister. Dr D. T. Niles, a leading figure in Sri Lankan Methodism, like many others, stayed for a while as a guest at MIH while engaged in consultations in Britain.[29] A Nigerian student worked for the Nigerian Broadcasting Company and then researched African music, while Mary Ludlow herself became head-mistress of a large multicultural school in north London, a type of community she had first learned to respect when at the Bayswater hostel. One South African trainee nurse went home, re-trained, and then became a professor of postgraduate training for nurses, while Doreen Potter married the Revd Dr Philip Potter and used her musical gifts in the production of *Cantate Domine*, a songbook published by the World Council of Churches, of which her husband was sometime General Secretary.

The year 1964 became a critical one for Hilda Porter for she retired. She missed much and found it difficult to let go of her work – evident by her living nearby and her frequent visits. But by now this 'human dynamo', as she was once dubbed, two people in one, so fast did she move, was ageing.[30] Students remembered her as well-dressed, but never stylish, with a laugh that echoed round the house, and also her ability to laugh at herself.[31] They remembered how hard she had worked[32] and how 'very, very visionary' she was,[33] yet as Stanley Sowton judged, 'tough in the right sort of way'.[34] One thing few knew was how she had once sold some of the family jewellery to buy books and send them to every student in one year.[35]

Of course she had infuriated some. Hilda up in arms was 'an army in banners' as Douglas Thompson has judged, adding she was also 'mistress of the *fait accompli*', seeing a need and expecting her friends to pay the bill.[36] Now that was all over, and in due course Hilda found herself in The Martins, a Methodist home in Suffolk opened in 1962. It was a turbulent time for her as her mind began to lose its cogency, 'best described', one writer has considered, 'by Confucius who said he could "never remember he was growing old"'.[37] Later, when Hilda needed even more care, she was transferred to a Methodist Home in Cheshire where, in 1976, she died, aged 84. A former student visiting Britain was the last person from her family, as she considered them, to see her alive.[38] Often she had claimed to be the 'richest woman in the world', and so it proved to the end. Gordon Newton, also a former student, summed it up with: 'Many of us share the legacy of her wealth.'[39]

Others besides Hilda Porter helped to provide hospitality for overseas students, 70,000 of whom it was estimated were in Britain in the mid-1960s. At that time, Methodist hostels were helping nearly 300 Christians, 91 Muslims, 72 Hindus and 24 Buddhists. Yet a decade later, such student work was plummeting, partly because African groups in particular bought houses and shared the premises; and universities began to provide more convenient accommodation. However, by 1968, MIH in Bayswater was still housing representatives of some 34 nations, though slowly in the 1970s such wide representation declined. Fewer came from Commonwealth countries and more from Spain, Germany and France, many of them to learn English. Moreover, the British Council itself found homes, as did some Embassies and High Commissions, Hong Kong in particular having its own student hostel.

In addition, Methodist Districts increasingly found it hard to maintain momentum as government legal requirements for fire and safety precautions meant costs escalated. MIH itself had to sell the house in South Kensington it had received as a bequest and used as a hostel for women, in order to pay for Inverness Terrace improvements.[40] Yet both Peggy Hiscock and Bernard Hall, successive wardens, found there was sufficient diversity and numbers with many, as Hilda Porter had written earlier, '. . . future world leaders. The impressions they form are incalculable.'[41] Bernard Hall in particular, however, noticed accommodation pressures lessening and that new attitudes were needed. 'We must treat students as adults,' he wrote, 'or they will walk out of our door.'[42] This meant a change of style 'which secular organizations have already achieved'.[43]

Despite altered structures and approaches, by 1987 only six houses remained in Britain, though Inverness Terrace at its fortieth anniversary had 144 students from 44 countries, including Bulgaria, Indonesia, Turkey, the Yemen as well as Japan and Korea. Yet Sunday worship now only attracted 25, who took it in turns to lead it, others preferring to visit central London churches, while many students had no Christian allegiance. By 1993 the warden, David Holmes, was reporting student representation had tilted yet again, with twelve from Spain, eight from Singapore, four each from Taiwan and Ethiopia, with seven from France.

The final crisis came in the mid-1990s when it was clear that students from developing countries were not coming because of educational opportunities at home and increasing fees. Thus more beds were taken by European students, often on grants. MIH's Mission Statement commented, 'Few are keen to be influenced by the Christian ethos of MIH.' There were other changes, too: in benefits legislation, in lay rather than clerical wardenship, and new economic realities. This came to a head when more binding regulations meant updating at too much expense.[44] The upshot of this sobering fact was the decision to sell Inverness Terrace and move elsewhere. Thus in 1998 emerged Methodist International Centre, near Euston Station, in a complex of buildings containing a conference centre whose fees help to subsidize student ones, though hotel guests are also welcome.

Within the Centre there are also offices, central dining facilities, with meals provided by a company on contract, a gym, a student room with IT, a laundry, TV lounge and other facilities. Some 82 students are in residence yearly, chosen from 300 to 400 who apply, men and women in equal numbers, with some rooms shared as before – not a facility greatly welcomed now.[45] There is now no Sunday worship, though some students attend central London churches. A monthly film club provides one of the few meeting points.

The Conference Centre itself is used by groups as varied as Save the Children Fund, the Prince's Trust, Camden Borough, and the Office of the Deputy Prime Minister. One special event has been in the summer when 12 disabled children have come free with their teachers, who pay reduced fees. In the International Centre's foyer is a Mission Statement: 'We will strive for excellence in everything we offer based on our commitment to Christian values. We will seek to enhance our provision for students and guests.' It is a far cry from Inverness Terrace, let alone from Wycliffe House in north London, which sustained some students long before Hilda Porter had her original idea. But pioneers go, consolidation begins, and groups that adapt continue to flourish, while others die.

This adage has proved true for hostels in London created by other pioneers. In the case of the Lambeth Student's Hostel, which begun at the Lambeth Mission in 1968, it was due largely to the energy of the then minister, Fred Poad, with British Council backing. It lasted for 20 years and saw some 2,000 students, 80 per cent of them from overseas. Yet from its start it had financial problems to such an extent that, though much money was raised before its opening, there was a £30,000 debt, only paid off with the help of the London Mission, which then owned it. The only hostel to adjoin a church – the site had been redeveloped after the war damage to include first a hall, then a church, then a hostel, which was 11 storeys high – the student mix was from both Christian and the other world faith communities, though at times some 20 per cent were of no faith. The Far East was particularly well represented, as was Africa, especially East African Asians. Christians tended to worship at the Lambeth Mission in a society that could trace its origin back to John Wesley himself. Many residents studied accountancy or printing. Doctors and dentists in training were also much in evidence. One student went home to be a barrister in Malaysia, while two English students met and married two Southlands students on a mission, and stayed in north Lambeth thereafter, partly drawn by the challenging nature of work in the inner city.

Because the Lambeth Mission had entered into a covenant with the British Council for 25 years, fees charged were related to grants, which meant the hostel never built up reserves, so when 'concrete cancer' was found in the hostel building structures, insufficient funds existed to deal with the problem. Nor could the London Mission itself undertake the radical refurbishment required. The hostel thus ended – but two decades of students had relished the chance to be in inner London and 'most look back with affection to their time there', considers Gordon Ashworth, a one-time chaplain and minister at the Lambeth Mission.[46]

Of course, young people came to London from other parts of Britain over many decades and Methodism responded to their needs in a number of different ways. In 1951, for example, Moullin House in Ealing was opened to provide secure accommodation for some 50 young people coming to the capital for the first time for work, training or study. The idea of a Methodist minister at Ealing Broadway Church, this caught the eye of Emma Moullin, the unmarried daughter of Thomas Moullin, one of the group in the nineteenth century involved in the creation of the Pearl Insurance Company, part of whose wealth she inherited. Her sister, Ada Moullin, who married a cousin, made some of that wealth available to erect a hostel built in Emma's memory, in Mount Park Road, not far from Ealing Broadway tube station. Because of post-war building restrictions, permission had to be given by the appropriate government department and for decades thereafter it served its purpose for Methodist young people. More recently, however, there have been fewer Methodist referrals and the hostel has become more international and inter-faith, with a further building, Havelock House, added in the 1960s. It contained seven self-contained flats for those wanting to settle into a permanent home after initial training, and these flats are available to them while they plan their next move. For many years the widow of the Methodist chairman, Peggy Simpson, was warden, living on the site until one day she wrote saying, 'I think at the age of ninety-five I should stop being Warden.'[47]

Another hostel, somewhat similar in intent, was opened in north London in 1960, and this was made possible by the successful city broker, H. Guy Chester, who gave both the land and initial funds. Its completion, however, was the result of an imaginative scheme whereby Methodist churches across Britain raised 'a million half-crowns'. The building in Muswell Hill was also the home of the Methodist Youth Department and then the Division of Education and Youth. There were study bedrooms for 80 people and, as with hostels set up by Hilda Porter and others, the mix of residents was varied, including medical students from the UK and abroad, trainees for the BBC and Ministry of Defence, Civil Servants – and even a young man training to be a baker. The founding warden was a Methodist layman, Glyn Amos, who had given up a career in banking under the influence of Jimmy Butterworth of Clubland and trained for youth work. With his wife, Ceinwen, he created a community that at its height generated drama productions, 'disco' nights, opportunities to develop public-speaking skills, with weekly visits from celebrities like Donald Soper and the Revd Harry Blackmore, who had proposed the fund-raising scheme to the Methodist Conference. 'Dozens of marriages resulted from the positive atmosphere,' his son, Tim Blackmore, has reflected, 'and residents regularly contributed to services in churches across north London.'[48] Like Moullin House, it provided a sense of security and enabled young people to adjust to London life before setting out on their own, many of whom made lasting friendships there. Under its new name, the Guy Chester Centre, it provides 120 study bedrooms, with a residential conference centre facility for 26.

Perhaps two of the least known of these ventures occurred in south London. After 1945, the Women's Fellowship sponsored Annesley House for young women at risk, which in the late 1960s became a hostel for young women in their first job in London, work then continued under the women's Network of the Methodist Church until the house was sold in January 2004. Revenue from the sale will be given in grants to applicants working with vulnerable women and families.[49] Also in south London, as a result of the concern of Mostyn Road Methodist Church in the 1950s and 1960s, Mostyn House was set up for single working young women at risk from exploitative landlords as many migrated from the Caribbean. They, too, needed a secure base in London as they began adult life and this they found, being passed on to MIH and elsewhere if Mostyn House was full. Norma Harrison, its first warden, would often meet boat trains as Hilda Porter and others had done before her, holding up signs that read 'Methodist' or 'Can we help?' She also made contact with others from the Caribbean living in the Brixton area. Such was the respect the hostel gained that Sir Hugh

Foot (later Lord Caradon), former Governor of Jamaica, and a well-known Methodist from the West Country Foot family, visited and praised it.[50]

Will all this hostel work survive as costs continue to escalate and in societies where parents increasingly provide the funding? It is difficult to see how voluntary groups will be able continually to underpin institutional responses unless undergirded with funds, as the Methodist International Centre is. Otherwise, it seems after a decade or two that such schemes run into insuperable difficulties, though they provide havens for their residents, and clearly are of value to them wherever in the world they later live and work.

Notes

1 See Pauline Webb, *Women of Our Time*, Peterborough, Epworth Press, 1963, pp. 71–2.

2 Webb, *Women*, p. 73.

3 Webb, *Women*, p. 73.

4 Webb, *Women*, p. 74.

5 Webb, *Women*, p. 75.

6 Webb, *Women*, p. 78.

7 Paul Lang, interview with author, 3 October 2004.

8 Webb, *Women*, p. 80.

9 Webb, *Women*, p. 82.

10 Webb, *Women*, p. 82.

11 Margaret Prothero, letter to author, 16 November 2004.

12 Prothero, letter.

13 London Mission Report 1951, pp. 29–30.

14 London Mission Report 1951, pp. 29–30.

15 Frances Smart, interview with author, 5 November 2004.

16 Mary Ludlow, interview with author, 17 January 2005.

17 Prothero, letter.

18 Ludlow, interview.

19 Frances Smart, *Notes on Methodist International House*, Bayswater, 1950–98.

20 Smart, *Notes*.

21 Smart, *Notes*.

22 Smart, *Notes*.

23 Smart, interview.

24 The Revd Peggy Hiscock, interview with author, 17 January 2005.

25 Hilda Porter, interview with Winifred M. Pearce in *The Life of Faith*, 28 March 1963, p. 291.

26 Professor Jiro Nagasawe, *MIH Silver Jubilee Brochure*, 1950–75, p. 13.

27 Smart, *Notes*.

28 Prothero, letter.

29 Smart, *Notes*.

30 Smart, *Notes*.

31 Webb, *Women*, p. 93.

32 Smart, *Notes*.

33 Grace Igwe, interview with Meg Hall for author, autumn 2004.

34 Stanley Sowton, 'Joyful News', *Layman's Forum*, 1952.

35 Smart, *Notes*.

36 The Revd Douglas Thompson, *Methodist Recorder*, 9 December 1976, p. 15.

37 Thompson, *Methodist Recorder*.

38 Smart, *Notes*.

39 The Revd Gordon D. Newton, *Methodist Recorder*, 13 December 1976, p. 13.

40 Hiscock, interview.

41 Hilda Porter, brochure issued after the opening of seven hostels in Britain.

42 The Revd Bernard Hall, Warden's Report, 5 April 1982.

43 Hall, Warden's Report.

44 Chris Maskell, Secretary-Treasurer to the Management Committee, Briefing Paper mid-1990s.

45 Maura Cooke, interview with author, 11 January 2005.

46 The Revd Gordon Ashworth, interview with author, 25 February 2005.

47 Colin Pratt, Warden Moullin House, interview with author, 22 February 2005.

48 Tim Blackmore, MBE, letter to author, 17 February 2005.

49 See *Magnet* no.70, Summer 2005, p. 37.

50 Claire Taylor, 'British Churches and Jamaican Migrants, a Study in Religion and Identity 1948–1965', unpublished PhD, Anglia Polytechnic University, 2004. (A copy of this can be located in the Minet Local History Library for the London Borough of Lambeth, off Knatchbull Road, London SE5.)

10

Living On a Large Map
Douglas Griffiths, Youth and Community Work

Like many of his generation, Douglas Griffiths's life was tempered by World War One – even though he was only in his late teens during the war. After appointments in the Home Counties, Liverpool and Hull, in the 1930s he found his ultimate vocation – in London itself. He had already set up a youth club in Hornsey by 1939, and during London's Blitz he met and talked with frightened and unruly youngsters in air raid shelters, finding he could communicate with them easily.[1]

In 1943, the Birmingham Methodist Conference agreed to establish a Methodist Youth Department, partly in response to government espousal of open youth clubs. Douglas was appointed secretary, and soon his fertile brain was suggesting novel approaches. One was to invite delegates from the youth clubs now being set up across the UK to meet annually for 'London Weekends', the first of which occurred on 2 June 1945 in Westminster Central Hall, where a Club Congress was held before the official launch in the Albert Hall.

'For many of us,' Pauline Webb, who was there, has written, 'it was the first time we had been allowed into the centre of London since the Blitz. There was heady excitement in the air as we prepared to celebrate peace and inaugurate officially the Methodist Association of Youth Clubs (MAYC), of which we had become enthusiastic founders in our local churches.'[2] Sir Stafford Cripps, soon to be Chancellor of the Exchequer in the newly elected Labour government, was one of the many eminent public figures to address MAYC – just as George Thomas and David Frost did later on. 'Through our clubs we are members of that great society of Christians whose job is to build the Kingdom of God,' he told the gathering.[3] 'He made us feel that Christian young people had a vital role to play in shaping the future of the nation,' Dr Webb recalled, becoming then the socialist she has remained.[4]

Some of the delegates from over 2,500 clubs had slept overnight in large air raid shelters in Camden Town, but nothing diminished their enthusiasm,[5] which 'Griff', as he was soon called, noted with satisfaction. 'Many wondered where the MAYC voyage would take us,' he recalled later, as 'some dreamed of service overseas, for we were already on a large map. All were startled at the depth and rollicking comradeship of the crew.'[6] On one point Griff was clear: MAYC was born 'amid fun and adventure and deep evangelical purpose'. Indeed, never before had any church mobilized so many young people with little, or no, Christian background and convinced them 'Christianity is caring, not necessarily succeeding, but loving and believing and hoping'.[7]

Douglas Griffiths had persuaded colleagues to support an annual Albert Hall booking as the focus for 'London Weekends' and thousands of teenagers from all over the UK for many decades descended on the capital to rekindle visions through worship, drama, sports and rousing debates. It was not always professional, but it was fun – as talented youth leaders brought their clubs and stimulated leadership in their communities and MAYC developed a motto: in life devoted; in faith equipped; in person fit; in church a family and in service world citizens.[8]

By 1954, there were some 20,000 MAYC members in Greater London clubs, often led by ex-army or national service personnel.[9] The Jewish youth worker Basil Henriques, however, regretted that Methodist youth work was weak in the inner city and called for more government co-operation in youth leader training. Dr Irvonwy Morgan, then head of London Mission, explained that Methodism suffered from damaged buildings and lack of money after 1945.[10] Moreover, attempts to support 'open' youth clubs, as the government had encouraged, was being ruined by the damage, Clubland being exceptional.[11] Leonard Barnett, one of those like Reg Bedford, who succeeded Griff – who in 1949 had gone to Springfield Hall in south London, re-naming it 'Friendship House' – argued that 'the real issue is the need for wise and experienced youth leaders'.[12]

Griff himself was experiencing similar difficulties as Teddy Boys in gangs expressed teenage alienation in the 1950s. However, when he joined the debate, he argued it was unnecessary to have full-time youth leaders because youth work was 'the church's job – it belongs to the people and the minister together'. The Friendship House club leader, he reported, was a builder's foreman, his assistant was an office worker.[13] Griff, of course, had a special charisma and was now able to take Springfield Hall, with a history since 1902 of social awareness under a number of leading ministers, into a new phase. During the war it had maintained a youth club, 80 per cent of whose members had no church connection.[14] 'What have you been doing to X and his pals?' queried a policeman at the time. 'They used to be the biggest nuisance in this neighbourhood and now they are setting an example to the whole area.'[15] But the club had not survived, so Griff restarted it with six young people, asking them for three loyalties: to the family of the Church, the club and one another. Soon some 45 attended worship regularly. But the previous winter, he admitted, 'we found we had to deal with four gangs of spivs'. Despite opposition, 'the spivs' became members, though it divided the club into groups and those attending worship declined in numbers.[16]

MAYC continued to be strong throughout the 1950s and 1960s, celebrating its twenty-first anniversary in 1966 in its usual rumbustious style.[17] 'The early enthusiasm had been justified,' Griff declared as the gathering met under the jazzy title: 'Get with it for God and our neighbour'. 'Are we all in this or is it for the select few?' Griff asked, telling the assembly that 'each of you is original' and that they 'met God in Jesus Christ in the Church, but God did not live there. God met people in market place, science lab, the political arena – everywhere and all the time.'[18]

The offering was for MAYC members' expenses who had recently gone as volunteers abroad, 13 of whom appeared at the Westminster Central Hall event. Pauline Webb, who attended, said she marvelled that a movement begun in the immediate post-war years still met the needs of current teenagers.[19] Now MAYC was keen to raise money for Christian Aid's Tractors for the Hungry project, and in due course 35 were sent.[20] It also raised money for a hospital in the Ivory Coast, a project begun in London MAYC, which eventually became nationwide.

By 1995, however, when MAYC celebrated its fiftieth anniversary, things looked very different. Griff had died in 1985, leaving London in 1959 for Rotherham, and then ten years of retirement, and did not live to see the slow demise of 'London Weekend'. But ticket sales crept down as youth culture changed, and there was more secular state involvement in the payment of youth workers, often full-time, and the anniversary seemed to 'give permission for older workers to retire, with no coherent policy to replace them'.[21] Yet MAYC's Albert Hall event still exhibited flair using music, dance and video presentations to wrestle with homelessness and racism, an experience undergone by a South African Methodist who was tortured and imprisoned, and Stephen Lawrence's friends, who explained how his murder affected them. 'Make homelessness an issue for the next election,' MAYC's world-action secretary urged.

Now different ventures were tried – the use of Trafalgar Square for one large event, for example – and in 1997 a series demonstrating different worship styles – like those at Iona and Taizé – was put on at Westminster Central Hall for London Methodists but, despite being noticed by *The Times*, no more than 150 ever came. Meanwhile a debate about MAYC's future raged, the eventual outcome of which was to end 'London Weekend' and sponsor the bi-annual 'Breakthrough' at different venues across Britain, focused on youth work rather than clubs.[22]

How would Griff have viewed such developments? He had been at the height of his powers when there seemed to be 'a liberal, evangelical social feel about Methodism', as Mark Wakelin has judged, which lasted until the 1960s.[23] Then patterns – theological and social – became more diverse, with some congregations seeming to want not teenagers present, but 'older younger people'.[24] This would have not met with Griff's approval, for essentially 'he was a prophet and a pioneer'.[25] He had most of all a capacity to be both friend and leader.[26] Friendship was a word that connected with society around him and Griff saw it contained both fellowship and love aspects of New Testament theology. 'It has occurred to me since,' a former colleague has reflected, 'that he took Weatherhead's motion of the Transforming Friendship and developed it – and youth and community practice reflected it.'[27] Moreover, his various slogans, like living on a large map, 'were effective pedagogy and theology'.[28]

It was indeed refreshing, as his colleagues discovered, to work with a Christian whose attitude was consistently 'Can Do' and 'Why Not?' – an outlook typified by his first booking of the Albert Hall when others were timid because of the costs. 'The way we behaved as leaders of youth clubs was a matter of theology,' colleagues learned.[29] Surely, then, this man 'of great strength of mind, compassion, understanding and humble'[30] would have responded creatively to changes needed in the 1990s just as he had responded to the need for new approaches in the post-1945 world?

Douglas Griffiths did not only pioneer work with young people. He developed a distinctive approach to Church and community work, arguing that mission could not be separate from the weekly celebration of Holy Communion, with preaching and prayer being central too. Despite the fact that one of his predecessors had in 1934 noted that since he had come to the Mission[31] some 400 members have moved to the new suburban areas, Friendship House still had many members and these he welded into a worshipping community out of the mission dependency of the past, giving young people a sense of belonging and a desire to work together as an evangelistic agency. To do this, he helped the church 'identify with its neighbourhood'.[32]

He also saw the need to create cells of Christians in what he called 'flat-fellowships'. He prepared church members first at Springfield, then in the flats themselves. First he, and then the deaconess, would visit with a few church friends invited to meet them in the flats. There was, he found, considerable resistance to flat-fellowships. People deliberately kept apart, not wanting others in their block to know they were church-goers. But Douglas was not daunted and tried to show them the joy of 'making a Christian community in the block, inviting others to share its life'.[33] More bravely, he tried to contact younger flat-dwellers, parents of young people in the church's youth groups, to form a club in the block, which Douglas would visit for talks and late evening prayer. Serious and difficult questions about faith and life were often raised on these occasions, but despite his enthusiasm and energy he had to admit 'we have only about six active groups in the flats'.[34]

If Douglas Griffiths, with all his charisma and determination 'to go to those who need you most',[35] found the going hard, how much more difficult it must have been for other leaders with less obvious gifts. Dagenham, planning for which followed on from the 1919 Housing and Town Planning Acts, with building starting in 1921 and ending in 1935, is a case in point, as new homes came first, and later Ford Motor Works, shops, community services and schools.[36] Methodism, with its specific mission stances, which Douglas Griffiths felt were so limited, responded by erecting two Central Halls, Becontree and Dagenham Heathway, now both closed and sold, though there are still two Methodist churches on the edges of the estate.

'The estates were in effect mission fields and the culture was inclined towards conventional, structured Christianity,' Trevor Lockwood, who worked in Dagenham, has judged. The exception was the Sunday School, which at Heathway reached 1,000, with hundreds on its wait-ing list. 'More than a few of today's late middle-aged church people and those who might not attend church but have a basic belief in God and support a Christian lifestyle,' he considers, 'owe a great deal to those who selflessly and sacrificially gave themselves to this work week after week and year after year.'[37] Despite this work and the cinema ministry that drew both adults and children, mission was often hard – though in 1955 both Central Halls were high profile when their ministers, one of whom was secretary of a group of objectors to the LCC's housing appli-cations policy, sought to get justice for Dagenham so children of its original residents could be offered accommodation there.[38]

Nevertheless, though they had a good record of supporting com-munities, especially in World War Two, few churches on estates pros-pered. Sometimes, however, a church was the only group with facilities available for community use – as at St Helier, now on the boundary of Sutton and Merton Boroughs – and this helped maintain contacts. Like many outer London churches, St Helier was the result of an initiative from an already established congregation, in this instance at Tooting. The area had been developed in the early 1930s, and as the London County Council erected 50 houses weekly, Tooting's minister, John

Broadbelt, gathered a Sunday School together, soon building a dual-purpose Central Hall, which was erected before even the cinema or the pub.[39] 'Slowly,' wrote his successor A. E. Binks, in 1934, 'a church is being established on the Estate.'

By 1936 it was strong enough to hold an open-air cinema mission,[40] which in 1937 involved 1,500 in a cinema group, called the Guild of Light. Such young people's work continued into the early 1960s, with a contingent taking part in the first MAYC Albert Hall celebration that Douglas Griffiths organized. Most significant, as the Christian community (some from inner London) grew, was the founding in 1948 of a club for blind people, which still meets regularly. As on other estates, however, housing policy impacted unhelpfully as properties were unavailable to the next generation, which had to move away, thereby denuding both Church and community of their skills.[41] Despite this, St Helier Methodist Church has survived, though severely curtailed in numbers, and is still able to offer its facilities for community use.

Downham, an estate for 40,000 to the north of Beckenham, was not so successful. Backed by Joseph Rank and others, who in the 1930s formed a support group to establish Wesley Hall, it also soon had a large Sunday School, though church finances were always precarious. Some 3,000, mostly children, used the premises weekly, with 1,500 attending cinema programmes and 500 'at Gospel picture services on Sundays. It became a counter-attraction to the local cinema itself,' one minister observed.[42] The church even produced a film that illustrated youth activities, which gained new recruits.

Downham was still holding its own in 1946, with many on its premises with no church connection. The year 1955 was a peak moment, too, when the boys' club was visited by Roger Bannister, who had become world famous in 1954 by running a four-minute mile.[43] But its life degenerated in the 1960s and was 'ever prone to vandalism, with church life the despair of the minister', one local vicar recalls.[44] It seemed, as on other estates, that someone had been appointed incongruent both in dress and language. When later a deaconess was in charge, Wesley Hall picked up, but by the early 1970s it was closed and sold.

The pattern of innovation, which Douglas Griffiths and others tried, succeeded for a time, but then communities changed and substantially altered, leading to failure and closure, a pattern crystal clear at Harold Hill Methodist Church, halfway between Romford and Brentwood. Funded with War Damage Commission money from an inner London church, it was opened in 1954, a communion table at one end, a stage at the other. In 1948, open-air services had begun in this new area of 15,000 houses, with other events held in any available buildings, including people's homes. Now there were high hopes that a Christian community would enable people, many uprooted and isolated from London friends and relatives, to find new roots.

To a certain extent, this occurred at Harold Hill, though there were other churches and organizations also vying for support. As at Downham and Dagenham, Sunday School was important, its red letter days being outings at a time when parents owned neither television nor car. Other young people's groups also developed, even a Guild. 'For three to four years we attracted some really tough types who seemed to appreciate the club with a difference,' Stan Cornish has recalled.[45]

The church was also fortunate in attracting good leadership – though from beyond the estate, a pattern repeated so often elsewhere. One was head of music at the local comprehensive school, and created a musical quartet that played before and after the service; another was a public school teacher and semi-professional footballer, who ran a successful youth club. However, the work was beset by two problems – the cultural differences between estate residents and 'outsiders' and, as at St Helier, the effect of housing policies, which meant that when couples married they had to leave the area, often depriving the church of two local leaders at once. Another problem was the rapid succession of ministers, and later the loss of a full-time deaconess, which implied a downgrading of support by the Circuit, though a team of lay preachers provided some continuity for a while. Vandalism became a recurring issue, as at Downham, with broken windows, smashed panels, graffiti and lead taken from the roof. But Harold Hill estate did settle down, becoming more self-sufficient as greater prosperity led to changing lifestyles. Yet increasingly, Harold Hill's Methodist leadership commuted in to the area, and the goodwill generated at the start did not translate into committed support, though residents were appreciative of the Methodist Church's attempts at community-building.[46]

Eventually membership dwindled below 20 and the site was sold for £140,000, some of it paid to the Greater London Council to release the church from its restrictive covenant which stopped the premises from being other than for Methodist use. The releasing of the restrictive covenant enabled a block of flats to be built. In 1979, a local paper wrote about 'the church that died fighting a losing battle', adding 'like its central figure the church has come and gone in just thirty years'.[47] On the last night, as the remaining congregation prepared to join Harold Hill Methodist Church, thugs gathered and warned they would damage the property, so the final act of the congregation's leaders was to phone the police and ask for protection for the building when it was finally closed.[48]

Harold Hill Methodists were naturally disappointed that their endeavour ended, but surely it was better to have tried and failed than not to have tried. It has been a common experience for Methodists in estates like those at Honor Oak Park in south London, where Lord Soper's Order of Christian Witness sponsored their Long Term Project in the 1950s and early 1960s, focused on a council flat from where several members attempted to build community. A similar, but more successful, struggle occurred at Old Oak Methodist Church in north London on a LCC Estate for 10,000. In due course, it felt it could no longer usefully operate its dual-purpose hall, and built a church on its site.

What lessons can Methodism learn from its attempt to sustain new communities on London's housing estates? First, that it is vital to understand an estate's sociology. It is surely not sufficient to appoint staff to create a worshipping community, with its ancillary services of the kind that flourish successfully in suburban contexts.[49] Moreover, staff need ongoing training for their situations as 'incarnation involves learning to live with culture and to speak its language'. Indeed, as in other continents, so in the UK 'Christians must learn to produce indigenous churches'.[50]

Second, work needs to be ecumenical, as when the Roehampton Christian Community Centre began in 1968, one of the earliest local ecumenical projects in Britain. Here, on an estate famed internationally for its layout, though later its walkways and tree-lined paths were to become a haven for muggers, residents were to experience many deprivations. To begin with, Anglican–Methodist co-operation was effective, yet over the years this has declined to the detriment of the community. Now only innovative approaches to worship on Sunday afternoons have stemmed the decline, which have included a Passover meal, a healing service, and an occasion when worshippers selected their 'Songs of Praise'. More recently, an evangelical organization has set up a weekday luncheon club for those over 60, though it was threatened with closure when Wandsworth Council cut grants for all such clubs. A temporary reprieve was gained after members took to the streets and held a protest outside the council's headquarters, blocking traffic for an hour and a half, having first obtained police permission for their protest. The Roehampton Forum, for professionals involved on the estate, now meets bi-monthly to consider problems such as this.

The relation of the estate to the wider community becomes more problematical if church members living on the estate choose to worship in a more prosperous area. Further complications have also occurred as a result of the sale of council houses. Landlords now buy up property when it is offered for sale and let it to students from the newly created Roehampton University nearby, thus causing a further source of tension and potential conflict.

A group not dissimilar from Roehampton's also operates on Broadwater Farm in Tottenham, largely a development after the 1985 riot there, partly caused when police invaded the home of Cynthia Jarrett, seeking her son, to apprehend him for non-payment of a licence, and Cynthia, a diabetic, died from the shock. The revolt, stimulated also by forces beyond Broadwater Farm, was set in the context of a death in Brixton, where there was also strong opposition to the stop and search policy of the police, which now escalated as Tottenham officers overwhelmed the area.

'Sadly the Church was largely absent from the Estate at that time,' a recent statement has admitted.[51] But since then, a Christian presence has emerged with a number of Christians from different traditions making their home there. One Anglican, who with his wife worked on the estate for ten years before moving to work on Iona, found the Roman Catholic, Free Church and Pentecostalist mix invigorating and has remarked that 'the presence of Pentecostalists mutually stretched our theologies and liturgies in the cause of reconciliation and witness'.[52]

A visitor entering Broadwater Farm is first greeted by the word 'Welcome' in several languages by the Garden of Remembrance, opened in 1989 and commemorating those who lost their lives in 1985, which also recalls the suffering of residents who have experienced poverty, neglect and prejudice. In the 1990s, the week after a tree was planted in the Peace Garden, Jenni Sweet, at Miller Memorial Church, near the estate, found a hope 'for more such events',[53] an indication that residents wanted 'to live without racial hatred or violence'.[54] Jenni found her pastoral visiting was most moving, especially 'visiting the women and listening to their stories'. While Winston Silcott, who had been arrested and found guilty of the murder of PC Blakelock, a conviction later quashed as unsound, was still in prison for an unconnected offence, Jenni shared in a house agape with Silcott's aunt, grandmother and neighbours, who also prayed for the Blakelock family, then returned home the same evening to have a telephone conversation with PC Blakelock's widow.[55]

The ecumenical group has been financed since 1990 by a grant from Methodism's Racial Justice Office, which has given nearly £30,000 for ongoing expenses. It supports the Residents' Association in dealings with the Haringey Council, the police and health authorities. There is now on Broadwater Farm a Health and Employment Centre and the ecumenical group relates to these. It also helps deal with internal racial and personality conflicts and joins in the celebrations – the annual carnival, the Christmas party and the gospel concert. English language teaching for adults is also supported and, perhaps most important of all, ongoing support offered for those families still affected by the riot.[56] It tries also to establish constructive relations with the police.

Some members of the ecumenical group have been on racism awareness courses and there was one away-day when members faced deep-rooted cultural and personal suspicions of one another and found reconciliation.[57] Successive Methodist ministers at Miller Memorial, especially Jenni Sweet and Cathy Bird, have been supportive – as have ministers from St Mark's in Tottenham High Road. Indeed, many of the Estate's children attended Miller Memorial's Sunday School, and the church's Women's Fellowship acted like yeast in bread on several occasions – including helping to plant small window boxes for older residents.[58]

But Methodist ministers come and go and the continuity has been provided by Francis Ackroyd, a United Reformed minister who has worked in Tottenham for over 26 years. Now, with people coming to Broadwater Farm from across the world, Christians have put their marker down for a new way of 'being church', on an Estate where more than 10 per cent of residents have some Christian allegiance, though often they worship in other areas. At the Second European Ecumenical Assembly in Graz in 1997, six men and women from Broadwater Farm from the pastoral group ran a workshop called 'Healing the City', challenging members to indicate what they would do in situations that had arisen for them. The team comprised 'three men, three women, three black, three white, one Roman Catholic, two Anglicans, three Pentecostals, one Caribbean, one Irish, two Ghanaian, two English',[59] a measure of the Estate's cosmopolitan nature.

The third and final point that emerges from all attempts at community work is to accept both failure and success equally, as on Broadwater Farm, which has undergone a personal and corporate death and resurrection, indicated by Yvonne Sinclair, who has lived there, and brought her family up, over 33 years. Despite the changes – it is now more multiracial than before the 1985 riots – she feels 'positive', as others do. Though there may still be iron gates on many front doors, and she herself has experienced two break-ins over 15 years, she feels now it is only 'the little ASBO crowd' that deliberately causes difficulties. Admitting the friendliness can be superficial at times, she still believes that the changes set in motion after 1985 have made residents much more positive.[60]

Sometimes success is not as apparent, as on Broadwater Farm, but is still to be celebrated – as at Manor Methodist Church in Bermondsey when in the 1970s the church found itself in the middle of two estates whose hostility was immense. Manor therefore brokered meetings between leasers of the two all-white groups, arranging for church hall bookings on differing days. It also ran a newspaper for the two estates, one of which had 600 residents, the other 2,400, including 400 children under 14 and 800 teenagers.

In due course, Manor roofed over a Sunday School building that had not been completed and soon there was a youth and community hall available, opened in February 1972 by Harold Wilson, then Labour Party leader, and his wife, Mary. The minister at the time, Peter Coates, felt that the local authority should be acting, but it was fully stretched and, in the view of some, inadequate.[61] It was therefore, Coates considered, 'the Christian duty to do everything it can to provide places where young people can be accepted'.[62] By 1978 his successor could write that 'Manor swarms with youngsters from Monday to Friday every week' with 'youth clubs, sports activities, a lunch club for the elderly and a group of fellow Christians who have no building of their own . . . '[63]

By the 1980s, however, with the Greater London Council and the Inner London Education Authority abolished by the government, and as costs escalated, the pattern had to change. The site itself was sold to find money to rebuild the church, but only after 20 years of valuable work had been achieved, though not without difficulties for club members were heavily into crime and police regularly called in. Nevertheless, a Scout Troop, still successful after many decades, has survived, and parents from several traditions and diverse cultures send their children to it.

Perhaps a recent scheme organized for Scouts by the London City Mission points one way ahead: nearly 30 young people were taken to Auschwitz to learn about the consequences for society when legitimate diversity is deliberately denied. Maybe, too, people might choose to live on or even retire to estates, as Brian and Zena Goss have done in east London after their experience of positive ecumenical co-operation in multicultural Tottenham. Sadly, Brian has also experienced the violence of estate life when his cheek bone was fractured in three places when he intervened to help a neighbour being targeted by 'wayward youngsters'. Despite this setback, however, both he and Zena feel they are 'in the right place where we live in Hackney'.[64] Another approach that could be imitated is the Small Churches' Group which came together in the 1980s to help six estates in Tower Hamlets and Newham.[65]

Yet the fact remains that Methodism is numerically strongest from Northwood to Ilford, Surbiton to Beckenham, where congregations have emerged with similar patterns of worship, uniformed organization and the letting of property to diverse community groups ranging from the Barking Team Ministry's survey of the Borough's needs in the 1960s, to Shirley's literary circle and church orchestra later. This strength is hardly surprising when it is realized, for example, that Ruislip-Northwood went from a population of some 16,000 in 1930 to 72,000 in 1954.[66]

Shirley Methodist Church, in the London Borough of Croydon, was strong and imaginative enough to undertake a course in community development with the help of Dr George Lovell. Barking went even further, when three ministers and two deaconesses met ten times for a meal and evening with Terry Walton, of the Greater London Youth and Community Service, and Barking borough leaders in social services, housing, leisure and education. 'Out of it,' Howard Booth, the then Superintendent, has written, 'came leadership roles for staff members'.[67] One became involved with community relations and consultations with the (then) Community Relations Commission, which led to the appointment of a full-time officer and secretary, and an office for many years at the Barking Methodist Church, with Howard Booth as its first Chair.

A second staff member became chair of the Dagenham Association for Mental Health, which used a former Methodist property as a base for its work. David Porter, a third team member, became involved in industrial mission through the formation of an industrial mission group, at the same time training with the Westminster Pastoral Foundation and then practising as a psychotherapist. There were also, Howard Booth has explained, 'a variety of co-operative products with the Social Services, including clubs on our premises for the deaf, blind and handicapped',[68] with church members acting as volunteers under social service leadership.

Marigold Oakley, a trained Sister with the National Children's Home, was seconded to the Team Ministry by them, with Barking Borough paying half her salary. She led a variety of children's activities, especially one for children whose fathers were in prison. In addition, there was a regular ministers and social workers club on Methodist premises, with the Council for Social Service retaining an office there for a weekly Citizens Advice Bureau.

How successful was this work, which lasted for some six or seven years? 'Failure?' Howard Booth has queried. 'If we did fail, it was because we had not had George Lovell's input sooner. Gareth Cooper and I went to his courses, but with hindsight we did not involve the laity enough in the decision-making. We were a strong staff and we led from the front.'[69] Unfortunately, when Howard Booth left for Harrow after eight years, little of this brave attempt at engagement with the public authorities survived either the vagaries of the Methodist appointment system or the early death of one of the team.

Like Trevor Lockwood in Dagenham, who created a collaborative ministry with his churches and used community development insights, on moving from Barking to Harrow, Howard Booth involved the entire Harrow Circuit staff in AVEC community development courses as ministers realized they needed to be free of their isolation and work with the laity in new and more co-operative styles.[70] Yet the positive insights stemming from this training did not address the Monday to Friday work lives of many suburban people as they impinged on so much of Greater London's life.

From 1921, one Harrow church helped to plant others in the expanding area so groups began in Ruislip, Kenton and North Harrow, which, with existing societies in Pinner, Eastcote and Northwood, helped Harrow Circuit become one of the strongest in Britain. Maybe the next stage for such Circuits is not only to acquire community development skills, but to join with other suburban churches to create a South East Region group to help the laity at work across the metropolis?

Post-1945 saw the creation of New Towns across the region to cope with its growth and the city's population density; but only one was built in London, on the Erith marshes at Thamesmead in Bexley and Greenwich Boroughs. Here Methodists have been partners with Anglicans and the United Reformed Church in shared arrangements, which sometimes have also included Roman Catholic communities. Indeed, it was a Roman Catholic priest who first realized how helpful community development approaches might be in developing awareness in and beyond the Thamesmead churches. These became necessary, too, because of the complex relations of a large staff struggling with issues of collaboration, consultation, autonomy and fellowship. Needing help they turned to the ecumenical agency, AVEC, as the Roman Catholic priest had done earlier. One of its workers helped them deal with their issues over a number of years.[71]

Maybe a future role for residential places like the Guy Chester Centre in Muswell Hill is to help foster new ministries for the magnetic southeast, as it has been termed,[72] for the laity in its secular existence and also for those in authority in the churches and their communities to explore new partnerships in both ministry and mission.

Notes

1 The Revd Douglas Griffiths, Obituary, Methodist Conference Minutes 1983, pp. 63–4.

2 Dr Pauline Webb, letter to author, 3 November 1997. See also Happy 60th Anniversary MAYC, Methodist Church 2005.

3 Sir Stafford Cripps, *Methodist Recorder*, 14 June 1945, p. 8.

4 Webb, letter.

5 *Methodist Recorder*, 14 June 1945, p. 5.

6 The Revd Douglas Griffiths, *Methodist Recorder* Supplement, iv, 4 May 1970.

7 The Revd Douglas Griffiths, quoted in *Momentum*, March 2005, p. 15.

8 See John Munsey Turner, *Modern Methodism in England 1932–1998*, Peterborough, Methodist Publishing House, 1998, p. 75.

9 The Revd Terry Walton, letter to the Revd Tony Holden, 31 September 2004.

10 The Revd Dr Irvonwy Morgan, *Daily Telegraph*, 24 March 1954.

11 *Methodist Recorder*, 18 March 1954.

12 The Revd Leonard Barnett, *Methodist Recorder*, 25 March 1954.

13 The Revd Douglas Griffiths, *Methodist Recorder*, 25 March 1954.

14 W. J. Smart, *London, 'Its tragedy and triumph'*, A Wartime London Mission Report, p. 19.

15 Smart, *London*, p. 42.

16 The Revd Douglas Griffiths, responding to questions asked by the Committee of London Methodism 1950–1953, London Mission Committee files.

17 *Methodist Recorder*, 19 May 1966, p. 5.

18 Griffiths, *Methodist Recorder*.

19 Webb, letter.

20 *Methodist Recorder*, 2 June 2005, pp. 10–11.

21 The Revd Mark Wakelin, interview with author, 9 February 2005.

22 For the debate about this, see *Methodist Recorder*, 21 March 1997, p. 1; 3 February 2005, p. 7; 24 March 2005, p. 11; 2 June 2005, pp. 10–11.

23 Wakelin, interview.

24 Wakelin, interview.

25 Dr Pauline Webb, letter to author, 4 March 2005.

26 The Revd Alan S. Tongue, letter to author, 4 March 2005.

27 The Revd Neville Davis, who worked with Douglas Griffiths in Rotherham in the 1960s, letter to author, 2 March 2005.

28 Davis, letter.

29 Davis, letter.

30 Griffiths, obituary.

31 The Revd W. G. Hughes, London Mission Report 1934, p. 23.

32 Griffiths, *Methodist Recorder*, 29 November 1951.

33 Griffiths, Minutes of the London Methodist Commission 1950–53, London Mission Committee files.

34 Griffiths, Minutes.

35 Griffiths, London Mission Report 1959.

36 Jeffrey Harris and Peter Jarvis, *The Church in the Council Estate* – A Consultation of Clergy and Ministers working on Urban Housing Estates held in July 1977 at the University of Surrey at Guildford, Methodist Home Mission Division 1978, p. 5. For specific studies of particular congregations see David Wasdell, Barkingside Methodist Church, and a Profile of Havering Road Methodist Church, published in 1983, being part of the Urban Church Project (Unit for Research into Changing Institutions). The two case studies were part of 25 – 15 Anglican and 10 Methodist – churches studied in the late 1970s.

37 Trevor Lockwood in Harris and Jarvis, *Church*, p. 23. See also Trevor Lockwood, *The Church on the Housing Estate*, Methodist Home Mission Division, 1993.

38 London Mission Report 1955, pp. 28–9.

39 Tooting Methodist Church, *Sixty Glorious Years 1910–1970*, p. 9.

40 The Revd A. E. Binks, London Mission Report 1936, p. 32.

41 I am grateful to Allan Dawson, who has been at St Helier Central Hall since 1940, for this information.

42 The Revd E. Ewart Dewhurst, London Mission Report 1934.

43 London Mission Report 1955, p. 15.

44 The Very Revd David Frayne, letter to author, 1 June 2005.

45 Stan Cornish, letter to author, 10 June 2005.

46 Cornish, letter.

47 *Romford Observer*, 20 July 1979, p. 24.

48 Cornish, letter.

49 Harris and Jarvis, *Church*, p. 10.

50 Harris and Jarvis, *Church*, pp. 27 and 32.

51 Note on Broadwater Farm Church Workers and Clergy Group, 2005, based on an earlier statement prepared by the Revd Francis Ackroyd.

52 David Hawkey, letter to author, 22 July 2005.

53 The Revd Jenni Sweet, letter to author, 1 August 2005.

54 Sweet, letter.

55 Sweet, letter.

56 Hawkey, letter.

57 Hawkey, letter.

58 Sweet, letter.

59 Hawkey, letter.

60 Mrs Yvonne Sinclair, interview with author, 24 July 2005.

61 Eddie Langdown, interview with author, 18 July 2005.

62 The Revd Peter Coates, *South Londoner*, 9 February 1972, cited in J. D. Beasley, *The Bitter Cry Heard and Heeded, The Story of the South London Mission 1889–1989*, South London Mission, 1990, p. 158.

63 The Revd Philip Luscombe in Beasley, *Bitter Cry*, p. 158.

64 The Revd Brian Goss, letter to author, 22 March 2005.

65 Rank Trust, London Mission Committee files 1984.

66 London Mission Report 1956, p. 33.

67 The Revd Howard Booth, letter to author, 16 August 2005.

68 Booth, letter.

69 Booth, letter.

70 See AVEC Archives, Annotated Catalogue, Box 10.

71 AVEC Archives, Annotated Catalogue, p. 41.

72 Jeffrey Harris, ed., *The Magnetic South: Living Churches in London and the South East*, Methodist Home Mission Division, 1988. The address of the Guy Chester Centre is: Chester House, Pages Lane, Muswell Hill, London N10 1PR.

11

Working With, *Rather than* For
George Lovell, Catherine Widdicombe and AVEC

On 14 July 1961 the *Croydon Advertiser* reported that a mixed club had been set up by the Parchmore Road Methodist Church and the local Council of Churches in Thornton Heath, backed by Croydon's Education Committee, who had recommended that 'Mr T. Walton should be appointed part-time youth leader'. The area had become high profile nearly a decade earlier on 2 November 1952 when Police Constable Sidney Miles had been killed pursuing two youths, Craig and Bentley, for which Bentley was hung, though it transpired his friend was the guilty one. It resembled an inner-city neighbourhood, yet it was set in a largely prosperous and suburban borough, sometimes described as the largest town in Europe.

The new club met in a secondary school on the estate where violence was still a factor. Indeed, damage to property soon caused its closure and removal to Parchmore Road. Here it eventually became part of what was known as the Ten Centres Youth and Community Project, the brainchild of Terry Walton of London MAYC, who had cut his teeth in youth work in 1950s Upper Norwood Methodism. Indeed, in due course the club there became one of the Centres, with non-churchgoing young people putting on *Jesus Christ Superstar* at MAYC's London Weekend. The youth work there still exists, but is now part-time.[1]

Terry Walton, who came from a tough Bermondsey background, had been evacuated to Cornwall during the war. In 1944, aged 13, angry and confused at being sent back to London as doodlebugs fell, he set up camp – along with a gang of other boys – in a house sealed off because of the bombing. For this, he was sent to an approved school. By the age of 16 he had been converted, and from then on seldom looked back, becoming involved not only in inner London youth work, but also by putting up in his own home Caribbean students, who later held high-profile jobs on their return to the Caribbean.[2] With the help of F. Ronald Ducker, who chaired the London South East District and invited Terry to be District MAYC lay secretary, Terry soon became known throughout London.

In the early 1960s, Ducker, along with others, negotiated with both Kent and Croydon Education Committees and with the Inner London Education Authority (ILEA) a development programme for young people, based on Methodist sites, as they responded to proposals recommended by the 1960 Albermarle report. Ducker also negotiated with Dr Irvonwy Morgan, secretary of the London Mission Committee, who had access not only to Rank Trust and other charitable money, but also War Damage Commission funds, available either for rebuilding Methodist churches on original or new sites, the latter being a concession he and others had negotiated with the authorities.

Part Puritan scholar and poet, part entrepreneur, Morgan and his wife lived with daily suffering as they had a disabled child to care for. He was always his own person and, with a firmness that enabled him to pursue a policy if he judged it viable, could also seize a moment whatever the difficulties. By the mid-1960s, therefore, he had agreed to setting up a Greater London Youth and Community Service (GLYCS), eventually based at King's Cross Mission, which became another of the Centres. Without him, the project would never have started, for he chaired its Management Committee.[3]

Initially the ILEA funded a part-time training and development officer for London MAYC with Terry appointed to the post, with an office in Bromley Central Hall. Convinced that church youth work needed to be more competent, he encouraged staff training, especially with the help of Dr T. R. Batten, Reader in Community Development at London University's Institute of Education. Dr Batten supported Terry in his work, which in 1963 included a survey for Dr Morgan of possible new initiatives in the newly created 12 inner London boroughs. Eventually this resulted in nine bases, one of which was outside London at Gillingham in Kent. Another never materialized for Dr Morgan did not think the declining church at Westridge Road, Battersea, was strong enough to sustain work with Ton-Up Bikers, who for several years had been given help by street youth workers. Focused also on Battersea Bridge, the Monarchs Motor Cycle club, which later became Hell's Angels, was assisted to maintain bikes by five Greater London Council instructors. Sometimes members helped to decorate old people's homes as well as enthusiastically taking part in sporting events.[4] Some later made good but they were a raw group and 'Friday night discotheques meant frisking young people to remove hatchets, knives, cycle chains'.[5] Little wonder that Dr Morgan feared, with such a small congregation, that if he entered a binding legal agreement with the ILEA, eventually it might end up owning the property.

Terry Walton introduced George Lovell, who in 1966 was appointed to the Parchmore Road Centre, to Dr Batten. Previously, in Sydenham,

Lovell had worked in a deprived area with 13- to 16-year-olds of average, or less-than-average, ability, but had found the going tough. Born in 1929, initially he had intended to be an engineer, but felt called to the Methodist ministry, though at the start of training the strain on him and his wife, Molly, was considerable as they had a small child to bring up. There was a third adult member in their south London home, Dorothy Household, a teacher who became enthused as George, now on a Batten community development course, explained its theory and practice. Indeed she returned to college to study education to help her make a complementary contribution to George's work as it developed at Parchmore. Sometime later, however, when Molly, two Lancashire nephews and Dorothy were visiting the Tower of London, a bomb exploded (for which nobody has ever been charged) that killed Dorothy, seriously injuring Molly and her nephews.

'Parchmore broke new ground during my ministry,' George Lovell has written, 'by establishing a Centre in which we worked *with*, rather than *for*, people in the church and in the community. This approach is at the heart of church and community development.' He added, 'We were thinking about what we were doing and why, what was going on around us and about each other's ideas. Our thinking was down-to-earth. It was about theory, theology and spirituality but it was not abstract – it was directed towards action.'[6]

The work was assessed in teach-ins and workshops, which focused on community and open youth work and the effectiveness of church activities.[7] First they considered what being one of the Ten Centres meant and the training that was needed; second, there was discussion on how to establish church youth work involving a comprehensive Christian education programme; third, how to reorganize administration and management; and, lastly, how to weld new and old together and create structures in time for George's departure. The entire process lasted from October 1966 to 1972.[8]

As Parchmore developed, so did other Centres – but not everything was plain sailing. One example was Railton Road, Brixton, where in 1965 a team ministry had been established after pioneer work by two earlier ministers had drawn many to it from the expanding Caribbean communities around the Centre. With George Pottinger, Byron Chambers and others was Gavton Shepherd from Guyana, a product of Georgetown Clubland, which had been modelled by the Revd Deryck Adams, later himself a minister at Railton Road, on Clubland in Southwark. Gavton was full time and employed by the ILEA. Soon he found himself running a 'black club' five nights a week with some 150 members. Activities included involvement in MAYC weekends and exchange visits with other clubs, though Epilogues were not always popular. By 1970, when its new premises were complete, Gavton, who was one of the first black youth workers in Britain, found the Club was known widely as 'Shepherd's'.

The team ministry, one of a number set up at the time, tried to highlight the problems of black youngsters, especially their treatment by the police. Some arrested were strip-searched, and others reported their heads were put down toilets that were then flushed. This led Gavton to hold a meeting with the accusers and the police, whose Chief of Police stormed out when it became too heated.[9] In spite of incidents like this, the Centre flourished, with Friday being its big night. Gavton himself moved on and, after further training, worked in other social and community work fields, but by 1975 there were three full-time paid youth workers at the Centre.

Meanwhile, Parchmore, whose youth centre had opened in May 1968, with some 60 members, both black and white, found Saturday night the liveliest, especially when members had earlier watched Crystal Palace play! For a while the youth centre experienced violence, with broken glass and broken bottles everywhere, which led to its closure. Where had George and the full-time worker gone wrong? There may have been a culture clash between the working-class young people and staff, although a more potent factor was the clash between the members themselves, heightened because the club was a safe space to express their anger and their views. The power to choose which adults worked with them, as they requested, was granted; ironically, the original helpers were invited back and asked what interests and skills they brought. What proved critical was that members themselves had taken the initiative. 'Church' youth, meanwhile, asked for authority to use the Saturday slot, vacant since the violence of 1968, which was granted. A worker was now appointed with street credibility which helped the club re-form, and after three months members asked for skilled coaching in football and table tennis,[10] as George found himself their 'vicar'.

The conflict in which George was involved was not untypical of others – at New Eltham, for example, where work had begun in 1965 in a dilapidated hut next to the church. When the new premises were opened in 1967, soon the large numbers attending from the community were a great challenge to this quiet suburban church. David Lemmon, its first youth worker, found he had to deal on Wednesdays with 40 'Rockers', and some 200 'Mods' and others on Thursdays. Fortunately, none chose the wrong night, so there were no punch-ups between the two groups as there had been on Brighton beach.

A range of community activities also began, including a playgroup and a coffee bar, and soon community groups learned that they could hire the premises. Misunderstanding of the Youth and Community

Centre's purposes now arose among some in the congregation. One effect of these ongoing disputes was that none of the professional youth and community workers, including David, stayed long enough to properly establish the work. A similar conflict ensued at Plumstead when the youth worker, John Goodwin, suggested to black members that their children might use the Centre and many, some from a nearby estate, turned up in such numbers that the Christian community felt overwhelmed.[11] 'The success of one strand mitigated against the success of another,' Eric Murray, training officer at the King's Cross Centre, has remarked.[12]

As a result of the ILEA's demise in the mid-1980s, the 28-year contract for youth work at New Eltham was honoured by the Borough of Greenwich. At the end of this period, however, funding was no longer available and the substantial youth work ended. For his part, Barrie Heafford, one of New Eltham's earlier ministers, wondered if sufficient thinking about implications of the Centres had been done. In New Eltham's case this included likely clashes between comprehensive and grammar school young people and commuter and inner-city mentalities. However he added, 'I benefited from the experiences and insight of six years spent grappling with the philosophy of working with people, rather than for them.'[13] This, he felt, helped his later ministries. Despite such problems, New Eltham Centre survived, and is sponsoring a daily club for older people and offering facilities for community hire,[14] including the south Greenwich Adult Institute.[15]

Like Barrie Heafford, George Lovell and his colleagues learned much from their crises, especially about the need to clarify boundaries, a point that emerged from five problem areas that their studies discerned: work with the retired; the handicapped; former psychiatric patients; those needing counselling; and help for children with homework difficulties. As George saw it, the key motivation must be a desire to help 'develop people's lives whether they become Christian or not'. Some might consider this compromised the Church's mission 'but it is realistic,' he felt, 'because it means we have a positive purpose in regard to *all* who come to the centre'.[16] It took some time for more traditional Christians to accept this approach but, like George, they soon found themselves learning new skills.

George himself was now studying at London University, preparing a PhD thesis based on his experiences and beginning in-service training sessions for Centre employees. Meanwhile Terry Walton was helping to implement the policy that he and Dr Morgan, with Methodist Conference backing, had devised. It often involved complex negotiations not only with Methodist structures, but with the Department of Education and Science and the ILEA. There were inevitable delays by statutory authorities as a result of funding problems and legal matters to agree, whereby London Methodism committed itself to arrangements for several decades. Out of these, the Church, of course, gained new and purpose-built plant or, as at Parchmore, property adapted for new tasks. It gained, too, new secular colleagues, so inevitably there were tensions when Church and secular personnel met to consider their respective roles and expectations.

The King's Cross development became 'a communication centre', according to Dr Morgan, where Terry and others established training courses with support from Dr Batten. 'It certainly sharpened our thinking,' Eric Murray has judged.[17] On Friday nights for several years there was the King's Cross Hovel Night Club, helped by Cy Grant and Steve Race, with counselling for teenagers available in the background. Its aim, Terry felt, 'was to provide a Methodist attraction point away from Soho and the drug culture which was emerging'.[18] By 1973 one estimate was that, during the past three years, training courses had increased from 5 to 29, involving 3,000, including 1,000 club leaders and others. By 1977, however, the cost of running the Centre, formally opened in 1972 by Margaret Thatcher as Secretary of State for Education and Science, was too costly and the GLYCS moved to Muswell Hill alongside the national office for education and youth.

In the meantime, by 1968 Terry, who had always lived on a large map, creating the Community Education for the Young European programme of youth exchanges between Britain and Germany, with King's Cross Hostel as a base for those doing community service,[19] had become unconvinced that Methodism cared about inner London. He therefore resigned as development officer, joining Kingsway College to direct a Community Education and Research Project, while retaining a consultancy role with GLYCS. By 1974 he had moved again, to Avery Hill College, and his association with the Ten Centres programme ended.

George Lovell saw changes, too. He left Parchmore in 1972 to join with Catherine Widdicombe, from the Roman Catholic Grail community, to run Project 70–75. Sometimes two people come together and their respective gifts and experiences make them joint pioneers. This happened to George and Catherine, acknowledged later by Archbishop Derek Worlock, as he became, who recognized 'they are naturally a working partnership which ought to be used and never lost'.[20]

The Grail, a group of women who commit themselves without time limit to God, is concerned with the apostolate of the laity in daily life. Founded in the 1930s in Holland, it was brought to England by Baroness Van Drakestein, and based in Pinner from the early 1950s.[21] Catherine had joined it in 1949 after becoming a teacher, attracted by its pioneering spirit and practical approach, as members took on laity education, and later group work, counselling, modern liturgy and community building. By 1962 Catherine was in Rome, as head of a small secretariat for the Roman Catholic Bishops of England and Wales at the Second Vatican Council. Drawn to many of its ideas, from 1964 to 1970 she explored them in various ways and committed herself to implementing the Council's approaches in Britain.[22]

From 1967 she set out to become more competent, first by taking part in sensitivity training courses, and then acting as a staff member on many of them. In 1969 she attended a course on non-directive community development run by the Battens and, walking down Gower Street at the time, 'was gripped by an intense insight into the significance and potential of this approach'. She was convinced that those in authority in the Church would find in it a way of turning Vatican II ideas into reality in ordinary parishes and communities.

She raised her concerns with the Battens who encouraged her to discuss them with George Lovell. Subsequently, with two clergy colleagues, one Anglican, one Roman Catholic, she convened several ecumenical groups of clergy and church workers at the Grail to take her ideas forward, first gaining support from her Grail community, which sent her on a three-month course that Dr Batten ran.[23] She soon realized that she needed an ecumenical team to help her implement an idea that she had conceived on the Batten course, which was eventually created with George and herself full-time.[24] Changed radically by her Rome experience, and now seeing truth as a process wider than the Churches, she was reaching out in ways that surprised her as she began to establish with the team[25] what has become known as Project 70–75.[26] It met over a year to create an action-research project for local Christians, though finance, as with many ecumenical ventures, was a problem. But with individual gifts, the Grail's support and George funded by well-wishers, they began negotiations with Crouch End churches in the London Borough of Haringey.

Initially the local churches did not relish the idea of being pioneers, but grew more keen as they realized how helpful to their work the acquisition of new skills might be. Eventually the team worked with individual clergy and laity and also with five churches: an Anglican parish that set up a visiting scheme; a community centre in another Catholic parish; and a project in a Baptist church.[27] The team also helped Hornsey community schemes estimate their needs, with one team member helping young mothers to act on what they had discovered.[28] Another programme during Project 70–75 involved open youth work, which led to a walk-in counselling centre staffed by professionals; this subsequently became an outstanding organization.[29]

After withdrawing in the autumn of 1974 by mutual agreement, the team spent two years assessing its work and preparing a final report, which was published in 1978. What emerged? Overall, both clergy and laity were impressed by changes that had occurred as a result of their work together, within both congregations and communities. They also valued increased understanding between them and felt that the community development approach was compatible with their witness and mission.[30]

In 1972 George was involved in training a group of ministers as they considered the relation of the community to the Methodist Church, and roles and tensions between ministers and lay workers. It also considered the theology implied and the structures necessary, for the Ten Centres youth workers often employed by local authorities, and misunderstandings that could arise between the different groups with which they were involved. The meeting, which included representatives from seven other Centres, was enthused as it realized Jesus himself used a community development model. It was 'even the meaning of the Incarnation': working *with* rather than *for* people; allowing them freedom of choice, decision-making and responsibility for consequences. Thus they were able to grow and become more mature. Moreover, as a teacher, Jesus took care to help people to clarify and structure their thinking too.[31] Subsequently, when in 1976 George and Catherine, using the French word for 'with', founded AVEC, they were invited to conduct a course for the Ten Centre staff. This they did in 1979–80.

The Revd Edward Rogers, author of *A Christian Commentary on Communism* and one-time head of the Department of Christian Citizenship, agreed to become AVEC's chair, which gave it credibility, stability and wider support. 'I live in Croydon,' he later wrote, 'and frequently visit the place of his [George Lovell's] initial experiment in Thornton Heath, and have seen for myself that a decade after his departure the way he pioneered proves effective.'[32] From now on, George and Catherine, with part-time colleagues, grew in professionalism and competency, working with AVEC which was based at Chelsea Methodist Church until the project ceased in 1994.

For Catherine, the support of Archbishop Worlock, whom she had first met at the Second Vatican Council, helped her work forward; though, despite being an AVEC trustee, he was not always able to obtain the support of other bishops. Catherine, however, did have the Grail's unwavering commitment, while George had a number of senior Methodist leaders backing him, though not always with money, and the backing of Chelsea Methodist Church.[33] Over the period they were able to set up 357 work consultations. There were day conferences, too, ongoing support for individuals and groups, and also a two-year postgraduate diploma. But the core of their training was their ten-day church and community development work and theory course. [34]

Staff also provided consultancy services for, or worked with, some 139 projects, mostly in the UK, with a few in Ireland and Africa. They were involved with 8,000 people from ten denominations, including 4,000 Roman Catholics, at parish, hierarchy and religious order level, 2,000 Methodists, and 1,500 Anglicans. [35] Courses were about Church and community work at all levels and ministry to specialized groups. All training and consultancy was regarded as an action-research programme. [36] Clustered around this were a number of independent programmes for higher accreditation – one in 1984 by Catherine on the implementation of the Second Vatican Council, and one in 1987 by their part-time colleague and Methodist minister, Charles New, on the use of community development in a local church and community centre. [37]

How did such work impact on London? At the personal level, individuals like Leslie Griffiths, [38] now at Wesley's Chapel, and Diane and Richard Clutterbuck, who first met AVEC as returning missionaries, felt their work was clarified by AVEC courses. 'It was very important for Richard and me, as a couple,' Diane has written, 'that we did those first two courses together.' [39] 'Richard had an idea for a Christian Arts Festival in Muswell Hill,' which he took to its Council of Churches. 'It has just taken off,' she noted, 'gathered a momentum of its own.' [40] One Roman Catholic bishop, Bishop Guazzelli, from Westminster Diocese, was overheard to say of an AVEC course that it was 'the most informative and formative course he had done in his whole priest's career'. [41]

Some, however, like Wendy Godfrey, who edited an ecumenical community work newsletter, was not so sure about George's and Catherine's approaches. Conceding their book on Project 70–75 reflected 'meticulous scholarship and deep care', she still felt 'there is something directive about non-directive intervention'. [42] 'What a contrast to the way we usually muddle happily through,' she commented. Was there a danger of 'getting bogged down by the consultative process'? She thus preferred a 'discovery and learn as you go approach', which was more flexible, less didactic 'and equally effective'. [43]

George, however – keen to learn from the social sciences – argues community development models are about maximizing human freedom. Just as 'Albert Schweitzer had reverence for life', so the community development movement exhibited 'a reverence for freedom'. It was 'more than self-help, for there was a philosophical, pastoral and theological position which affirmed the freedom given by God 'and whether we allow that to other people'. [44] George does, however, concede that community development includes 'both environmental and social improvement', yet is 'more than either or both of these things'. [45]

By the early 1990s (Edward Rogers had been succeeded as AVEC's chair by the Revd Nigel Gilson in 1988), the question of George's and Catherine's successors arose. They had become a formidable pair, with Catherine more the entrepreneur, as she had been over Project 70–75, and George more the theoretician who thought things through. Both had become effective practitioners, trainers and consultants and gave each other confidence as they listened, encouraged and challenged one another. George, ever the engineer, would ask: 'Does it work?' then 'How does it work?' or 'Why isn't it working?' 'If it doesn't work,' he would add, 'what must be done to put it right?' All these were questions that could be put to a project, a group, or an individual organization.[46]

Despite their work there were continuing funding problems, and though key Roman Catholic figures, including Cardinal Hume, had been supportive, had it not been for the Grail, Catherine would have found little security. How, then, could successors be found? George ceased as director in 1991, becoming AVEC's research worker, then part-time senior research fellow at Westminster College, Oxford. Catherine, who left after George, continued her life at the Grail, at one point becoming its president. Both found they were invited to run courses and were sought out for advice. AVEC's trustees did find a successor to George – an Anglican priest; but money was not sufficiently forthcoming for the long-term to persuade them that AVEC had a viable future and in 1994 it closed. Despite grant aid, churches and their workers had been unwilling to pay economic prices, and as Nigel Gilson observed, 'Some people may have been challenged or threatened by new understandings of authority', conceding also that 'doubtless we made mistakes'.[47] Compared with the church leaders who backed AVEC initially, fighting its corner when others had reservations, there seemed few, if any, on the board ready to think laterally – apart from requesting George and Catherine to 'harvest' the work they had done, and make AVEC's experience and resources more readily accessible for others to use.[48]

Over ten years, seven new books were produced and a church and community development archive set up at the Wesley Studies Centre, now at Oxford Brookes University, which includes an analysis and listing of the material they have gathered in a digestible form. Another spin-off was 'the AVEC Association'. However, this was short-lived, but AVEC Resources, which continues, has provided useful publications and theoretical material.

Analogous crises hit the Ten Centres programmes, particularly in the 1980s recession. By now, Walham Green and Green Lanes had come to grief. Despite having some 1,000 young men and women of Caribbean background at Waltham Green's start, with one full-time and five part-time youth workers, its young radical minister, with community development experience, often found himself involved in conflicts stemming from five housing estates near the Centre. Violence had become a problem, too, with some prepared to use knives, others on probation, and yet others involved in serious crime.[49] Some members took part in summer schools out of London,[50] but trouble broke out when the Centre was set on fire, though this seemed to cement members' support. As elsewhere, conflicts arose between ILEA staff and the Church: it seemed that, despite regular meetings with Methodist authorities and ILEA officials, the aims and goals of the two in supporting the Centres had not been thought through fully, though ILEA staff were appreciative of Methodism's attempt to reach out in often deprived areas.

'No blueprint is possible for the Centres as a whole,'[51] Tony White, Terry Walton's successor, once wrote, a dictum that proved correct at Green Lanes. Here lack of staff continuity, insufficient Circuit support (though 16 members had attended a King's Cross course),[52] laity who commuted in, and one minister not even persuaded of the community development approach,[53] proved difficult obstacles to overcome. A dynamic young black minister appointed to Green Lanes soon attracted more from the African–Caribbean community and, discovering ILEA plans to use the premises full time, summarily gave its youth workers their marching orders. 'I changed Green Lanes through the Church Council meeting from a youth and community centre,' he wrote, 'to an ecumenical centre.'[54] Soon it was used by two Pentecostal congregations, and on Saturdays by an Asian group for social gatherings.

If George Lovell and Terry Walton were to revisit their pasts, what would they now be told? At Brixton, Terry would learn that during the 1981 Brixton riots, when Railton Road burned, the Centre was not touched. And that its minister, Graham Kent, and two youth workers had given evidence to *The Scarman Report*. Scarman himself, along with his wife, had visited the Centre and heard about the 'Sus' laws and the way that young black people were often stopped and searched.[55] Just as earlier the Brixton Advice Centre and a local clinic had begun at Railton Road, so more recently Terry would have found the Metropolitan Police had used it for racism and cultural awareness training events, and Methodism's Racial Justice Unit had been funding ongoing running costs since 1992, because Lambeth had reduced grants.[56] Gavton Shepherd, Terry would learn, was still at the church, wondering now how new street ministry could be started.[57]

Terry would also have found a record of good work at Plumstead, where during the 1970s and 1980s a large black club had thrived, despite some problems with drugs. A few had become youth workers, and in Woolwich a 'Simba Club', a large African–Caribbean Centre for the whole area, had been formed and survived for over a decade.[58] One minister, David Cruise, had felt there was insufficient church youth work, so had set up a Sunday night group, of which Stephen Lawrence was a member, with his family becoming involved in the church and his mother a member. David has continued to help the Lawrence family in its subsequent struggles and campaigns.

With a membership of about 100, Plumstead has allowed youth work to flourish for 30 years and hundreds of adults to use a property that is one of the best equipped in Greenwich. Work has varied according to changing patterns and needs, and has included support for single parents; employment and skills projects; and work with Vietnamese and other refugees from the nearby Barnfield estate. With a Tamil school at one point and an Iranian Youth Agency based at the Centre, the church has been international, itself arranging exchanges over five years, including trips to Brazil and the Czech Republic. Its 'Chatterbox' lunch club for the elderly is still run by church members who caught the original Youth and Community Centre vision; with, more recently, projects concerned with domestic violence and help for teenagers in trouble at school gaining the ascendancy.

George's visit to Parchmore now would have resulted in a surprise. There is no longer a youth centre as such. In the 1990s, a time of local authority retrenchment, a major conflict developed between a paid youth worker and another group using the Centre. None of the attempts to resolve it ended satisfactorily and the people involved were asked to leave. A little later, Croydon Borough stopped supporting Centre-based youth work. The effect of this on the ever-changing congregation, now mainly African–Caribbean, was to ask itself 'Who are we?' and 'Where are we going?'[59] To survive, it discovered it had to develop work for which funds were available and accept conditions laid down by funders. In 2004 Parchmore was still a stable congregation, but had also become a highly successful Healthy Living Centre – in addition to being a place where people came for recreation and education. It is, says the minister and team leader, 'a place of welcome but also a place where friendship and support goes out into the community'.[60] There are several paid staff at Parchmore involved with over 50 groups.

The Healthy Living Centre has many facets, including fitness, health problems, multicultural cooking and Health Awareness Days. It involves health professionals and is supported by the Patient Care Trust. Many volunteers are involved in the various activities, both on the site and in the community, including the daily 'Meals on Legs' service. It is over 30 years since Parchmore's building was remodelled, and the congregation now has to work out how to renew it physically – a process already begun with the installation of solar power for its water needs. Some

1,700 use the property weekly, from a neighbourhood that now has a Hindu temple and a mosque. Fortunately, the Centre is in a strong and supportive Circuit, but the group knows it must adapt or die – a challenge needing both wisdom and creativity. As in other Centres, these two gifts had to be combined, which sometimes proved difficult.

Notes

1 John Goodwin, interview with author, 17 January 2005.

2 The Revd Terry Walton, Aide Memoire for Brian Frost, 21 October 2004, p. 26.

3 Walton, Aide Memoire, p. 27.

4 London Mission Report 1966, pp. 4–5.

5 The Revd Chris Cheeseman, letter to Terry Walton, 22 September 2004.

6 George Lovell, Garth Rogers and Peter Sharrocks, *The Parchmore Partnership*, ed. Malcolm Grundy, Chester House Publications, 1995, p. 5.

7 *The Parchmore Partnership*, p. 6.

8 *The Parchmore Partnership*, pp. 8.

9 Gavton Shepherd, interview with author, 12 October 2004.

10 George Lovell, Parchmore Church, Youth and Community Project: An Account of the Development and Progress of the Youth Centre's Work, Chapter 1, AVEC files, Wesley Studies Centre, Oxford Brookes University, Oxford (Harcourt Hill Campus).

11 Goodwin, interview.

12 The Revd Eric Murray, interview with author, 30 June 2005.

13 The Revd Barrie Heafford, letter to author, 20 April 2005.

14 Steve Offord, letter to author, 27 February 2005.

15 London Mission Committee, Rank Trust Files 1991.

16 George Lovell, *Methodist Recorder*, 22 February 1968.

17 Eric Murray, letter to Terry Walton, 2 October 2005.

18 Terry Walton, letter to Eric Murray, 28 September 2004.

19 London Mission Reports, 1967 and 1968.

20 Catherine Widdicombe, interview with author, 7 June 2005.

21 On the role of Baroness Yvonne Van Drakestein, see 'The Grail', *In Touch*, series 2, no. 62, 30 November 1994, pp. 1–6.

22 See Catherine Widdicombe and George Lovell, 'Our Church and Community Development Stories', AVEC Tenth Anniversary Brochure, 1987, p. 2.

23 Widdicombe and Lovell, *Community Development Stories*, p. 3.

24 Catherine Widdicombe, 'Memorandum on the use of the non-directive approach', 1969, AVEC Archive no. 180.

25 Widdicombe, 'Memorandum'.

26 Widdicombe, interview.

27 See George Lovell and Catherine Widdicombe, *Churches and Communities. An Approach to Development in the Local Church*, London, Search Press, 1978, pp. 74–95.

28 Widdicombe and Lovell, *Churches and Communities*, pp. 124–57.

29 Widdicombe and Lovell, *Churches and Communities*, pp. 96–123.

30 Widdicombe and Lovell, *Churches and Communities*, pp. 195–205.

31 Report of the Conference of Ministers of the Ten Centres at Aylesford, Kent, 30 June–1 July 1972, AVEC Files. See also Grundy, *Parchmore Partnership*, pp. 82–3.

32 The Revd Edward Rogers, Foreword, in George Lovell, *Human and Religious Factors in Church and Community Work* (based on the Beckley Social Service Lecture 1981), London, Grail Publication, 1982.

33 The Revd Dr George Lovell, interview with author, 7 June 2005.

34 George Lovell and Catherine Widdicome, AVEC Archives, *Annotated Catalogue* 2002, p. 11.

35 Widdicombe and Lovell, *Annotated Catalogue*, p. 11.

36 Widdicombe and Lovell, *Annotated Catalogue*, p. 12.

37 For full list, see AVEC Archives, File 146. See also *Annotated Catalogue*, pp. 56–62.

38 See George Lovell, ed., *Telling Experiences, Stories about a Transforming Way of Working with People*, London, Chester House Publications, 1996, pp. 15–28.

39 Diane Clutterbuck, in Lovell, ed., *Telling Experiences*, pp. 158–60.

40 Clutterbuck in Lovell, ed., *Telling Experiences*, p. 160.

41 Widdicombe, interview.

42 Wendy Godfrey, Review of George Lovell and Catherine Widdicombe, 'Churches and Communities', *Epworth Review*, May 1979, p. 119.

43 Godfrey, *Epworth Review*, p. 120.

44 George Lovell, interview with author, 7 June 2005.

45 George Lovell, 'The Mission of the Church and Community Development' in *The Social Sciences and the Church*, ed. C. L. Mitton, Edinburgh, T&T Clark, 1972, p. 209.

46 George Lovell and Catherine Widdicombe, joint interview with author, 7 June 2005.

47 The Revd Nigel Gilson, Foreword in George Lovell, *Avec, Agency and Approach*, an AVEC publication, the Grail, 125 Waxwell Lane, Pinner, Middx HA5 3ER, 1996.

48 AVEC Resources Brochure. Resources for people working and consulting in church and community, An Annotated Book List, the Grail, 2000, p. 1. AVEC Resources is a group set up in association with the Grail by a small charitable trust to make more generally available papers and books on community development, in-service training and work and vocational ministry and mission.

49 Dr Irvonwy Morgan, London Mission Report 1972, p. 15.

50 Morgan, London Mission Report 1972, p. 18.

51 Tony White, Brochure for the King's Cross Centre Opening, 1972.

52 London Mission Report 1967, pp. 25–7.

53 Meeting of Ministers, King's Cross Centre, 24 March 1971, AVEC Files.

54 Robinson Milwood, *Liberation and Mission. A Black Experience*, London, African and Caribbean Resource (ACEC) Centre, 1997, p. 14.

55 *The Scarman Report, The Brixton Disorders 10–12 April 1981*, Harmondsworth, Penguin Books, 1982, especially pp. 43, 69, 222–3.

56 'Reflection and Renewal, Review of the Multi-Racial Projects Fund (MRPF)' *Methodist Church* 2003, p.25.

57 Gavton Shepherd, interview with author, 12 October 2004.

58 John Goodwin, interview with author, 17 January 2005.

59 The Revd Andrew Shepherd-Dart, interview with author, 17 May 2005.

60 The Revd Andrew Shepherd-Dart, The Parchmore Centre, Annual Report 2004, p. 1.

Part 4

Public Advocates

Introduction by Stuart Jordan

Many of the examples of Methodist social passion described so far have shown an acute awareness of human need and of the possibilities for an effective response. Now, in this final section, the focus moves away from the direct meeting of individual need to those concerned with addressing some of the underlying causes of injustice – away from social or community provision to the realm of public advocacy.

While the ministry of Donald Soper, with its public commitment to socialism and pacifism, is well known, the names and political significance of Henry Broadhurst, Arthur Henderson and Philip Snowden will be new to many. The breadth as well as length of Soper's own ministry encompassed many dimensions and often transcended the boundaries and thinking of his Wesleyanism. None the less, the emphasis here on his political involvement should be seen alongside his successive pastoral appointments within the London Missions, where his political commitments were grounded in a wide range of practical engagement with social reality.

The same commitment to a local congregation and community also roots the passion for justice seen in the account of Pauline Webb and David Haslam. Their campaigns were part of a growing international awareness among Christians of the legitimate demands for liberation heard in many parts of the world. Within the UK context, the challenges they issued and the protests they organized were bound to provoke controversy among the Churches, as well as the major financial institutions that were their main targets. At the same time, the issues of justice they espoused resonated for many Methodists and other Christians with the tradition of which they were part. Meanwhile, their witness, embodying as it did a well-organized strategy, helped many to appreciate the need to move beyond abstract principles to effective action.

The issue of racism awareness to which Sybil Phoenix has contributed so much was, of course, informed by her own personal experience and that of the black community of which she is part. Her story again embraces different dimensions, as her involvement moves from local youth and community projects that met immediate needs, to the longer-term task of addressing the causes of racism through the provision of awareness training.

The individuals whose stories are recounted here have been outstanding advocates of major issues in which many others have also shared, not least as a result of the leadership and inspiration they have provided. They exemplify the possibility that political conviction can be combined with graciousness and humour to good effect. As for all the pioneers whose stories have been told, it is clear that they are regularly sustained by the worship and witness of local congregations and that, for them, their social passion is explicitly rooted in the Christian gospel.

The Magnificat Puts the Communist Manifesto in the Shade
Donald Soper and Christian Socialism

In the late 1980s an elderly, disillusioned trade unionist, who had seen too much selfishness in the Amalgamated Engineering Union, in which he had been a shop steward, saw Lord Soper on television. Turning to his wife he commented: 'A good man; but very left'. The trade unionist, who had abandoned the Church in the 1920s, had yet retained an ethical stance, and Donald Soper had reached him through the genius of his communication skills.

Donald Soper was born in 1903 into a prosperous middle-class family in Wandsworth. At Cambridge University, studying for the ministry at Wesley House, after a first degree in history, it seems he first became aware of the Methodist minister S. E. Keeble, and his Christian Socialism, during the 1924 Birmingham Conference on politics, economics and citizenship (COPEC), to which he was a delegate. Certainly, as was his practice always, he picked up ideas from wherever he found them and re-minted them for a wider audience. But, more significantly, William Temple, Chair of COPEC, made his often quoted remark 'Christianity is the most materialistic of all the world's religions',[1] which Soper later observed 'put a theological cat among a number of religious pigeons'.[2]

In some ways COPEC was a turning point for Donald Soper as he became convinced 'social policies and personal ethics were the obverse and reverse of the same model', a view similar to that of an earlier Christian Socialist, Philip Snowden. Soper had a further crucial experience one lunchtime in Derby on a Student Christian Movement mission, when 'unfledged and unknowing' he made a visit to a local engineering works. Here he 'saw industrial life at firsthand' and 'came out at the end emotionally a socialist', he recalled.[3] 'When I was young,' he once reminisced, 'socialism was the light of my life.'[4] The 1926 General Strike soon gave him the opportunity to show his colours and, unlike many students, he sided with the strikers, addressing meetings in their support. With a friend from Wesley House, Cambridge, Soper opened a centre for the strikers in a Primitive Methodist Chapel downtown where, he later claimed, he discovered through debate 'the fellowship of controversy'.[5]

Donald Soper's 'conversion', for such it was, highlights an experience many early Christian Socialists also knew as they struggled with unjust work conditions and poverty. This had begun in the second half of the nineteenth century as they forsook Liberalism for Labour, though at the start some were called Lib-Lab in their outlook. A key date in this shift occurred in 1885 when a member of Hugh Price Hughes's Brixton congregation, Henry Broadhurst, was asked by him to write on religion and the working classes for the first edition of Hughes's new weekly, *The Methodist Times*. Life had been tough for Broadhurst, especially in the late 1850s, when as a stonemason he tramped miles for work in the south of England as a result of an economic depression. By 1872 he had become chair of the masons' committee when there was agitation for better pay in the building trade, and soon became its spokesperson. They obtained better conditions, which led to Broadhurst working full time with the Stonemason's Union. Thus, if one Christian Socialist strand was middle class, as intellectuals like Donald Soper turned towards the working class, another was the rising up within it of trade unionists like Henry Broadhurst, who were also Methodists.

The year 1872 also saw Broadhurst as the Union's delegate to the Trades Union Congress and elected to its parliamentary committee, where he played a leading role. The next year he was elected Secretary of the Labour Representation League. Formed to send trade unionists to Parliament, in 1875 the TUC made Broadhurst its secretary. Later public work led to direct contact with Gladstone and, after becoming a Liberal MP, by 1886 he was Under-Secretary in the Home Department, the first working man to be a government minister. Association with the Liberals, however, meant trade unionists became dissatisfied with him. He lost his seat, but in 1894 he became an MP in Leicester, where he continued in Parliament until 1906 as a leading member of the small, but significant, group of Lib-Labs.[6]

The Lib-Lab tension played a significant role in Methodism for many decades, but a growing number of Methodists, like S. E. Keeble, turned to Christian Socialism. They were, however, in a minority and in the 1906 Parliament, comprising some 200 Nonconformist MPs – the exact figure is disputed, depending on how Free Church membership is defined – most Methodists were Liberal.

Among the 1906 Labour intake, however, were Arthur Henderson and Philip Snowden, both of whom had undergone the same kind of 'conversion' as Soper. Henderson was a Wesleyan and a member of Clapham High Street Methodist Church from the time that his work brought him to live in London.[7] Snowden, also brought up in Wesleyan Methodism, retained no specific allegiance, but was deeply influenced by Keeble. Yet while only three of the nine MPs of the Labour Representation Committee (which later became the Labour Party) had traditional Free Church loyalty,[8] the Liberal Party itself had high-profile Methodists like Henry Fowler (later Viscount Wolverhampton and the first Methodist in the House of Lords) and Sir Robert Perks. Despite this, Free Church MPs were in a much weaker position than their supporters believed, because in the 1906 Liberal landslide they were smaller in number than their 1900 predecessors.[9] Moreover, because of their dual allegiance, to party and Church, most of them easily succumbed to government wishes.[10] In addition, the divisions caused by their diversity led to reports that in Wales in particular Nonconformists were becoming Labour supporters.[11]

No such difficulties encompassed Henderson and Snowden. Henderson, who had grown up in Glasgow, where he read *The Methodist Times* in the 1880s, was already a trade unionist and secretary of the local branch of the Iron Founders. Becoming his union's district delegate in 1892, he was later sponsored by the Labour Representation League, which after a London Conference of Socialist and Trade Unionists in 1899 had become the Labour Representation Committee. Becoming its treasurer in 1903, it backed Henderson's desire to be an MP and by 1906 he was in Parliament. Succeeding Keir Hardie as Labour Party leader in 1911, he replaced Ramsey MacDonald as party secretary. Known affectionately as 'Uncle Arthur', Henderson held the post until 1934 and thus was at the heart of early Labour Party history.

It is difficult to over-estimate the achievement of the Methodist who remained a lay preacher and faithful worshipper all his life, while at the same time dealing with national and international issues of grave concern. 'For Arthur,' his brother once said, 'life began with his conversion.' Surely never had the travelling evangelist Rodney 'Gipsy' Smith, who had seen Henderson converted at 16, made such an impact.[12] Henderson never mapped out his theological convictions; rather, he lived out love of neighbour at several levels, serving first in the Asquith 1914 War Cabinet, advising on labour relations, then in Lloyd George's War Cabinet of five. His courage was evident when attacked at a Labour Party Conference over the working of the government's Munitions Acts, to which he replied: 'I'm not here either to please myself or you; I am here to see the war through.'[13]

It has been customary for Labour left-wingers like Lord Soper to register ambivalence towards right-wing trade unionists as they perceived them, yet Henderson resigned from Lloyd George's Cabinet when it would not endorse his attempt to involve international socialists in a Stockholm Peace Conference after he had visited the Kerensky government in Moscow in 1917. Remaining Labour Party leader, as one historian has written, 'he had learnt his lesson. Never again, he declared, would he join a Government in which Labour did not predominate. From that moment "Lib-Lab" was dead.'[14]

In 1916 the Labour Party Conference adopted a resolution from Philip Snowden calling for the nationalization of railways, mines, shipping, banking and insurance,[15] and now, after a major Party reorganization by Henderson, a Conference in 1918 at Westminster Central Hall agreed to 'common ownership of the means of production'.[16] Clause Four, as it became known, caused endless debate within and beyond Labour Party circles and was often used as a reason for not voting Labour. Yet over many decades, socialists like Donald Soper, Aneurin Bevan and Tony Benn, along with many others in the left-wing Tribune group, defended it stoutly. In 1995, however, at a specially convened conference, again at Westminster Central Hall,[17] Tony Blair achieved acceptance for a new Clause Four, despite opposition from Soper among others, who organized meetings against it.

Philip Snowden learned to compromise in a way other left-wingers did not. Starting life in a two-roomed cottage in Keighley in 1864, where his father was a weaver in a mill, he was exposed at an early age both to radical Wesleyanism and the Bible, with Gladstone given equal attention. To escape from the mill he became a pupil-teacher and then an insurance office clerk, passing an examination at 22 for the civil service. An accident at 27 left him disabled and invalided out of the civil service. For the next two years he studied socialism and during this period – 1892–3 – was decisively influenced by S. E. Keeble's 'Great Thoughts'.[18] For the next ten years he became an Independent Labour Party (ILP) propagandist, as a speaker second only to Keir Hardie. MP for Blackburn from 1906, Snowden was an outstanding debater, interested in the effect of the drink trade and financial affairs. He lost his seat in 1918, but by 1922 he was an MP again and in 1924 Chancellor of the Exchequer, though more Free Trade and Gladstonian than socialist. In 1927 he left the ILP, but spoke for trade unionists against a government bill, though not sympathizing with the 1926 General Strike as Soper had done. In 1929 he was again Chancellor, but then his parliamentary life was overshadowed by the Great Depression.

Unlike Henderson, Foreign Secretary in the 1929 Labour government and now preoccupied with the League of Nations and chairing the 1932 World Conference on Disarmament, Snowden became a member, with other Labour MPs, of Ramsey MacDonald's National Government and in one budget was forced to suspend the Gold Standard. The year 1931 saw the end of his life as an MP and he became Lord Privy Seal in the House of Lords. He died in 1937, his stature curtailed by his infirmity and lack of teamwork skills. In 1934 Henderson was awarded the Nobel Peace Prize, but no such acclaim reached Snowden. Yet he could articulate what he believed, like Donald Soper, arguing that 'personal salvation and social salvation are like the palm trees which bear no fruit unless they grow side by side'.[19] Snowden's idealism, however, was tempered by realism. 'The only way to regain the earthly paradise,' he judged, 'is by the old, hard road of Calvary', through persecution, poverty, temptation, 'by the agony and bloody sweat', the crown of thorns, the agonizing death. In language reminiscent of Soper later, Snowden talked of the 'resurrection to the New Humanity', purified by suffering but 'triumphant through sacrifice'.[20]

Thus in the late 1920s Methodism had three people living out in the political realm what they perceived to be New Testament theology – Henderson, Snowden and Soper. The last two were aware of S. E. Keeble, who had left Scott Lidgett and even Hugh Price Hughes behind politically, though he had reviewed Hughes's *Social Christianity* favourably. Keeble was familiar with the writings of Karl Marx and had already argued that 'a purified Socialism is simply an industrially applied Christianity'.[21] Falling out with Hughes over his support for the South African War, Keeble founded the short-lived *Methodist Weekly*, which supported Labour, but Wesleyan tastes were different and it lasted only from 1900 to 1903.

Nevertheless, with Arthur Henderson, and ministers like Henry Carter and J. E. Rattenbury, in 1905 they created the Wesleyan Methodist Union of Social Service (MUSS), in parallel with the body created by the Primitive Methodists.[22] As early as 1912, Keeble was writing a pamphlet for MUSS favouring 'A Legal Minimum Wage',[23] followed by *The Citizen of Tomorrow*, also written for MUSS, which was used throughout Wesley Guilds.[24] It became a key element, leading in 1918 to the creation of the Temperance and Social Welfare Department, disbanded in 1926 through insufficient support, though the annual Beckly lecture was then set up by a Keeble enthusiast. Like Soper, Keeble acted as a catalyst for new thinking, influencing people like George Thomas who used Keeble's book on *The Social Teaching of the Bible* in his 1959 Beckly lecture.[25] However, Keeble never became admired in the way Donald Soper did, arousing the wrath of Methodists like Fowler, Perks and others who created the Nonconformist Anti-Socialist League, with Fowler writing in the *Methodist Recorder* on 'The Perils of Socialism'.[26] 'He was,' it was said of S. E. Keeble when he died in 1946, 'a pioneer whom his Church could not follow.'[27]

Donald Soper had little time to absorb the activities of Henderson, Snowden or even Keeble, for grassroots pressures overtook him in the late 1920s when he went to a church in the Old Kent Road and then in 1929 to the recently opened Islington Central Hall. In Southwark he came across both Roderick Kedward, who for a while became Bermondsey's MP, and also Charles G. Ammon, the secretary of the Brotherhood at his church, who invited Alfred Salter MP to address it and also Keir Hardie.[28] Increasingly, too, weekly open-air meetings on Tower Hill preoccupied him, which continued until Soper's death in 1998. Early on he was floored by questions about Marxism. With Kedward's help, he now navigated his way through the writings of Marx and Lenin, wondering whether to join the Communist Party.[29] Soper returned to Tower Hill equipped to answer communist questioning and heckling, often from dockers, who increasingly flocked to his lunch-time soapbox. He did not become a communist, but joined the Labour Party instead, remaining always on its left-wing. 'The Magnificat puts the Communist Manifesto in the shade,' he concluded.[30] Nevertheless, he now realized that economics, though not necessarily the key to everything, 'undoubtedly plays a dominant role in our lives', and therefore had to be taken 'into the most serious account'.[31]

A visit to South Wales during the 1930s depression confirmed Soper's socialism when he heard of the high unemployment rates among miners. In 1932, while in Islington, he set up a rest room for self-support and a limited form of bartering for unemployed men, which ran for several years.[32] Such action he justified theologically, often rooting it in his conception 'goodwill on fire', writing: 'The love of Christ was goodwill on fire, indefatigable, undefeated.'[33] Like Philip Snowden, Soper focused on the Crucifixion, writing: 'We believe the reformation of society and the establishment of social justice can never be achieved without the fire of enthusiasm and self-sacrifice which is found in the Cross of Jesus Christ.'[34]

It was Christ's action on the cross that convinced Soper that pacifism and Christian faith went hand in glove, so in the 1930s he teamed up with Dick Sheppard, the dynamic vicar of St Martin-in-the-Fields, and others in the 'War We Say No' Movement, which became the Peace Pledge Union. He also played a key role in the Methodist Peace Fellowship, created in 1933 by Henry Carter, and also the ecumenical Fellowship of Reconciliation, whose roots went back to World War One.[35] Even the conflict with Hitler did not deflect him; in fact, he was banned from the BBC during it, but continued to proclaim his views from Hyde Park.[36]

As the 1950s unfolded, Soper was among those prominent in the campaign against the H-Bomb and then the Campaign for Nuclear

Disarmament (CND) and its annual Aldermaston March, though he always stated his total pacifist beliefs rather than taking only an anti-nuclear stance. Thus, from the 1936 Dorchester Rally for peace with Vera Brittain and George Lansbury among others, to the Westminster Central Hall gathering for a nuclear-free world in 1993, Soper was always at the forefront, his socialism and pacifism linked in his discipleship. Even when writing from the 1950s for the left-wing journal *Tribune*, to which he contributed over 500 pieces, Donald linked discipleship and the secular world. 'Holy Week and Passion-tide proclaim the ultimate victory not of violence, but of non-violence,' he wrote shortly after Martin Luther King's murder in Memphis, Tennessee, on 4 April 1968. 'At the foot of the Cross on Good Friday, the way of Jesus, of Ghandi, of Martin Luther King, may look like defeat, but Good Friday is not the end of the Christian year, but only the beginning. The end is Easter morning when even death is swallowed up in victory.'[37]

During the 1950s, controversy split the Labour Party when followers of Aneurin Bevan took a left-wing approach to many issues, as decades later many did when they responded to Tony Benn's views. Matters were made worse when at the end of the decade Bevan, then Shadow Foreign Secretary, ceased to be a unilateralist, a change of heart that Soper found hard to forgive, as he had been a 'Bevanite'.[38] Despite Bevan's views, the 1960 Labour Party Conference voted for unilateral nuclear disarmament, partly as a result of CND's campaigns. For Donald, 'a pacifist revolutionary', as he once called himself,[39] this was the high tide of left-wing influence on institutional Labour, but it lasted only for a year before Hugh Gaitskell, Labour's leader – who had told the 1960 Conference he would 'fight, fight and fight again' to reverse the decision – in 1961 overturned the unilateralist vote.

The year 1960 was another peak one for Soper was elected president of the 'Victory for Socialism' group,[40] of which he was a vocal member, along with Bevan and his wife, Jennie Lee, Michael Foot, Kingsley Martin (the editor of the *New Statesman*) and Sydney Silverman MP, a key figure in the campaign to abolish the death penalty. It was a formal recognition of his commitment, which in the 1959 election had seen him speaking at Reading for Ian Mikardo and in Blackburn for Barbara Castle, both *Tribune* members. He had also joined with Gaitskell and Bevan in a Party Political Broadcast, when he was interviewed by the Christian Socialist MP, Tom Driberg, even though he was unhappy with their espousal of the mixed economy.[41]

In 1959 Driberg had edited *Papers from the Lamb*, written by a group set up to answer the question: 'Should an attempt be made to form a new organisation of Christian Socialism in which existing organisations could, if they wished, unite?'[42] In theory, the answer depended on response to the document but Donald, a recently appointed alderman on the London County Council, called a two-day meeting at his Kingsway Hall base. So, on 22 and 23 January 1960, those interested gathered, and drafted a Constitution,[43] aware they were the inheritors of previous groups – including not only S. E. Keeble, but nineteenth-century Anglicans like Charles Kingsley, F. D. Maurice, Stewart Headlam and Scott Holland,[44] as well as William Temple whose 1942 Penguin Special *Christianity and Social Order* no doubt had contributed in 1945 to the election of over 100 MPs who became members of the Parliamentary Socialist Group.[45]

The meeting agreed that a revived Christian Socialist Movement (CSM) would commit itself to common ownership of the world's major resources; a classless and just society; human and racial equality; the unity of all Christ's people; friendship between East and West; abolition of all nuclear weapons, disarmament and world peace. The steering committee, the *New Statesman* observed, seemed to guarantee 'these Christians will be uncompromisingly Socialist without being sectarian'.[46]

After a debate, independence rather than Labour Party affiliation was preferred by most of those attending.[47] The 600-strong gathering heard speeches from Father Groser and Canon Stanley Evans, but it was tense as it set up an executive comprising those previously influential in the parent organizations. Soper was invited to chair it. At the meeting, the platform was enhanced by the presence of R. H. Tawney himself, now nearly 80,[48] whose books *Religion and the Rise of Capitalism* and *The Acquisitive Society* had so influenced Donald Soper and William Temple and many others from the 1920s onwards. 'Tawney did not necessarily convert me to socialism,' Soper later explained, 'but he provided for me seminal thinking and principles about the Christian Socialist Movement which have moulded my thinking ever since.'[49]

While at Kingsway Hall, the Christian Socialists heard that Aneurin Bevan was seriously ill. Prayers for him were said and a message of support sent.[50] By July, Bevan had died and his widow, Jennie Lee, invited Bishop Mervyn Stockwood and Soper to take part in planned ceremonies, though Bevan had not been a Christian, despite a Baptist background in childhood. Accordingly, one cold night at Maun Pound, high above Ebbw Vale, in wild countryside where Bevan had addressed many open-air meetings, Donald addressed a memorial gathering of miners, steelworkers, MPs James Griffiths, James Callaghan and Michael Foot, and prominent trade union leaders. 'No-one else could have spoken as a socialist to colleagues, many of whom were not religious or agnostics, with such command of appropriate language, sentiment or sympathy,' Michael Foot remembered later.[51]

CSM had to survive for the next two decades alongside other radical groups and its membership then was never over 450. But in the 1980s – Soper had been its president from 1975 – after a recruitment drive, it grew substantially. In 1986, after 13 years, the Labour Party decided to reopen its ranks to 'Socialist Societies' and CSM was asked to affiliate, a logical development for a group that claimed 17 MPs as members. With the former GLC councillor Peter Dawe as chairman, CSM flourished and in 1993 the new Labour leader, John Smith, agreed to give the Tawney Lecture, inaugurated by CSM in 1962 after Tawney's death. Soper was in the chair as 400 in Bloomsbury Baptist Church heard John Smith speak on 'Reclaiming the Ground: Christianity and Socialism'. 'I heard again the dry voice and spiritual clarity of Tawney,' Soper said in his vote of thanks, 'and also the voice of William Temple.' 'Be faithful for a new dawn,' he urged attenders,[52] telling *The Week in Politics*: 'He's done us good,' when asked to assess John Smith's lecture.[53]

But ideals such as Soper's, as Harold Wilson once remarked, rarely survive the rough and tumble of political life.[54] This became clear after John Smith's unexpected death when Tony Blair and Gordon Brown, both CSM members, spelt out their vision of 'New Labour', a vision very different from Soper's and his friends. Soper was unconvinced by what Professor Ronald Preston called 'Middle Axioms', proximate policies for a complex world, though sometimes he could admit the need for compromise in politics. 'Jesus had to compromise,' he once argued. 'He could not have proceeded at all without the protection of the Roman Empire which "his kingdom was to overthrow".'[55] Nevertheless, Soper remained uneasy with many 'New Labour' outlooks.

However, just as the CSM had always been split between pacifist and non-pacifist members, now it found itself divided over reform of Clause 4, with its executive in the main supporting retention of the existing wording, with over 75 per cent of CSM members favouring change, 'effectively voting to ditch Labour's commitment to common ownership', as Chris Bryant has indicated.[56] 'The Labour Party owes more to Methodism than Marxism,' Lord Healey wrote in a speech he prepared for Morgan Phillips, then General Secretary of the TUC, to give at a Socialist International Conference in Copenhagen in the early 1950s, as the Labour Party's international secretary.[57] Now it seemed the pragmatic side of the Party was asserting itself over its dogmatic strand, with a concern for ethics rather than metaphysics of the Marxist variety. 'It is a strange fact,' Kenneth Greet has remarked, 'that a Methodism founded by a High Tory has come to feel so much at home in the Labour Party.'[58] This is not to say Methodism has lost all links with Liberalism – Alan Beith, one-time deputy leader of the Liberal Party, would belie that. Nor, of course, that there have not been prominent Methodist Conservatives like Sir Kingsley Wood, elected to the LCC in 1911 and from 1918 MP for Woolwich West, who reformed the Post Office and as Chancellor (1940–43) introduced the PAYE tax arrangements. More recently, Rhodes Boyson, also a London MP, has had strong Methodist links, as had Selwyn Lloyd, one of three Methodist MPs who became Speaker.[59]

Nevertheless, from Cabinet to local level – Hilary Armstrong and Paul Boateng would be examples of Methodists in the Cabinet – to Donald Anderson, linked with Notting Hill Methodism and one-time chair of the House of Commons Select Committee on Foreign Affairs, Lord Healey's dictum seems to hold water. At a local London level, too, there have been others, like Arthur Downes, a Soper protégé in Tower Hamlets, and John Hart, who came into Methodism via the Brotherhood Movement in East Ham, and rose to be a member of the council for 54 years, part of the time Labour leader of the council and then mayor and deputy mayor. At one point he found he was working with at least eight others on the council from East Ham Central Hall. Two other London Borough mayors have been Councillor Peter Lemmon, a Methodist minister in Brent, and Peter Dawe, a lay preacher in Waltham Forest. Trade unionists, like Len Murray, general secretary of the Trade Union Congress from 1973 to 1984, have also been part of Greater London Methodism. Yet the Conservative link with Methodism has also continued, with Brian Coleman on the Greater London Authority from Barnet, and David Wilshire, a member, along with MPs from every party of the Methodist Parliamentary Fellowship. Serviced on a monthly basis by the Westminster Central Hall Superintendent, it also meets annually with the president and vice-president.

The most high-profile Methodist parliamentarian of an earlier generation was Ellen Wilkinson, the Jarrow MP who fought for the unemployed and led the Jarrow March.[60] She it was, Soper once claimed, who 'gave to the Labour Movement and to the political world the concept that unemployment is intolerable'.[61] Clearly, though Soper was the most well-known Methodist in political and social affairs for a number of decades, there were many others. He must therefore be seen in a long tradition going back to the time when the East End Mission made space for dockers in their 1894–95 strike, allowing trade unionists to hold regular meetings in Paddy's Goose,[62] a link that was still in evidence in 1913 during the Great Dock Strike,[63] and in 1915, when dock labourers were still holding weekly union meetings there.[64] In 1919, when the UK was racked by a serious railway strike, the Progressive Party politician on the LCC and Methodist patriarch, Dr Scott Lidgett, was part of an appeal instigated by the Archbishop of Canterbury, along with Cardinal

Bourne and a Free Church leader, Dr F. B. Meyer, in which they pleaded for the same solidarity with industrial workers recently shown in the war, though they did not endorse the strike itself.[65]

What, then, has been Donald Soper's unique contribution? While others like F. W. Chudleigh have served on a borough council (Stepney from 1909), lay workers like the one-time Methodist trainee and later MP, Arthur Sherwell, became socially alert through his time at the WLM,[66] and some have been engaged in detailed care work (as Percy Ineson when he chaired the LCC Care Committee),[67] Soper was able to link theology and socialism, as perhaps only S. E. Keeble had done before him. Also, through his immense media skills, including the use of humour and the striking phrase, Soper was able to present a human face to the Church, while using his formidable intellect to interpret what others have judged as Christian Socialism. Yet the prayer he suggested for use by the 1966 Labour government in a service of dedication in the House of Commons Crypt Chapel, and subsequently cited by Harold Wilson at a Labour Party Conference, when he said he hoped his government's record would be judged on its contents, was probably strong on vision but weak on pragmatism.[68] As Lord Callaghan once asked, conceding that Donald Soper's principles were much admired: 'Is he a practical man?'[69] And the Methodist peer, Lord Peter Archer of Sandwell, wondering if Soper knew how to win in politics, has raised the question as to whether he 'sees things *too* clearly'?[70]

Notes

1 Donald Soper, *Calling for Action*, An Autobiographical Enquiry, London, Robson Books, 1984, p. 77.

2 Soper, *Calling for Action*, p. 77.

3 Brian Frost, *Goodwill on Fire: Donald Soper's Life and Mission*, London, Hodder & Stoughton, 1996, pp. 20–2, citing Donald Soper, 'The time of my Life, 1921–6', 5 January 1969, British Library National Sound Archive, BBC P317R.

4 Donald Soper, Hyde Park, 5 July 1987, cited in Brian Frost, ed., *Vintage Soper: God, Faith and Society*, London, Hodder & Stoughton, 1997, p. 10.

5 Douglas Thompson, *Donald Soper: A Biography*, London, Denholm House Press, 1971, p. 16.

6 See John A. Vickers, ed., *A Dictionary of Methodism in Britain and Ireland*, Peterborough, Epworth Press, 2000, p. 44.

7 London Mission Report 1954, p. 32.

8 Kenneth D. Brown, 'Nonconformity and the British labour movement: a case study', *Journal of Social History*, 1975, vol. 8, Issue 4, pp. 119–20.

9 James Munson, *The Nonconformists: In Search of a Lost Identity*, London, 1991, p. 282.

10 D. W. Bebbington, 'The Free Church MPs of the 1906 Parliament' in S. Taylor and D. L.Wykes, eds, *Parliament and Dissent* as part of *Parliamentary History*, XXIV, no. 1, Edinburgh University Press, 2005.

11 *British Weekly*, 25 July 1907, p. 378.

12 J. G. Wickham Legg, ed., *Dictionary of National Biography 1931–1940*, Oxford, OUP, 1949, p. 420.

13 Legg, *Dictionary*, p. 420.

14 A. J. P. Taylor, *English History, 1914–1945*, Oxford, OUP, 1965, p. 90.

15 Marwick, *The Deluge*, 1965, p. 190.

16 Margaret Bondfield, *A Life's Work*, London, Hutchinson, 1949, pp. 157–8. See also *The Times*, 27 February 1918.

17 See *The Observer*, 30 April 1995, p. 1. Also, Andrew Grice, *The Sunday Times*, 30 April 1995.

18 Philip Snowden's letters, cited by Michael Edwards, 'S. E. Keeble and Nonconformist Thinking 1880–1939', unpublished M.Litt, Bristol University 1969, p. 12, note 50. The key sentence is: 'The early articles in the book are those which appeared in "Great Thoughts" about nineteen years ago, and which are responsible for first turning my mind to the study of socialism.' Philip Snowden, cited by Edwards, p. 131. At his last meeting with S. E. Keeble, Philip Snowden asked not to refer to their relationship 'a reticence he later observed in his recent "Autobiography"' wrote S. E. Keeble on Snowden's death. (S. E. Keeble, *Methodist Times*, 1937, cited by Edwards, p. 131.)

19 Philip Snowden, in *The Labour Prophet*, April 1898, pp. 169–70.

20 Philip Snowden, *The Christ That Is To Be*, Independent Labour Party, 1903, p. 13, cited by Chris Bryant, *Possible Dreams: A Personal History of British Christian Socialism*, London, Hodder & Stoughton, 1996, p. 134.

21 S. E. Keeble, *Industrial Day-Dreams*, 1896.

22 See Vickers, *Dictionary*, p. 65.

23 Edwards, *S. E. Keeble*, footnote 107. See also S. E. Keeble, *Christian Responsibility for the Social Order*, Peterborough, Epworth Press, 1922, and Maldwyn Edwards, *S. E. Keeble, Pioneer and Prophet*, Peterborough, Epworth Press, 1949.

24 Edwards, *S. E. Keeble*, p. 10.

25 George Thomas, *The Christian Heritage in Politics*, Peterborough, Epworth Press, 1959, p. 36, quoting S. E. Keeble, *The Social Teaching of the Bible*, 1909, Methodist Union of Social Service, p. 7.

26 *Methodist Recorder*, 30 January 1908, p. 4.

27 *Methodist Recorder*, 12 September 1946, p. 17.

28 Frost, *Goodwill on Fire*, p. 27.

29 Donald Soper, 80th Birthday Interview with Ronald Eyre, BBC February 1983.

30 Donald Soper, *The Advocacy of the Gospel*, London, Hodder & Stoughton, 1961, pp. 119–20.

31 Soper, *Calling for Action*, pp. 89–90.

32 Frost, *Goodwill on Fire*, p. 37. See also *Methodist Recorder*, 13 December 1962.

33 Soper, *Advocacy*, p. 115.

34 Donald Soper, The London Mission Report 1938, p. 9.

35 Frost, *Goodwill on Fire*, pp. 38–9.

36 See Frost, *Goodwill on Fire*, the chapter called 'Peace Maker and Pacifist', pp. 46–67.

37 Donald Soper, *Tribune*, 12 April 1968, p. 3, cited in Frost, *Vintage Soper*, p. 9.

38 Frost, *Goodwill on Fire*, p. 77, quoting a comment by Lord Soper to the Revd Len Barnett in an interview at Central Methodist Church, Bromley, 1983.

39 Donald Soper, Hyde Park, 5 July 1987, cited in Frost, *Vintage Soper*, p. 24.

40 *Tribune*, 4 March 1960.

41 Donald Soper, *Tribune*, 11 December 1959, p. 4.

42 *Papers from the Lamb*, Christian Socialist Movement, 1960, p. 2.

43 Bryant, *Possible Dreams*, pp. 259–61.

44 Frost, *Goodwill on Fire*, p. 79.

45 David Ormrod, 'Christian socialist organisations', in *Facing the Future as Christians and Socialists*, CSM, 1985, p. 29.

46 *New Statesman and Nation*, 20 April 1960.

47 *CSM News*, no. 2, September 1960, cited in *Possible Dreams*, p. 261.

48 *Methodist Recorder*, 28 January 1960.

49 Donald Soper, 'Socialism – An Enduring Creed, R. H. Tawney Lecture, March 1981', published in David Ormrod, ed., *Freedom and Equality*, London, CSM, 1990, p. 42.

50 *Methodist Recorder*, 28 January 1960. See also Frost, *Goodwill on Fire*, p. 77.

51 Brian Frost, interview with Michael Foot, 5 August 1993, cited in Frost, *Goodwill on Fire*, p. 77.

52 Donald Soper, closing remarks, Bloomsbury Baptist Church, 20 February 1993.

53 Frost, *Goodwill on Fire*, p. 243.

54 William Purcell, *Odd Man Out*, London, Mowbrays, 1983, p. 184, a re-issue of *Portrait of Soper*, London, Mowbrays, 1972, with an Epilogue added.

55 *News Chronicle*, 24 December 1986, cited in Frost, *Goodwill on Fire*, p. 260. See also 'Here I Stand – The Place of Compromise in the Christian Life', Alex Wood Memorial Lecture, Fellowship of Reconciliation, 1959.

56 Bryant, *Possible Dreams*, pp. 271–2.

57 Lord Healey of Riddlesdown, letter to author, 4 February 2005. See also *The Oxford Dictionary of Quotations*, where it is attributed to Morgan Phillips, via James Callaghan's autobiography, *Time and Chance*, 1987.

58 The Revd Dr Kenneth Greet, interview with author, 11 November 2004.

59 The other two were Lord Mowbray-King and Lord Tonypandy, both from the Labour Party.

60 For Ellen Wilkinson, see Vickers, *Dictionary*, p. 394.

61 Graham Dale, *God's Politicians: The Christian Contribution to the Hundred Years of Labour*, London, HarperCollins, 2000, p. 118, citing Betty D. Vernon, *Ellen Wilkinson 1891–1947*, London, Croom Helm, 1983, p. 137.

62 London Wesleyan Mission Report 1895, p. 9.

63 Peter Thompson, London Mission Report 1913, pp. 12–13.

64 London Mission Report 1915.

65 *The Times*, 20 October 1919, cited in G. K. A. Bell, *Randall Davidson*,

Archbishop of Canterbury, vol. 2, Oxford, OUP, 1935, pp. 951–2.

66 Christopher Oldstone-Moore, *Hugh Price Hughes*, University of Wales Press, 1999, p. 282.

67 See Vickers, *Dictionary*, p. 175.

68 The prayer read:

> O God, grant us a vision of our land, fair as it might be:
> A land of righteousness where none shall wrong his neighbour;
> A land of plenty where evil and poverty shall be done away;
> A land of brotherhood where all success shall be founded on
> service and honour and shall be given on excellence alone;
> A land of peace, where order shall not rest on force,
> but on the love of all for the common life and weal;
> Bless our efforts to make the vision a living reality;
> Inspire and strengthen each one of us that we may give time,
> thought, and sacrifice to speed the day of its coming.

(*Methodist Recorder*, 13 October 1966). See also Frost, *Goodwill on Fire*, p. 279, note 142. The prayer, with a slight modification, came from Walter Rauschenbusch, *Prayers for the Social Awakening*, published in America in 1918.

69 Lord Callaghan of Cardiff, interview with author, 8 December 1993, cited in Frost, *Goodwill on Fire*, p. 253.

70 Lord Archer of Sandwell, interview with author, 17 June 1993, cited in Frost, *Goodwill on Fire*, p. 253.

13

A *Small* Cog *in a* Big
Anti-Apartheid Wheel
Pauline Webb, David Haslam and End Loans to
South Africa (ELTSA)

In early 1969 David Mason, a key figure in the creation of the Notting Hill Team Ministry in 1960, which had transformed an inner-city Methodist Church in North Kensington into a thriving multiracial congregation, bounded into the office of the Director of the Notting Hill Ecumenical Centre at the former Bayswater Methodist Church, which the team had set up earlier. He had, he indicated, invited the World Council of Churches' (WCC) Consultation on Racism to Notting Hill. Could the Ecumenical Centre cope?

Eventually the building was ready for the delegates who arrived from every continent in what turned out to be 'an emotional and often confrontational meeting', according to its organizer. At it, 'representatives of the racially oppressed demanded, among other things, a boycott of institutions supporting racism', a fund to pay for 'reparations' for injustices suffered over centuries, 'and support for the armed struggle of oppressed blacks in situations where all other means had failed'.[1]

Besides the general-secretary of the WCC, Dr Eugene Carson Blake, delegates included Senator George McGovern, later Democratic candidate for the presidency in the USA; Garfield Todd, former Prime Minister of Rhodesia; Dr Nathan Todd, involved in Black Studies in America; Mark Bonham Carter from the British Race Relations Board; and representatives from Fiji, Japan, Hungary, Russia and countries in Latin America among others. Archbishop Michael Ramsey chaired one session and was confronted by the black power activist Roy Sawh. At a ticket-only evening in Church House, Westminster, addressed by Oliver Tambo, among others, Bishop Trevor Huddleston was shouted down by the National Front, which had infiltrated the event, and the gathering was suspended for 20 minutes while the police, who had been called, cleared the vocal protestors from the hall.

Later that same year, Consultation reports were referred to the Central Committee of the WCC, meeting at Canterbury, with proposals for action. They ranged from consideration of 'the realities of racism today' to 'the spiritual and moral issues involved in opposing racism'.[2] Though some of the Notting Hill demands were not met, they influenced the Central Committee's recommendations, which set up a Programme to Combat Racism (PCR) and gave it a five-year mandate, renewed in 1974 and thereafter. It became a sub-unit of the WCC's Unit on Justice and Service.

Dr Pauline Webb had begun her professional life as a teacher, before moving on to the Methodist Missionary Society, where for several years she edited its magazine *The Kingdom Overseas*. In 1965, at an unusually early age, she became vice-president of the Methodist Conference, having already been dubbed 'an angry young woman' by some in the secular press for her earlier Conference speeches about world poverty and injustice. A Methodist delegate to the WCC's Uppsala Assembly in 1968, to her surprise she was elected vice-moderator of the WCC Central Committee, a post she held until 1975.[3]

Delegates, Pauline included, were made deeply aware of racism, for at the Assembly's opening service there was a substitute preacher 'for Martin Luther King who had fallen to an assassin's bullet'.[4] Soon Pauline found herself chairing the Programme to Combat Racism. 'We need action that will speak louder than words', it was felt, and Pauline, now head of the recently formed Methodist Board of Lay Training, agreed, defending the PCR's decision to give grants to the medical and philanthropic work of the Patriotic Front of Zimbabwe and the South African National Congress (ANC) in exile from special funds donated by Churches from all continents. Many British church leaders, however, remained deeply ambivalent about its role and activities, though not the Baptist ecumenical leader, Dr Ernest Payne, who defended the World Council's policies and appeared in defence of Pauline and the PCR in the BBC radio programme *You the Jury*.

In 1973 David Haslam went on a sabbatical to the USA and visited the Inter-Faith Centre for Corporate Responsibility, set up by the National Council of Churches in 1971 to research the activities of trans-national companies. While there he learned that since 1970 an European-American Banking Consortium (EABC), based in the USA, had lent money to the Rhodesian and South African authorities, including 210 million dollars to the South African government and its agencies, British bankers providing 35 million dollars, with Midland Bank being the largest donor.[5]

Brought up in a Methodist family in Lancashire, as a teenager David had responded to an evangelistic appeal and was confirmed. After studying chemistry in Birmingham, followed by a year's primary school teaching, he returned to the city to study theology and became a Methodist minister. While working in his first church in inner-city Coventry, he became 'aware of racism encountered by immigrants from the Indian sub-continent'.[6] In his next job, on a council estate in Southampton, and following on from his 1973 American visit, he determined to act on the new insights gained in Uppsala, at the WCC Assembly which he had attended, and in the USA. He discussed the issue of corporate responsibility with a number of people, including Pauline, especially in relation to southern Africa. Three months later a small group of some seven or eight, mostly Methodists, decided to picket the Midland Bank AGM at Poultry in the City of London's financial area. They gave out leaflets to shareholders as they arrived,[7] which urged them to encourage the Bank to withdraw its investments from South Africa.

Such action was almost unknown at an AGM, and shareholders were both astonished and amused, though already by 1971 other shareholders had gone to company meetings 'armed with information about company activities in such areas as South Africa, asking some very pertinent questions about company policies'.[8] And in August 1972, the WCC had published its booklet *Time to Withdraw*. Clearly part of the first worldwide struggle for human rights, David Haslam, with help from the Alliance of Radical Methodists, among others, was about to form End Loans to South Africa (ELTSA), which was to prove a very significant, though small, pressure group in the international struggle against racism in Southern Africa. By March 1973, and already an executive member of the Anti-Apartheid Movement (AAM), David was writing in *The Guardian*: 'It seems quite clear that it is totally out of order for Christian organisations to have money invested in companies profiting from what amounts to slave labour.'[9]

In July, at the Methodist Conference, of which he was a member, David urged the Methodist Board of Finance's Report be referred back. 'What was the Methodist Church doing in response to the action of the WCC and the British Council of Churches?' he asked. (Earlier that year, the BCC had issued a booklet on Investments in South Africa.) Britain had 64 per cent of investments in South Africa and was therefore 'the main economic support of the apartheid regime'.[10]

In 1974 David Haslam and his family moved to Harlesden Methodist Church from Southampton, but not before he had organized another irruption at Midland's AGM. 'Protests included one from the newly formed ELTSA . . . of which Miss Pauline Webb is chair and the Revd David Haslam is the vice-chair,' the *Methodist Recorder* reported. 'A statement adds "We trust that the Midland Bank will remember the damage that such a campaign will do to its good name and that it will, therefore, withdraw its loans to the South African Government with assurance not to make others in future!" '[11]

AAM itself was already campaigning against Barclays Bank, which had over 1,000 South African branches, so ELTSA had to bear this in mind when it produced a Newsletter to inform its growing circle of supporters. It held talks now with Churches who were shareholders in banks. Martin Bailey, the son of the Quaker activist Sydney Bailey, was an original ELTSA member – and through him Bernard Rivers became the first of several paid workers, like Terry Shott (a South African conscientious objector, who organized a group of them in London), and David Craine, a Methodist lay preacher, at one time also ELTSA's Treasurer.

'The sanctions campaign', Nerys John has written, 'brought into the open the issue of corporate ethics, investor responsibility and public accountability, which had never before been faced in so acute a form.'[12] It is easy, of course, to regard as a stunt ELTSA's climbing the walls of Westminster Central Hall and pinning a banner across it in the 1970s because the Midland Bank branch there dealt with Methodist Church finance. But by such action and planting counterfeit deposit slips in branches overprinted with 'deposit your money on apartheid',[13] the publicity generated caused controversy, thereby helping develop awareness of the issue. Indeed, after 30 minutes of protest at the Central Hall, when an official emerged to remonstrate with protestors, Dr Webb declared herself willing to meet its trustees to urge the case for disinvestment in South Africa by the Midland Bank.[14]

David Haslam and others in ELTSA now grew increasingly restive as approaches to the Midland Bank by church bodies, some of whom were shareholders, received the response that bankers could not decide on 'the morality of the purposes for which they lent'.[15] They even refused to say if they would have lent money to Nazi Germany in the 1930s. In 1976, therefore, ELTSA organized the first ever Resolution to a British Company on a social or moral issue,[16] having found 100 shareholders, holding over 10,000 shares between them, to support it. The Methodist Church Central Finance Board was the leading sponsor and called on 'the Directors to cause to make the Midland Bank to make no further loans to the South African Government or its departments, agencies or state corporations and not to renew or extend any such existing loans'.[17] Support was also obtained from the Church Commissioners, universities, local authorities and charities,[18] though many colleges and even church bodies refused to support the resolution.[19] Rejected by 47 million to 3 million,[20] the *Financial Mail* in Johannesburg noted that this indicated opposition to apartheid was now more substantial and vocal.[21]

In 1976 there were serious riots in Soweto, the large black township on Johannesburg's edge, triggered by an attempt to enforce the teaching of Afrikaans in black schools. Young people who resisted were killed in the rioting that ensued and many others were injured. ELTSA decided to bring a further Resolution before Midland's AGM, identifying 1,000 of its largest shareholders and key individuals in churches and trades unions, who were invited to support a letter to Midland. In its Annual Report sent to shareholders, Lord Armstrong, its chair, stressed Midland would continue to observe a policy of 'strict political neutrality and asked them to oppose the Resolution, which was tabled by the Greater London Council'.[22] This time it received 6.9 per cent support – 49 million to 3.6 million votes.[23]

Intense pressure now bore down on Midland from action taken by the WCC-PCR and Dutch Banks in EABC who wanted to discontinue loans to South Africa.[24] By 1977 seven of the nine American banks had done the same and, in June, EABC agreed to grant no further credits, except those financing current trade transactions.[25] At that year's AGM, when a further Resolution gained 7 per cent of the vote, Midland's chair stated 'in convoluted fashion, that the Bank was not now making any loans to the South African Government'.[26] ELTSA's action certainly contributed to this, but how much influence campaigning has is always difficult to estimate.

Following informal discussion with Midland, ELTSA decided not to bring a Resolution to the 1978 AGM but to await developments.[27] *The Citizen*, a black newspaper read widely in Soweto, reported Lord Armstrong had announced Midland Bank's cessation of loans to the South African government.[28] Groups that had sprung up in other countries now took part in days of action, which David Haslam felt were important in making clear the international aspect of campaigning against the bankers.[29] ELTSA's own campaigning, especially against Hill Samuel, a key organizer of South Africa's much needed loans,[30] perhaps reached its high point when David appeared, along with Desmond Tutu, before the United Nations Special Committee against Apartheid in New York in June 1979.[31]

ELTSA now turned its attention to other UK banks involved in South Africa: Barclays, and Standard Chartered, the second largest. The campaign against Barclays had been running for some years under the AAM, with a particular focus on students, who were urged not to take out accounts with Barclays. Now ELTSA took over the main thrust, as AAM continued to engage in its other range of activities. Barclays National, established in South Africa in 1971, by 1972 was identified by a UN report as the major UK bank lending to South Africa.[32] It soon became apparent that its loans from 1979 to mid-1982 amounted to 347 million dollars, and indeed by 1985 they were some £750 million: £300 million direct to state corporations, £450 million inter-bank financing from Barclays to Barclays National.[33] ELTSA now escalated its campaign, establishing a 'Barclays Shadow Board of Directors', which first met on 26 January 1981.

'It would seek to provide alternative information on Barclays' involvement with South Africa which was *not* contained in the Bank's Annual Report,' wrote Michael Dummett, Professor of Logic at New College Oxford, who was elected chair. On the board, which also considered activities in Namibia, were the High Commissioners of Zambia and Grenada, MPs Robert Hughes (also AAM chair) and Neil Kinnock, the Bishop of Manchester, several academics and the actress Julie Christie, which ensured publicity. Donald Woods, the exiled South African journalist and friend of Steve Biko, joined in 1982, as did Ethel de Keyser from AAM. Subsequent chairs included Dr Colin Morris, followed by the Dean of King's College, London, Richard Harries, later Bishop of Oxford. Bishop Colin Winter, the exiled Bishop of Damaraland, was company secretary until his death in November 1981, when David Haslam took his place. Board members changed, too, as Adelaide Tambo joined for the ANC Women's League, Ken Gill from the trades unions and Russell Profitt, from Lewisham Council, who later chaired the board.

Shadow board members attended Barclays AGM on 29 April 1981 when Julie Christie, on the Board's behalf, asked the retiring Barclays chair, Sir Anthony Tuke, to explain the decision to remain in South Africa and 'improve conditions' from within and also asked 'what new measures Barclays had taken during the past year to challenge the basis of the apartheid system?' Sir Anthony admitted that 'our powers of changing a system in a country, however much we dislike it, are limited'. Nevertheless, Barclays would not withdraw from South Africa but would 'carry on as we do now'.[34]

In 1981 pressure was also applied at a more local level and the bank was forced to issue a briefing paper for branch managers as it continued to lose both retail customers and individuals. The Methodist Conference itself approved a resolution urging members to withdraw their Barclays accounts. Also that year, the Labour Party Conference pledged that the Party would encourage Labour-controlled authorities and affiliated organizations to refuse to bank with Barclays. By 1985 nine local authorities had joined the boycott, the first eight Labour-controlled, as the campaign escalated after the 1985 State of Emergency in South Africa.

During the time of the Shadow Barclays Reports (1981–6), many activities against banking on apartheid were organized. Such campaigning, as David Haslam has pointed out, demanded 'thousands of leaflets, endless efforts at publicity, permanent fund-raising, painstaking research, speaking, writing, phoning, persuading, encouraging, demanding'.[35] But it produced fruits, for in March 1985 the then Barclays chair, Sir Timothy Bevan, and his South African counterpart met at Leeds Castle with 20 chief executives of the largest Western contributors to discuss how to fend off criticism of their role in South Africa.[36] In August the British bank failed to take up a share issue in Barclays National, reducing its shares from 50.4 per cent to 40 per cent, an indication it was beginning to withdraw.[37] Barclays capital position in the UK too was weakened because the Bank of England declared it would treat Barclays National as if it were a subsidiary when deciding Barclays capital adequacy, judging the UK bank to have a moral responsibility for its partner bank.[38] 'The decision of Barclays Bank to withdraw from its South African investments was a personal triumph for Harlesden Methodist minister, the Revd David Haslam,' wrote one journalist. 'Mr Haslam, who was interviewed on national radio on the morning after the announcement last week, has spear-headed the disinvestment campaign against Barclays for years.'[39]

On 27 June 1987 a National Convention for Sanctions Against South Africa was held in London, where delegates agreed to work for the withdrawal of Standard Chartered from the country.[40] ELTSA produced briefing papers that no loans be made and that the bank itself withdraw. The Merchant Bank Hill Samuel was also targeted at this time. Nearly a decade earlier, in May 1978, ELTSA had written to all Arab governments outlining Hill Samuel's South African involvement.[41] Still more pressure was exerted on Hill Samuel, and in October 1986 it announced its intention to reduce its stake in its South African subsidiaries from 71 per cent to 20 per cent. By August 1987, partly no doubt due to the campaign but also because it had broader financial difficulties and a concern not to antagonize surrounding African countries, it withdrew completely.

On 20 July 1985 Chase Manhattan Bank, the USA's second largest, announced an end to loans for South Africa and refused to renew or make new ones to the South African government.[42] Other banks followed suit and a retired Swiss banker was appointed to mediate between the South African authorities and the 30 banks that held over 70 per cent of South Africa's debts. A settlement was agreed in February 1986 and the following year a three-year agreement was reached, to expire in June 1990. Now bans on government loans were also imposed by Commonwealth states, the USA, the Soviet Bloc, the Nordic countries and several others. The USA and the Commonwealth, excluding the UK, also imposed bans on private loans.[43] AAM and ELTSA had appealed to the 13 UK banks involved in the re-scheduling discussions to boycott the debt talks in October 1985, but they were unsuccessful.[44] Just before the February 1986 talks, Neil Kinnock himself wrote to Prime Minister Thatcher calling on UK banks not to help South Africa over its debt crisis,[45] but the British government refused to intervene.[46]

In 1987 David Haslam left Harlesden for the British Council of Churches' Community and Race Relations Unit, and accordingly took a lower profile in ELTSA. David Craine, who had joined in 1983, now helped the pressure group forward as a paid employee. It was less Methodist, even less Christian-based, than before, though Craine belonged to Harlesden Methodist Church. Money for tasks still came in haphazardly, from Methodist sources, small and large individual donations, the trades unions and from PCR itself, which funded the newsletter. David found Pauline Webb was still involved in giving advice both on strategy and media responses, though not as a member of ELTSA's committee. Working then for the BBC's World Service as religious services organizer, her role was that of an experienced campaigner in the background – especially helpful when emergencies arose.

By 1990 gold too had become a concern, and in July Ratner's, the world's largest jewellery retail group, agreed to stop using South African gold after a picket campaign outside its UK shops by anti-apartheid groups. Cosmos Desmond, the 1960s author of *The Discarded People* about South Africa's forced removals policy, and ELTSA's chair, observed that it was the biggest advance in peoples' sanctions since Barclays disinvestment in 1986. In the past there had been occasional tension between AAM and ELTSA. David Craine now tried to strengthen links between the two, for which there was already a precedent as a former ELTSA worker, Stuart Bell, who had written *Apartheid's Debt to the West, The Banks and the South African Lending Crisis* in the mid-1980s, was working for AAM.

David Craine found Harlesden Methodist Church to be supportive. Members put up posters like 'Victory to the ANC' and used Church Notices to recruit for the latest picket against Shell, which became another ELTSA protest campaign. Members also had been willing to wear 'Boycott Barclays' stickers, and join local protests against the bank. Such members were not 'activists' in the sense that Pauline Webb, David Haslam, and their colleagues at ELTSA's start from the Alliance of Radical Methodists had been, but they believed in the work their minister was doing and wanted to support the cause.[47]

At the time that South Africa's debts were being re-scheduled, ELTSA visited 14 banks involved and picketed them jointly with others, a necessity as ELTSA had few foot soldiers. One fascinating encounter occurred with NatWest, partly because of the involvement of the Dean of King's. He and other activists met senior figures to discuss South Africa's future when the Democratic Front was strong in South Africa and internal unrest seemed to be making the country ungovernable. The senior bank figures, shocked to learn of Richard Harries's belief in the doctrine of the Just War, nevertheless were interested to hear the opinions, which varied, as to how the opposition to apartheid within and without South Africa saw the future and how in particular the ANC would react if internal changes occurred there.[48]

The year 1990 was a key moment in ELTSA's campaign against Shell, the Royal Dutch Petroleum Group. Sanctions, now that Nelson Mandela had been released from prison, became part of the negotiations. Accordingly, 40 people went to Shell's AGM. ELTSA had already sent a letter to Shell's company secretary, suggesting a debate at the AGM, instead of a question and answer session, which was the normal procedure. 'We want to acknowledge the changes,' ELTSA indicated. Among the 40 were Denis Goldberg, one of those tried in 1963 with Mandela for treason, and also a prominent trade unionist and a leading church representative. Sir Peter Holmes, who chaired Shell Transport and Trading, indicated, after previous noisy shareholders' meetings, that the 1990 AGM would include 30 minutes devoted to southern Africa, during which three anti-apartheid speakers would each be allowed seven minutes before he replied and took further questions.[49] For David Haslam, one paper reported, there was no question 'that economic and political pressure had led to current changes'. He therefore urged Shell 'to suspend its operation completely in South Africa until apartheid is dead'.[50] Sir Peter Holmes countered that the company's clear stance on ending apartheid 'had won the company respect and support of the black community'. Accepting that some sanctions, like those on bank credits, had been effective, he argued that 'most trade restrictions would be detrimental not just to the economic but also political condition of black South Africans'. Thus he was 'totally opposed to disinvestment'.[51] The debate was yet another example of ELTSA's capacity to use protests as a 'Teach-in'. 'Honour has been satisfied on both sides,' wrote a journalist, 'the meeting broke up to general applause, plus a few scattered chants of Amandla.'[52]

The 1990s also saw a process whereby sanctions against South Africa were lifted. David Haslam was finally able to visit Durban in July 1991 as a guest of the ANC at its 48th Conference. In the report he wrote, he concluded sanctions had to be maintained *pro tem* and that vigilance was still needed with respect to bank loans, oil and gold. Monitoring processes needed to be in place, too, to ensure investment codes were implemented.[53] In the event, matters moved so rapidly that by 1994 sanctions were over and attention turned to debt relief globally as part of the Third World Debt Campaign that led to Jubilee 2000, a very different issue from the South African debt complexities.

'By the end ELTSA had become one of the most effective pressure groups the United Kingdom has ever seen for its size and resources,' David Craine has judged.[54] Banks needed to listen to it; and even when disruptive (on occasions Craine was physically evicted from AGMs), was capable of generating unfavourable publicity for bankers rather than protestors. At the level of shareholder action, ELTSA was helped by members of other groups, buying a block of shares, which were then divided out.[55] Stuart Bell later went into the Pensions Investment and Research Centre, part of a number of newer groups that emerged in the 1980s, like EIRIS, Ethical Investment Research and Information Service. Indeed, latterly Pauline Webb also took up this issue, becoming a member of the Ethical Advisory Committee of Credit Suisse. Thus earlier work by people like the Revd Elliott Kendall, who ran Christian Concern for Southern Africa, on whose Executive David Haslam sat, came to fruition following on from a major House of Commons investigation of the ethical investment of British firms and their employment practices in South Africa.

ELTSA effectively ended in 1994 with South Africa's new constitution and all-party elections, the product of complex negotiations over a long period. Its style had been largely confrontational, though even David Haslam, who persisted when others flagged, found the task of resisting Goliath-like institutions formidable. Nevertheless, 'to stand outside the company headquarters of international banks in the City of London', he has observed, 'doing street theatre about how putting money into the South African "piggy bank" always makes a profit, and facing the disinterest, the ridicule, the outright hostility of bank employees',[56] proved to be an illuminating theological experience.

He found, of course, that 'such financiers, and the majority of the church which supports them' were not on the same side 'as those with a radical theology who work in groups like ELTSA. They support the status quo, or, if necessary, a mild modification of it . . . '[57] David and his colleagues, however, believed that what they were doing was part of the Church's mission, 'participating in the Kingdom of God'. This puzzled some Marxists with whom they worked, who could not understand that their need to 'get alongside the poor and crucified'[58] came from a theology of liberation as they had learned about it from Latin American theologians.

'To some,' a journalist wrote, 'David Haslam is the epitome of the modern-day trendy, turbulent priest more concerned with El Salvador than salvation.'[59] But David could not have stayed faithful without the help of others and the intellectual equipment and eloquence he had, which aided his analysis. As in his article 'Mobilising the European Churches',[60] where he gave a succinct yet comprehensive account of the British Churches' failure to meet the moral challenge of investment in apartheid,[61] he was always ready to use both head and heart. Inevitably the personal cost was high, but, as David has explained, 'just when you thought you might give up, some other horror would occur'.[62]

ELTSA, 'a small cog in a big anti-apartheid wheel', as Brian Brown of the Christian Institute, saw it, was but part of a wider picture. 'It was', he has judged, 'the unrelenting and sacrificial struggle of South Africa's oppressed that was crucial in causing apartheid's demise. But it was the things for which ELTSA stood which were complementary in bringing about the talks with the ANC leadership and the other process of transition to democracy.'[63] What right had he to suggest that blacks were ready and willing to pay such a price for their emancipation demanded David Haslam's critics, of whom there were many, some with a keen focus on improving conditions for black workers in British firms. David's answer was that those at the forefront of the struggle and who took a greater risk encouraged him to act as he did.

The experience he gained gave him a grounding for a bigger struggle – the liberation of the Dalits in India, and elsewhere. Backed by Methodist sources and Christian Aid, his new task began while he was working for Churches Together in Britain and Ireland, the successor to the British Council of Churches. His analytic power is again present in *Caste Out!*,[64] his account of the situation of the 170 million of Indians, from a total of a billion, who are 'untouchable' as they were once termed. It is not because he thinks there are no racial justice issues in the UK to which Churches and others need attend. Rather, as he chairs the Dalit Solidarity Network, it has become the next stage of his international ministry, though he continues to be a local minister, this time with two congregations. There is indeed a rightness about this development for, of the 2–4 per cent of Indian Christians, the Dalits are three-quarters.

David Haslam has already met with senior representatives of a number of banks to discuss why new jobs they are creating in India do not allow reservations for Dalits when public sector reserved jobs are rapidly disappearing.[65] In addition the ethical investors, governments, the Churches and firms, have been encouraged to look more seriously at the corporate responsibility of companies outsourcing to India. The wheel has turned a further circle.

Notes

1 Baldwin Sjollema in *Dictionary of the Ecumenical Movement*, Geneva, World Council of Churches Publication, 1991, pp. 825–6.

2 London Mission Report 1969.

3 Sjollema, in *Dictionary*, pp. 825–6.

4 Harold E. Fey, ed., *The Ecumenical Advance: A History of the Ecumenical Movement*, Vol. 2 1948–1968, London, SPCK, 1970, p. 413.

5 See Nerys John, unpublished research paper, 'The campaign against British bank involvement in apartheid South Africa', quoting R. Stares, 'British Banks and South Africa', *Christian Concern for Southern Africa* (CCSA) mid-1990s.

6 David Haslam, interview with author, 28 September 2004.

7 Haslam, interview.

8 *Methodist Recorder*, 14 October 1971, p. 5.

9 David Haslam, *The Guardian*, 20 March 1973.

10 David Haslam, *Methodist Recorder*, 5 July 1973.

11 *Methodist Recorder*, 10 April 1974.

12 Nerys John, 'Campaign', p. 4.

13 Nerys John, 'Campaign', p. 10.

14 Dr Pauline Webb, interview with author, 26 November 2004.

15 David Haslam, 'The ELTSA story', in Rex Ambler and David Haslam, eds, *Agenda for Prophets: A Political Theology for Britain*, London, Bowerdean Press, 1980, p. 44.

16 Haslam, 'The ELTSA Story', p. 44.

17 Stares, quoted in Nerys John, 'Campaign', p. 54.

18 See *The Times*, 24 February 1976.

19 Haslam, 'The ELTSA Story', p. 44.

20 *The Guardian*, 17 March 1976.

21 *Financial Mail*, 15 April 1976.

22 *Financial Times*, 18 March 1977.

23 Stares, in Nerys John, 'Campaign', p. 54.

24 E. T. Shoenan, *South Africa Sanctions Directory: South Africa's Relations in Transition 1985*, a Chronology, Johannesburg, 1993, p. 11.

25 *Financial Times*, 5 October 1977.

26 Haslam, 'The ELTSA Story', p. 45.

27 *ELTSA Newsletter*, 14 January 1978, p. 12.

28 *The Citizen*, Johannesburg, 20 April 1978.

29 David Haslam, interview with Nerys John, in Nerys John, 'Campaign', p. 13.

30 Haslam, in Nerys John, 'Campaign', p. 13.

31 Haslam, 'The ELTSA Story', p. 45.

32 Barclays Shadow Report, ELTSA 1983, p. 6.

33 Barclays Shadow Report, ELTSA 1986, p. 6, cited in Nerys John, 'Campaign', p. 3.

34 Barclays Shadow Report 1981.

35 Haslam, 'The ELTSA Story', p. 45.

36 Nerys John, 'Campaign', p. 19.

37 Nerys John, 'Campaign', p. 21, quoting *Africa Research Bulletin in Economic, Financial and Technical Services 1985–86*.

38 Nerys John, 'Campaign', p. 21.

39 *Brent Chronicle*, 5 December 1986.

40 *Cape Herald*, Cape Town, 29 June 1987, cited in Nerys John, 'Campaign', p. 21.

41 ELTSA Newsletter, May 1978.

42 Nerys John, 'Campaign', p. 28.

43 Natross and Ardington, eds, *The Political Economy of South Africa*, Oxford, OUP, 1990, p. 277.

44 *The Guardian*, 22 October 1985.

45 Barclays Shadow Report, ELTSA 1988, p. 7.

46 World Council of Churches, *The Sanctions Mission*, p. 58, quoted in Nerys John, 'Campaign', p. 32.

47 David Craine, interview with author, 11 January 2005.

48 Craine, interview.

49 Andrew Bolger, *Financial Times*, 18 May 1990.

50 Bolger, *Financial Times*.

51 Bolger, *Financial Times*.

52 Bolger, *Financial Times*.

53 David Haslam, 'The time is not yet, a visit to the 48th National Conference of the ANC, Durban 2–6', July 1991, p. 11.

54 Craine, interview.

55 Craine, interview.

56 Haslam, 'The ELTSA Story', p. 56.

57 Haslam, 'The ELTSA Story', p. 56.

58 Haslam, 'The ELTSA Story', p. 46.

59 Mark Leslie, *West London Press*, 24 July 1987.

60 David Haslam, 'Mobilising the European Churches', in Pauline Webb, ed., *A Long Struggle: The Involvement of the World Council of Churches in South Africa*, Geneva, WCC, 1994.

61 See also David Haslam, *Go, Sell*, Peterborough, Epworth Press, 1975.

62 Haslam, interview with author.

63 The Revd Brian Brown, e-mail to author, 25 January 2005.

64 David Haslam, *Caste Out!*, London, Churches Together in Britain and Ireland, 1999.

65 'Dalit rights', *The Newsletter of the Dalit Solidarity Network UK*, Spring 2004, p. 4.

(More material on ELTSA can be found in the Bodleian Library of Commonwealth and African Studies at Rhodes House, South Parks Road, Oxford OX1 3RG. wttp://www.bodley.ox.ac.uk/dept/rhodes/eltsa.)

14

Only One Race – The Human Race
Sybil Phoenix and Racism Awareness

Sybil Phoenix was born in Guyana in 1927. 'We lived in Georgetown, at that time still British Guiana,' Sybil has recorded. 'My mother died in my ninth year. As my father worked in the quarries outside the city and returned home only for a few days each year, I suddenly was for all purposes orphaned.'[1] Because of her predicament it was decided that Sybil should move to a manse where her grandfather, who served in the local Congregational church, lived with another minister, a deacon and their families. When she was ten, a measure perhaps of her precociousness, Sybil climbed on her grandfather's knee and told him she wanted to participate in Holy Communion. He asked why a child should be allowed this privilege, so Sybil retorted: 'You are like the disciples who turned away the children from Jesus.' The outcome was that her grandfather told Sybil she could attend classes for full church membership.[2]

It soon became clear that Sybil had 'willing hands',[3] and a 'God-loving heart', as she puts it. Within a short space of time she had become the youngest Sunday School teacher that her community had ever known. When, in later decades, people in London and beyond applauded Sybil's work, but did not warm to her religious sensibilities, they perhaps did not fully appreciate that her passion both for justice and community came from her early understanding of Jesus' gospel. As she has written: 'My whole existence has been and is rooted in prayer. It is my firm belief that prayer changes things. It changes us and as we are changing, so does the world.'[4]

A mystic, without realizing it, Sybil came eventually to appreciate 'there was such a thing in life as presence'. Indeed, there were times in Guyana when she felt 'suddenly inexplicably engulfed by the presence',[5] as she became sensitive to nature – the lemon grass tea when it boiled and 'infused the whole house with its lovely scent', the diverse forests and the flamboyant trees in Georgetown itself, which shed their red petals over the avenues.[6]

At school, Sybil learned 'next to nothing about African culture and history or even about Guyana itself'. But she knew 'everything there was to know about England'.[7] European ministers and their wives were 'the mini-Gods of the country,' she observed subsequently[8] – so, too, she discovered, were the magistrates and other officials. Her aunt, who gave her a home when her grandfather died (she was then 12), made her respect her elders, 'including your betters,' she said firmly. Sybil therefore became passive, accepting the situation of black people, though some cousins were more assertive, despite being 'thumped' for such responses.[9]

Sybil now became more aware of class than racial divides, though one relative had become Guyana's first black judge. At the local church (the African Methodist Episcopal Zion Church – AME), to which her uncle belonged, where she had an administrative job, there were two forms that gave access to a doctor, one pink, the other form white – for church members. Sybil ensured that friends of hers from the local market received the latter form because, even if you had paid for the pink form, it did not confer great access to medical help. 'I was always upset by that,' Sybil has admitted.[10]

In Guyana there had been a long history of complex relationships between different racial groups. When the indigenous Amerindians resisted slavery, sometimes preferring to drown themselves instead, English colonialists had brought in European, Indian, Chinese and African workers, thus creating a seedbed for later conflicts. These occurred partly because the indentured Indians and their families, who had been brought to Guyana, were the bosses of the labourers in the sugar fields. Sybil became very aware of such tensions, the more so when a cousin with a stable job told her he would leave his current girlfriend for a Portuguese woman because he wanted his children to have access to white society.[11]

Sybil found her own ancestry was as varied as Guyana's, though her aunt was displeased that she had discovered this and hit her so hard she fell against a door. Her grandfather had been in the Anglo-Boer War and escaped by boat with a Scottish colonel. He then married a sister of the colonel, though only out of respect for him. Nevertheless, they had 21 children, one of whom was Sybil's grandfather. Sybil had thus to recognize that she had both an African and a Scottish dimension in her family history. This Sybil came to feel was the root of her aunt's antipathy to Sybil's mother, who had been fair-skinned – a fact more likely to get her a better job.[12]

By the 1950s Sybil was working for the political success of Cheddi Jagan and Forbes Burnham, then colleagues, despite the tensions that existed between the Indian and African communities. Aware of these, and of those between even Chinese and Indian shopkeepers, she gained respect for her work, and members of the Indian community, many of them Hindus or Muslims, brought her presents – as they did for Europeans. 'Now I was one of the betters,' Sybil has reflected.[13]

Sybil discovered that she had a good singing voice and this led to her involvement with the Philharmonic Choir, which was usually reserved for Europeans. Though her aunt disliked her singing, she could not stop Sybil becoming well-known. At the same time, as a member of Georgetown Clubland, Sybil learned youth club insights, as well as honing her social work skills through her church job. But it was learning always gained against the backdrop of her aunt's cruelty. When in 1994 Sybil visited Guyana with computers for a school's project, a blind woman asked to see her. 'Your aunt,' the old lady observed, 'how did you manage to give that woman such a good funeral?' Sybil admitted her aunt had been cruel, but added 'she made a woman out of me',[14] as Sybil had learnt how to cope with suffering from an early age. She also had a friend who taught her about humility. After her great success in the Philharmonic, with half a page devoted to her in a local paper, a lady that Sybil called 'Mom' said: 'You see this? Don't let it go to your head. You know what these white people do? They build you up and they pull you down.'[15]

At 22, Sybil planned to earn her living as a professional seamstress and hat-maker. She bought two sewing-machines and, with Joe Phoenix (later her fiancé), whom she met in a youth club that she was running, set up a business. It prospered, but in 1956, because she wanted to learn how to be a milliner and develop her social work skills further, she set off for England, arriving by boat in Portsmouth.[16] With hindsight, it is now possible to see that the gifts that were to be of such use to Sybil in London were already there in embryo – her faith; her social and youth work skills; her capacity to cope with suffering; and her awareness of race and class issues. She did not yet of course understand their comprehensiveness, nor could she foresee the massive burden of administration that she would have to cope with and that at times almost overwhelmed her.

On her arrival in Britain, Sybil's first surprise came at Victoria Station. Her eyes fixed on a white woman who was sweeping the platform. From Sybil's background, this seemed incredible.[17] After staying with friends and relations for a while, Joe and Sybil decided to find a home to live in once they were married – Joe being unaware then of where his future wife's commitments would lead. But over the next decades he tried to support her as best he could, even though her sense of extended family responsibilities often tested their family sorely.

They were shocked when they looked for a place to rent. One notice read: 'Double-room; no dogs, no children, no Irish, no coloureds need apply'.[18] 'My Britishness was worth nothing,' Sybil discovered, 'as white society saw my blackness and not my Britishness and my blackness was not part of England.'[19] Even the Methodist Church, to which she went in west London now that they had found temporary accommodation, made no response, though its members were pleasant enough on Sundays when she hailed them at the bus stop. It was but one of many rejections she experienced over the decades, which became more complex when she was worshipping with whites, yet listening to stories of black people who were being seriously mistreated.

By 1972, when Sybil was awarded the MBE, a recognition for being a foster-mother to many in the home that she and Joe had bought in Lewisham, clearly Sybil had become a black woman accepted by the white establishment in Britain. She was now, however, extremely sensitive to the injustices and deprivation of black people around her and had given up attempts to hide her blackness, a previous outlook of which she now became ashamed. One catalyst of her anger was an assault on a 64-year-old woman by a porter at Lewisham station. 'I've had enough,' Sybil told herself.[20] Then, through a local Anglican priest, she was asked to take on a club for black youngsters. At first she refused, but after much pressure agreed to run the Telegraph Hill Youth Club, re-named 'Moonshot' after a competition involving club members to find a new name. Soon, with 500 attending nightly, it moved to Pagnell Street, Deptford. Tensions were often high, especially between black youngsters and the police, but Sybil learned how to handle these and also the fights that broke out between club members.[21]

While at Moonshot, Sybil became involved with several projects and realized anew the animosities existing among diverse groups. Thus Africans would treat West Indians badly, Indians would curse Africans and prefer West Indians. It was a conflict made worse by competition for scarce resources, and Sybil had to work hard to handle the tensions. 'I found myself mediating between Africans and Indians,' she has explained.[22] Invited by the head of Deptford School to take assemblies, she also found herself involved with parents. To help their growth in awareness, she would encourage different groups to celebrate their own traditions, especially through food. There were celebrations, too, for Guyanan and Jamaican Independence Days. Sybil set up education classes for young blacks at Moonshot, with staff provided by the Inner London Education Authority and poverty classes funded by Cadburys. Parallel to this, and her fostering, which continued, she undertook more training in counselling and youth work.

It was 1977 and Moonshot's sports teams were winning trophies. There were classes in mechanics, woodwork, photography and the arts, as well as more academic subjects. Now Prince Charles paid a visit, following up a previous one by Princess Margaret in 1973. But that

November, an article appeared in a national paper saying the National Front had held a meeting and was determined to burn down the building in Pagnell Street, for which an extra appeal for extensions had recently been made.[23] A few weeks earlier it was also reported that people had been heard boasting in a local pub that they would burn down Moonshot.[24]

And so it was. On 18 December the police called Sybil at 4 a.m. to say that Moonshot was on fire. 'I shall never forget the blaze of red flames,' Sybil has recorded.[25] Ignoring advice, Sybil rushed into the building and found the charred accounts and then withdrew hastily. She did not lose heart, however. 'My name is Phoenix,' she declared, 'and, so help me God, out of the ashes I will re-build Moonshot.'[26] The Prince of Wales reopened it in 1981, but no one has ever been caught for the crime.

In 1980 the Revd Vic Watson, soon to be firmly behind Sybil's formal racism awareness work, wrote that the Pagnell Street Centre 'was one of the most significant of community organizations in Britain. It has allowed black people to assert their right to resources and self-management in their community.'[27] The Rt Revd David Sheppard, Bishop of Liverpool, whom Sybil had got to know when he was Bishop of Woolwich, noted in his Foreword to one of Sybil's books that 'the chain of bitterness' stopped with her and she 'soaks up those bitter feelings'.[28] He realized, from his visit to Moonshot to experience at first hand how young black people felt, that Sybil could interpret their needs and also specify action required by both local and national government, a point that Vic Watson had also made clear.[29] Thus what had begun as a youth club, in ten years had grown into a multi-purpose centre, an indication, he felt, of Sybil's 'professional skills, resourcefulness and courage'.[30]

The Centre finally gave Sybil a base for her work of speaking out, begun earlier, for example, on the David Frost show in 1973, or on *Thought for the Day* in 1974, or during a debate with Joan Lester, later an MP, on the future of education in Britain, where Sybil argued for a rewriting of some history books.[31] Increasingly, Sybil sought to interpret how black people felt to a wider society, one year addressing the women's section of the Labour Party meeting at Brighton.[32] This was especially so when she explained black attitudes to the police; however, Sybil never denigrated their function, as she realized that police officers played an important community role.[33]

Thus early in the 1970s Sybil became involved with Scotland Yard in helping to establish Help on Arrest schemes. This led to the appointment of police community liaison officers. From 1968, she had regularly visited the Hendon Police Training School to take sessions with its cadets, a commitment involving six weekly seminars. Here she explained how ethnic communities often felt about British society. 'Could Britain respond positively to the changes that are occurring?' she would ask. Such lectures were replicated at the South London Training School. Even though, as Sybil readily admits, there were bad police officers at the Lewisham Borough level, she found she had to 'remain friendly with the police if I was to serve the community'.[34]

Gradually, partly as a result of her work with Lewisham's Council for Community Relations, and feedback that she received from her preaching, speaking and lecturing, and also from students from both Oxford, Cambridge and beyond, who worked with her in Lewisham, Sybil became convinced that there was a need to train people in racism awareness. 'Racism permeates every part of British society,' a report written for Cardinal Hume by a group of which Sybil was a member concluded.[35] Sybil had already been aware of this through her work with the Anglican Diocese of Southwark when she had helped advise a group preparing a Lent course for its Bishop, Mervyn Stockwood. Not liking some of its contents he wanted to jettison it, but Sybil intervened when the Anglican clergy with whom she had worked felt unable to influence him. Arriving without an appointment, but knowing he was at home, Sybil challenged him about his attitude and threatened to make it public if the course did not go ahead. Her intervention proved critical, for soon David Sheppard, Dr Stockwood's colleague, dealt with his objections and the course was used.

This involvement led Sybil to work with an Ecumenical Unit for Racism Awareness (EURAP), launched in central London in the early 1980s. The programme, which took Sybil and her Anglican colleague, the Revd Jack Pawsey, to many parts of the Anglican Church in England, had twin foci – exposing both inherited white attitudes to black people as inferior beings and the power they had held for centuries 'to enact this view in the institutional processes of the societies they controlled'.[36] After a while, as the courses developed, there was a shift of emphasis, with EURAP's title changing to Training and Consultancy for Racial Justice.

Parallel with this work, in 1981 Sybil left the re-opened Pagnell Street Centre and began work with Methodism, which had decided – partly through Vic Watson's advocacy and others in central positions of authority in Methodism – to establish at his church in Walworth the Methodist Leadership Racism Awareness Training Unit (MELRAW). This involved Sybil in weekend conferences and courses to help people understand the human family and its essential unity, as she termed it. 'God has created only ONE world,' she repeated continually, 'and there is no third or fourth world. And there is only one Race, the human race, made in God's image.'[37] However, she accepted past memories had to be dealt with, otherwise the future could easily be damaged, sometimes irrevocably. In so doing she felt 'we bring the two great principles of justice and freedom into ever closer relationship'.[38] Soon Sybil moved beyond Clubland, her base, to work with the staff of the Division of Social Responsibility, Methodist ministers in training at Wesley College, Bristol, and also with groups in Birmingham, as well as Methodist leaders at District and area level. This work was later expanded to include other Christian traditions, institutions and community groups.[39]

Sybil also attended the Methodist Conference, speaking out in debates, and sometimes causing much annoyance. Some felt that with her preaching gifts she would make more impact through the pulpit. But after deciding to become a Methodist minister, she was persuaded instead to work for MELRAW. 'Some people wish I didn't exist,' she wrote later, 'because I'm always opening my mouth and I refuse to be quiet.'[40] Indeed, at the time she began MELRAW work, she was dubbed 'a dangerous woman'.[41]

The formula for its weekend courses varied, but always included a theological rationale and role-playing as well as talks on how black people in the UK lived. Worship was also a focal part of the courses, which mostly attracted white participants. For any black course members, Sybil stressed 'mercy, compassion and justice' as interwoven themes. Black people were in a position to forgive, she contended. Despite the fact that they had been hurt, the principles of justice *and* mercy were essential.

Between 20 and 30 trainees came to the programmes that MELRAW ran specifically for the police. Sybil organized one-day courses and follow-up days too, a procedure that lasted two to three months until all cadets had attended. Later there were visits to the police training centre at Crystal Palace. Her racism awareness training expanded further when she was invited to create a course in Düsseldorf in Germany for Protestant pastors, work that continues.

Sybil's courses were but one of various attempts to deal with racism in the UK. There were many other international movements concerned with the issue, partly highlighted by former colonies as they received independence, the obduracy of white governments in southern Africa, and the rise in the USA of the civil rights movement, led by Martin Luther King Junior. Leaders now emerged to proclaim 'black is beautiful', as African–Americans claimed their inheritance. Some, like Malcolm X, argued that black people should stand alone, a view that King thought unrealistic because of their minority status in US society. The 1970s saw a movement in South Africa, led by Steve Biko, called black consciousness, earlier movements having lost leaders like Nelson Mandela to life imprisonment. Such movements had an impact in the UK, especially London, because refugees from apartheid and elsewhere lived in the capital. Sybil herself took a keen interest in South Africa, and raised money for projects there.

In essence, however, what she and others had to argue about were the best policies for the UK. Thus the Zebra Project, begun in east London in 1975, and headed for a while by the Methodist minister Tony Holden, aimed to bring together black and white Christians in dialogue and partnership and to raise awareness and encourage co-operation so that the UK could become more of a plural society without racism. Its core work was in Newham, Tower Hamlets, Waltham Forest and Hackney, reaching out especially to black and often Pentecostal Christians, who used Methodist and other church property until they found sites of their own.

Meanwhile a number of the few black ministers in London focused on the need they perceived to develop a sense of self-confidence and self-reliance within the black Christian community, especially among young people. Church-based educational facilities and programmes designed to improve individual attainment and community pride were created. In Stoke Newington, the Revd Dr Robinson Milwood consciously engaged with what he believed to be 'the slave mentality' adopted by many of those who had come from the Caribbean to work in London and else-where, and set up black studies and other courses in his urban Christian Institute to aid this awareness. The Revd George Pottinger too, in Brixton, and the Revd Kingsley Halden, in Hackney, from their perspectives also tried to respond to their situations, the former in a large school in Tulse Hill, and the latter exploring the meaning of forgiveness; he also allowed the Citizens Advice Bureau to have an office at his church.

A community-based church emerged in Harlesden, where the late Keith Johnson was based from 1964 to 1974, before working with both the Commission for Racial Equality as its first police liaison officer and dealing with the Metropolitan and other police forces. This included a nursery and advice centre for social problems. Brent Council and the church sponsored a youth and community centre and an after-school club for 11–16-year-olds to help with the acquiring of skills. A similar approach occurred at Peckham Methodist Church with a work and schools project, and at Crossover, started by a member of the Bow Mission. However, finance for this scheme offering life skills came to grief when government funding was reduced. One centre, in a Methodist church in Ilford, serviced schools in five London boroughs offering teachers and community groups courses on the world faith communities, which involved partnership between voluntary and statutory services.

Schemes like this received grants from the Joint Inter-Divisional Fund for Multi-Racial Projects,[42] from 1995 paid for by Central Methodist Church Funds – a significant change because it meant such schemes were affirmed at the centre of the Methodist Church's life. Thus work begun earlier at national level and argued for in both committees and the Methodist Conference itself, in documents like Heather Walton's *A Tree God Planted*, came to fruition. There was, too, a growing awareness of Muslim, Hindu and Sikh presence, epitomized by the Central Mosque in Regent's Park, and small local ones elsewhere; a Hindu Temple in Neasden and a Sikh one in Southall, the largest outside Amritsar itself.

In east London, Intercom forged links with Newham's diverse religious groups and helped churches understand and accept an Asian community where many languages were spoken. The Revd Charles Watson, a presbyter from the Church of North India, offered a special ministry to Asians until his retirement – not only through Intercom, which he created, but also through Trinity Community Centre, where a congregation of great vivacity emerged. Unlike the Roman Catholic Church, which has regularly established chaplaincies for specific cultures, Methodism has not done so. A Ghanaian Fellowship and Chaplaincy was, however, inaugurated in September 2002, one of a number of African fellowships that have sprung up. It has also encouraged the growth of an Urdu-speaking congregation at King's Hall, Southall, work with South Koreans based in New Malden, a Tamil-speaking congregation in Hammersmith and ministries among Chinese speakers.

Starting with contacts made by Stephen Wong with Chinese students and nurses after 1945, and developed by Vernon Stones, who had a roving commission from the Methodist Missionary Society to make links with the Chinese Community in Greater London and beyond, Methodist involvement has grown from the formation of the Anglo-Chinese Association for those with mixed marriages, which had an office at the Methodist church in Shepherd's Bush Road. Stones's colleague, John Wong, enabled Chinese students to help restaurant workers learn English from this base, and they also put on popular Chinese films in Brixton.[43] This earlier work has led to the emergence of a Chinese church at King's Cross, used formerly by the German Mission, itself a development from arrangements for German-speaking Christians made in north London before 1914.[44] Here there is a weekday advice centre and a 200-strong congregation. A second major Chinese congregation worships at Epsom Methodist Church and new congregations have been started in a number of towns across England.

A Welsh-speaking church had by 2005 ended, but American Methodists attend Whitefields Memorial Church, part of the ecumenical Protestant community there. Members of the African Methodist Episcopal Church also worship in London in their own congregations. Clearly, culture, language and even the customs of ethnic communities are important, for large societies often seek either to absorb or alienate them through injustices or lack of generosity.

When in 1978, for example, London Entertains, a multicultural ethnic arts festival began, backed by Cardinal Hume, Lord Soper, Bishop Huddleston and artists like Cleo Laine, Donald Swann and Miriam Karlin, the Methodists – who with others co-founded it – did not fully appreciate how leadership models, decision-making processes and procedures would affect the running of an annual festival. It was one thing to hold lunchtime City crowds spellbound with African drumming on St Paul's Cathedral steps, or watch Spanish or Filippino dancers at the Trafalgar Square Finale, but quite another for groups to get under one another's skin or understand how a particular culture had developed. How much did Sybil contribute to such ventures? Certainly at one key moment in London Entertains, when two senior figures on its committee wanted to stop the venture almost at birth because of finance difficulties, Sybil's intervention, with that of another member, prevented such action.

In Methodism, as Ivan Weekes (along with Leon Murray a former Methodist vice-president) has observed: 'The agenda for racial justice within the Methodist Church has had a wider origin and support than is sometimes realised,'[45] as senior figures secured money for 'an agenda not easy to promote'.[46] Yet Sybil has stood out through her persistence. 'Sybil has been, and remains, the presiding genius of the work,' Dr Brian Beck has observed, 'a mother in Israel to hundreds of people, including myself, always seeking reconciliation and healing, but not at the price of sacrificing justice.'[47]

Much earlier, too, came the work of the Revd David Mason – the main figure, with Lord Soper, behind the Notting Hill Team Ministry in 1960 – as the Notting Hill Carnival (for some years headed by a member of its congregation) gathered momentum. David's work at a London, national and international level, specifically for East African Asians, and his race relations report to the Methodist Conference, and subsequent commitment to the Race Relations Board, were pioneer contributions. Another was Rowland Joiner's work in East Ham who, with the Congregational minister Clifford Hill, created the Newham Community Renewal Programme, which in his ten years there came to employ some ten full-time staff, running many community projects, including the Trinity Centre. Together, too, they encouraged men and women from Asia and the Caribbean to share their joint venture in two congregations and housed the first club for young Asians in Newham 'at a time when Paki-bashing was considered a popular sport'.[48] Before he left, Rowland ensured the continuation of the project and the Methodist minister Paul Regan was employed by the Programme, which he ran for many years.

'There was a clear progression from race awareness, through racial training to racial justice,' Gavton Shepherd, a former race relations officer and staff member of the Community Relations Commission, considers.[49] MELRAW itself, which Sybil had to leave for family reasons in 1991, despite finding finance a worry, continued under different leaders and then became part of the Methodist Church Committee for Racial Justice. 'Sybil's work,' Naboth Muchopa (who succeeded Ivan Weekes as secretary) has written, 'impacted greatly on some of the work we do today'.[50] 'Out of the Phoenix we rise,' suggested one of the training units' many brochures, a training that has been going for 20 years.

Not everyone of course is convinced that church structures embody racial injustice, and the writer A. Sivanandan, from a Marxist perspective, is convinced it stems from an abuse of power rather than lack of personal awareness. The Churches have had 1985 years 'to assess whether or not changed minds changed society,' he has argued,[51] a cautionary stricture when assessing the impact of church training schemes, despite Methodism being the first group nationally to embed such programmes at its heart. However, with the appointment of Inderjit Bhogal as its first Asian president in 2000 and the Ermal Kirby as its first black District chair, Methodism has indicated its commitment to representing diversity at all levels. With the growth in London of multi-ethnic Methodist congregations and the increasing ethnic minority representation on many committees, there is an indication that issues of power and awareness are being tackled.

Where, then, does Sybil Phoenix's work lead as she continues in a quieter vein with schemes that combine networking, fund-raising, personal ministry and ecumenical outreach? Clearly, training work must continue, involving more fully suburbs around London and other large cities, where Methodism still has a reasonable base. But the joy of celebration needs enhancing too, as in London boroughs that annually raise awareness of black history in particular.

The issues are, however, deeper, with serious discrimination in housing, employment and before the law. As Neil Richardson, a recent president of the Methodist Conference, has pointed out, 'We must accept that racial justice is not just a matter of political correctness but is central to the gospel.'[52] Perhaps, as Gavton Shepherd has suggested, the church should support a quota system for employment in the UK. It should certainly stimulate more discussion and debate about the creation of a plural society and world.[53] However, churches do not usually like hard-nosed policies, and clearly there are no instant answers for racial conflicts.

Yet it is also clear that love involves more than just personal caring. In 2007 the Bi-centenary of the British Parliament's Slave Trade Abolition Bill occurs and events are planned to celebrate this. The culmination of a three-year United Nations Programme, begun in 2004, with its year to commemorate the abolition struggle and Haiti's independence bi-centenary, this will surely be an appropriate time for Methodists – especially in London – for stock-taking, reflection and action.

Much has happened in race and cultural relations within and between nations since the early nineteenth century, but the struggle for racial justice has a long way to go, especially in the heavily urban context of London, with its rival groups with different attitudes to power and its use. But, as more migrants arrive, not least from mainland Europe, it is important for churches, among other groups in society, to learn to live beyond prejudice and discrimination, eschewing hatred and violence. Given that the world needs peace and justice so urgently, and Britain's opportunity in the European Union and the creative diversity of its cities, especially the capital, Sybil Phoenix's pioneering and persistent work may yet reap a further harvest.

Notes

1   Sybil Phoenix, *Willing Hands*, The Bible Reading Fellowship 1984, p. 11.
2   Phoenix, *Willing Hands*, p. 11.
3   Phoenix, *Willing Hands*, p. 14.
4   Phoenix, *Willing Hands*, p. 14.
5   Sybil Phoenix, *All My Love*, 1992.
6   Phoenix, *All My Love* , p. 16.
7   Phoenix, *Willing Hands*, p. 16.
8   Sybil Phoenix, interview with author, 1 November 2004.
9   Phoenix, interview.
10   Phoenix, interview.
11   Phoenix, interview.
12   Brian Frost, *Women and Forgiveness*, London, Collins-Fount, 1990, p. 54.
13   Phoenix, interview.
14   Phoenix, interview.
15   Phoenix, interview.
16   John Newbury, *Living in Harmony*, Religious and Moral Education Press, 1985, p. 6.
17   Frost, *Women and Forgiveness*, p. 56.
18   Frost, *Women and Forgiveness*, p. 57.
19   Sybil Phoenix, in Roger Hooker and John Sargent, eds, *Belonging to Britain: Christian Perspectives on a Plural Society*, London, Council of Churches for Britain and Ireland (CCBI) for the Committee for Relations with People of Other Faiths, 1991, p. 99.

20 Phoenix, interview.

21 Frost, *Women and Forgiveness*, p. 65.

22 Phoenix, interview.

23 Frost, *Women and Forgiveness*, p. 65.

24 Newbury, *Living in Harmony*, p. 19.

25 Phoenix, *Willing Hands*, p. 19.

26 Phoenix, *Willing Hands*, p. 40.

27 The Revd Vic Watson, *The London Experience*, the Review of the 19th Year of the London Committee, 1980, p. 27.

28 The Rt Revd David Sheppard, Foreword, in Phoenix, *Willing Hands*.

29 Watson, *The London Experience*, p. 27.

30 Watson, *The London Experience*, p. 28.

31 Frost, *Women and Forgiveness*, p. 71.

32 Frost, *Women and Forgiveness*, p. 71.

33 Frost, *Women and Forgiveness*, p. 72.

34 Frost, *Women and Forgiveness*, pp. 72–3.

35 Introduction to 'With You in Spirit'. See Frost, *Women and Forgiveness*, p. 74.

36 The Revd Jack Pewsey, letter to author, November 2004.

37 Talk by Sybil Phoenix, n.d.

38 Phoenix, Talk.

39 Discussion Paper on MELRAW, 'Past Present and Future', 1992, p. 3.

40 Hooker and Sargent, *Belonging to Britain*, p. 104.

41 Elizabeth Waldron, letter to author, 7 November 2004.

42 See Tony Holden, *People, Churches and Multi-Racial Projects*, Division of Social Responsibility of the Methodist Church (an account of English Methodism's responses to plural Britain), 1985.

43 This paragraph is based on notes provided by the Revd R. Keith Parsons, 28 January 2005.

44 London Committee Report, 1943, p. 19.

45 Ivan Weekes, letter to author, 13 November 2004.

46 Weekes, letter.

47 The Revd Dr Brian Beck, letter to author, 11 November 2004.

48 The Revd Roland Joiner, letter to author, 2 November 2004.

49 Gavton Shepherd, interview with author, 25 November 2004.

50 Naboth Muchopa, letter to author, 23 September 2004.

51 See Tony Holden, 'Racism Awareness Training', a paper prepared for MELRAW, 1985.

52 The Revd Dr Neil Richardson, quoted in *Beyond Duty*, Racial Justice Office, October 2003, p. 3.

53 Shepherd, interview.

Postscript

Stuart Jordan

The preceding chapters record the achievements of some exceptional individuals who, driven by their own social passion, have all excelled in their ability to conceive and implement a vision. The range of their work is naturally very varied because, over a period of more than a century, they have each responded to the most pressing needs of the moment, as they have seen them.

Some of the work described here had no precedent anywhere else and still remains unique. Some was part of a wider movement and finds parallels in other individuals or agencies. Some was derivative, drawing on the existing insights and practice of others, before being introduced into Methodism for the first time. In every case, however, the projects described required a combination of complementary gifts in their champions, not least the fusion of visionary and organizational skills that enabled them to discern the key issues and to implement the most effective response.

All this demanded a depth of faith and the pioneers' unswerving belief in themselves and in the task they had undertaken – often at significant personal cost. The need to stay focused on their goal could easily have restricted their lateral vision, though in fact these sketches regularly indicate an impressive breadth of approach and engagement, with proper attention given to individuals and to issues, to people and to policies.

Clearly, all of these pioneers and the initiatives they embraced are sustained by an explicitly Christian conviction, but does their particular Methodist allegiance provide any distinctive element in the mix? Given the parallel developments that can be found elsewhere, probably not, though there is a consistent, if unsurprising, congruence with the tradition that Wesley himself both embodied and bequeathed. Here are echoes of those wide-ranging experiments in practical divinity that typified Wesley's own ministry: new incarnations of his own, often innovative, responses to the needs of the young and the old, the poor and the enslaved. Here again are examples that mirror his own social passion, rooted in the basic gospel imperative to love one's neighbour, driven by a pastoral and pragmatic spirit and spawning a variety of organizational forms and activity.

There is no single theological paradigm that dominates in these different accounts. Instead, where theological motivation emerges at all, there is a range of convictions and emphases at work from models of individual redemption, via modes of incarnational presence to the language of kingdom theology and social liberation. What they all embrace, however, are two fundamental aspects of Wesley's own theology that are of enduring significance: his Arminianism – the belief that God's grace is offered to all, with its radical consequences for an inclusive Church and society – and his conviction that holiness must be embodied both in personal and social realities.

At another level, while creative work driven by such individual enthusiasms is unlikely to be determined for too long by institutional forms, it may be that the shape of Methodist church practice in London contributed in some way to the successful outcomes described. Linked by circuits and, more particularly, by the network of London Mission circuits, churches and their ministers were regularly relating beyond individual congregations and aware of wider patterns of need, practice and opportunity across the capital. The very creation of the Missions, as already noted, gave implicit encouragement to innovation and social engagement, while the co-ordinating work of the London Committee enabled personnel and financial resources to be identified and redistributed as needed – an element in the survival, let alone flourishing, of a number of the projects described. Meanwhile, Methodist connexionalism helped provide a platform and infrastructure that enabled many of these projects to increase their national profile and scope – as, of course, did the ecumenical involvement which is increasingly evident in the more recent of these accounts and, as in the case of various projects, agencies and campaigns, an essential part of their self-understanding.

Methodism's vigorous missionary tradition has also played its own significant role in a number of these developments, and the experience of working with the Church overseas explicitly shaped the vocational choices and direction of several of the British-born pioneers. Meanwhile, the fact that two of those described were formed in part by their experience of Clubland in Guyana – itself consciously modelled on the Walworth Road prototype – before they settled in London is but one small example of the wider process of global interdependence and migration that has transformed London Methodism in recent decades.

While certain strengths and emphases in the Methodist tradition have helped to fuel and sustain the social passion reflected in these accounts, they may also share some of its limiting characteristics. While strong on pragmatism and a readiness to respond to the immediate need, Method-

ist activism is not always sustained by contemplation and an appreciation of the sacramental, or its concern for relevance and immanence by
a sense of the transcendent. While pastorally sensitive to individual
needs, its commitment to remedial action can sometimes outstrip
attention to structural causes – notwithstanding the notable exceptions
recorded here. Its emphasis on the gathered community of members has
led to a model of the congregational, neighbourhood Church that, for
all its strengths, may also have inhibited engagement with the increasing
complexities of London life. The fact that many of the pioneers
described here were originally appointed as local ministers is a testimony to their personal capacity to transcend those in-built constraints
and to live on the larger map that, at its best, the Methodist connexional
system is designed to encourage.

Those driven by social passion are not easily daunted and are often
able to rise above circumstances. Nonetheless, as we contemplate the
current situation and future possibilities, it is clear that a series of
changes and developments have taken place that affect, if not determine,
the future shape and characteristics of all Christian social witness,
including that of the Methodists.

Some of those changes are already well illustrated in the preceding
chapters. Although not arranged in a strictly chronological order, the
stories of individual pioneers chart the changing focus of Methodism's
social passion, reflecting similar developments in other denominations
and other non-Church bodies. They traced the progress of that passion
from the pragmatic and pastoral response to evident individual need,
via the provision of services not covered at the time even by the emerging Welfare State, to the attempts to move beyond needs to preventative
community building and, finally, engagement with some of the economic and political causes of injustice. That journey from the individual
and pastoral to the structural and prophetic follows a trajectory that can
be mirrored in many secular agencies, but also reflects developments
throughout the period in an understanding of the Church's own role
and of the theological and biblical sources by which it is nourished.

In the midst of these obvious changes, however, it is interesting to
note in passing how many basic themes from earlier years have been
reshaped and reclaimed decades, and sometimes a century, later.
Whereas once nineteenth-century Sunday Schools included the teaching
of basic literacy, by the beginning of the twenty-first century a network
of supplementary education, or Saturday Schools, had grown up to support those felt to be under-achieving in the formal educational system.
While once the Slate Clubs offered temporary financial assistance to the
poorest, now some churches are engaged in credit unions or offer debt
counselling. The need for the Poor Man's Lawyer may have been miti-

gated by the provision of Citizens Advice Bureaux and the system of legal aid, but ministers and others are still called on to help find affordable and trustworthy professional help for those negotiating the immigration system and all its potential pitfalls.

In other instances, however, although the scale of the problem may have diminished or the profile of the constituency changed, the same fundamental human needs remain. The Queen Victoria Seamen's Rest still exists – though it now increasingly provides longer-term residential accommodation for retired seafarers. The Whitechapel Mission still offers meals and other facilities to a large number of homeless people, while networks of winter shelters – typically organized on a rota basis by groups of local churches – are regularly over-subscribed.

Despite these apparent continuities, however, a number of underlying differences predominate. First, it is evident that although the previous chapters describe the efforts of able, committed and often highly driven individuals, much of the work they pioneered depended for its effectiveness on cohorts of collaborators and volunteers. Sometimes their names are recorded – as with some of the Sisters and Deaconesses who periodically emerge into the limelight – but many more remain anonymous. Their presence was, however, always vital and the amount of time and energy they offered as part of their Christian discipleship was often heroic. Subsequently, however, social patterns have changed dramatically. Even where congregations have retained a significant membership, working patterns, lifestyles, multiple commitments and the 24/7 economy have all eroded the availability of volunteers, to the extent that even the core worship and regular programmes of many congregations have been reduced or redesigned.

In this context, finding adequate support for social or community projects is often a major challenge. One common response to the problem has been to employ paid workers – a natural and often appropriate route to take. But that solution also comes with associated risks, not least the endless round of fund-raising applications, the requirements of external funding bodies, and the need for more skilled management procedures and committees, all of which generate further demands on sometimes unsuspecting congregations. If the project grows and is able to sustain itself, the new professionalism it properly pursues can raise a new set of issues about its original ethos and the local church's ownership and engagement. These issues doubtless already had to be negotiated as part of the emergence of the major agencies described in Part 3. Today, along with the increasing raft of legislation governing the sector, they are likely to impact on even the most modest of church attempts to meet local need and to require responses beyond the inspired amateurism that has driven so much social passion in the period described.

Although the churches' combined contribution to the life of London's communities is still very significant,[1] they exist alongside many voluntary, let alone statutory, bodies committed to social welfare. At a time of shrinking human and financial resources, that fact alone has been enough to raise important questions about priorities and appropriate models of engagement. At its best, the Church's involvement in social care has often been seen in its use of pastoral instincts, grassroots involvement, wider networks and relative autonomy to pioneer pieces of work that may later have been taken on by other agencies. Despite the extensive range of high-quality statutory services on offer, that vocation is sometimes still necessary – and it is significant that there is some recent evidence of disaffected professionals applying for appointments in church projects, rather than in their own public sector, out of a conviction that they represent greater opportunities for innovative, people-centred work.

At the same time there is an increasingly urgent conversation to be had about possible ways of reframing the Church's engagement with social and community issues within a more holistic understanding, both of its mission and of the nature of human beings. While this may take many different forms,[2] it will often require a higher degree of intentionality and theological perception to ensure that social engagement is integral to the Church's internal life and sense of purpose.

Whereas the previous chapters tell primarily of individual energies and focused concerns, the changing social ethos and political climate have more recently encouraged the language and practice of partnerships that can often only be delivered by wider neighbourhood or agency alliances. Such partnerships appear to offer churches new opportunities to play an active role in community programmes that they may feel have been recently denied them, especially when those programmes become the means to access public funds. Such partnerships can be both creative and effective, though are again often associated with constraints, demands and uncertainties that need careful assessment. Either way, the dominant culture is one that, despite the impact of a small number of social entrepreneurs, encourages collaboration rather than individualism, integrated solutions rather than single-issue enthusiasms. Within the church context, at both a local and regional level, a desire to engage with social issues should by now automatically trigger an ecumenical question: could this work be done more effectively if Churches were to act together, a question that increasingly evokes a response across the theological, as well as the denominational spectrum.[3]

Given the ever-increasing diversity of London's population throughout the whole of the period described, the ecumenical dimension has been broadened further with the increased presence in London of communities practising many different world faiths. While this is not a new phenomenon in some parts of the city – the chapel in Spitalfields where the Methodist Covenant Service was first celebrated in 1755 was originally built for French Huguenots before later becoming a nineteenth-century synagogue and then, in 1976, a mosque – its extension across so many parts of London certainly is.

The opportunities and challenges arising from this complexity are as much cultural and social as they are religious – and religious labels used too readily as terms of convenience often only obscure the more nuanced issues of identity. What is clear, however, is that a proper attention to the religious needs of London's multi-ethnic populations within the civic arena has given a higher profile to the significance of all faith communities than has existed for some time – a trend further accentuated, of course, after the dramatic events of 9/11 in the USA and, more recently, the London bombings of 7 July 2005, both of which led to public manifestations of inter-faith solidarity.

Within this changing context, there is still a pioneering spirit abroad in the innovative programmes of some Methodist projects, but it is more likely to emerge within broader-based coalitions that draw on different traditions in addressing complex urban issues. It is only through ecumenical partnerships, for example, that some of the major issues – the environment, the Church's mission to London's economy, the impact of major development proposals for the Thames Gateway or the 2012 Olympics, or engagement with the Mayor and Greater London Authority – can be addressed. Meanwhile, an outstanding model of innovative collaborative action is seen in the London Citizens movement, which uses well-honed skills in community organizing to channel the values and social passion of faith groups, schools, student and trade unions into highly effective campaigns.[4] Within this broader context, any specifically Methodist contribution is likely to be modest. None the less, its long-standing witness to universal grace and social holiness, combined with an instinctive pragmatism, might still offer some useful additional leaven to the overall process.

In all this, one of the most obvious changes has been the new demographic realities of London itself, a pre-eminent global city whose population has become progressively more culturally diverse than ever. Such changes have already been reflected in its increasing multi-faith awareness and in the burgeoning growth of black-majority independent churches. Just as importantly, they have also had a major impact on the historic denominations in London, predominantly, but not exclusively, through two waves of immigration: from the Caribbean in the 1960s and 1970s and from West Africa since the 1980s – precisely those areas in which Methodist missionary activity was at its strongest. In the course of that process, the world Church has gifted many of its members and their families to London congregations. As a result, London congregations are experiencing numerical stability and often growth, in contrast with national trends, with currently over 50 per cent of all Methodists in the 32 London boroughs originating from black and ethnic minority backgrounds – one in four from West Africa alone.

The extent of this cultural diversity, the issues it raises and the need to discern its future identity have been among the major factors that have led London Methodism to claim its distinctive identity, redefine its boundaries by the creation of a new London District in 2006 and, more importantly still, explore new ways of working. Opportunities abound, as do issues of empowerment, ownership, and the release of gifts and vocations. The present demographic reality could not easily have been predicted even 20 or 30 years ago, and its future trajectory is, of course, equally uncertain.

Similarly, the implications of this cultural transformation for Methodism's social engagement remain to be seen. Some of the earliest distinctive initiatives, from supplementary education to racism awareness training, have already been noted, but more subtle and ambiguous dynamics are yet to surface. Writers about the global city identify as one of its distinguishing features the recurrent need to negotiate the 'contested space' of different expectations that rub up against one another.[5] There is no reason to suspect that the Church in the global city will be able to avoid that same challenge. Indeed, the more the hitherto marginalized voices are empowered, the more that negotiation will be needed, as different expectations of the Church, its priorities and its engagement with the community are expressed. Within this variety, there may well be a significant need to reclaim and test the Methodist heritage itself – not least Wesley's own holistic theology and practice – as a key resource for the Church's emerging identity and renewed sense of personal and social mission.

But perhaps the very presence of multi-ethnic congregations represents another reality of wider social significance. Here, within our congregations, are microcosms of the global community, laboratories of the Spirit in which we have opportunity to learn from one another, if we will, how differences can be negotiated for the enrichment of all. For that to happen we need to move beyond the mental shorthand that too readily describes such congregations as 'multicultural', as if the aspiration were already reality, for in practice the diversity is held together within what is still predominantly a mono-cultural (white British) framework. While, thanks mainly to the historic vigour of the Methodist missionary movement, that framework still generates just enough of a unifying factor in worship and ethos, other, more intentional and qualitatively different, steps are necessary if genuinely multicultural congregations are to emerge. In a context of global mobility, it may be that community building is once more becoming a significant part of the Church's social vocation as congregations learn to focus on who they are and might become, just as much as on what they do.

One further opportunity that a new district might help facilitate is to identify, encourage and celebrate the various contributions to community life already made by church members who work in London, whether they themselves live in the city or are part of the ebb and flow of daily commuting. Ideally, of course, that would be part of a co-ordinated ecumenical venture that paid attention to particular sectors of the city's life,[6] but it may need to begin within the existing denominational networks. Even the apparently simple task of identifying and gathering individuals, however, presents more than a major logistical challenge. It also requires a theological vision that transcends the normative model of the gathered congregation and encourages an understanding of the city as itself an arena of God's presence, and hence of the Church's mission.

It is something of that vision that has provoked the varied examples of Methodist social passion to which attention has been drawn throughout this book. Inspired by Scripture, encouraged by Wesley's own convictions, sustained by worship, the protagonists have engaged with the reality of London, whether in its local, regional, national or global manifestations. The results of their efforts have been as diverse and particular as the individuals themselves and their contexts. Sometimes their work has merged seamlessly into that of their successors; at other times it has achieved a distinctive profile and organizational reality that has stood the test of time.

Methodist social passion still exists, though today it has to negotiate ever increasing complexities – of diverse communities, limited resources and funding conditions, management and legislation – in pursuit of effective solutions. Meanwhile, individual pioneers, with all their strengths and weaknesses, are less likely to emerge in a context that both exalts and demands collaborative partnerships.

As London Methodism prepares to write a new chapter, it is timely to recall the contributions made by those outstanding individuals who have embodied their social passion in effective action for the sake of the wider community. For some of the reasons suggested, it is unlikely that many of their models or ways of working will again be possible or appropriate in such a rapidly changing context. New challenges and opportunities will, however, surely emerge and, as they do, new vision and innovative practice will be required of contemporary London Methodists, just as much as their predecessors.

Postscript

Those challenges will require responses increasingly informed by different perspectives and disciplines. Within any search for a sustainable urban future, technical responses and resources will be essential, but so will be other, more dissonant voices: voices that speak the language of wholeness as well as health, justice as well as profit; ecological imperative as well as growth; voices that recognize the dignity of the marginalized, address questions of lifestyle, or anticipate the issues associated with extended life expectancy.

From their own storehouses of spirituality and tradition, the Churches and other faith traditions in London may have a significant contribution to make in this process, though only to the extent that they help one another move beyond internal constituency interests to address their common concerns.[7] Within that wider spectrum, the recurrent Methodist social passion rehearsed in these chapters may again have a creative role to play. Should that happen, those whose achievements are celebrated here would receive their most fitting tribute.

Notes

1 See *Regenerating Communities: Faith Communities and Social Action*, 2002, a survey undertaken by the London Churches Group for Social Action which identified the extent and type of faith-based projects across London and predicted on the basis of evidence gathered that 'faith communities could be running more than 7,000 projects in London, employing 10,000 staff and involving over 45,000 volunteers' (p.5).

2 See, for example, the creative opportunities for community ministry advocated by Ann Morisy in *Journeying Out: A New Approach to Christian Mission*, London, Morehouse, 2004.

3 In London, the London Churches Group for Social Action is an agency that promotes ecumenical co-operation around matters of social and civic concern, both at a pan-London level and, through its network of Ecumenical Borough Deans, at the borough level too. In 2000 and 2004 it worked closely with the Evangelical Alliance to produce joint materials and events in connection with the mayoral elections.

4 London Citizens is based in Whitechapel – see their website at www.londoncitizens.org.uk.

5 See, for example, L. Sandercock, *Cosmopolis II: Mongrel Cities of the 21st Century*, London, Continuum, 2003 or the discussion in A. Davey, *Urban Christianity and Global Order*, London, SPCK, 2001.

6 An embryonic project gathering Christians in eight key sectors of London's life was initiated in 2003–4 as a means of compiling an ecumenical submission to the mayoral election process. The reflections of these eight focus groups were compiled as *Faith, Work and City: A Christian Contribution to the Mayor of London Election 2004*. Details from the London Churches Group, 1 Central Buildings, Westminster, London SW1H 9NH.

7 For the Churches' most recent contribution to this process at a national level, see *Faithful Cities: A Call for Celebration, Vision and Justice*, the report of the Commission on Urban Life and Faith, May 2006, available from Methodist Publishing House www.mph.org.uk.

Select Bibliography

Cornell, G., *A Living Spirituality and Theology for the City* www.wlm.org.uk/churchatthecentreofthecity.html.

Crucible, 'On the Faultlines of the Global City' (journal issue dedicated to London Issues), July–September 2004.

Dupuis, J., *Christianity and the Religions: From Confrontation to Dialogue*, London, Darton, Longman and Todd, 2002.

Frost, B., *Citizen Incognito*, London, Sheed & Ward, 1971 (meditations on London).

Harris, J., *The Magnetic South*, Methodist Church Home Mission Division, 1988.

Heitzenrater, R. P., ed., *The Poor and the People Called Methodists 1729–1999*, Nashville, Kingswood Books, 2002.

Inwood, S., *City of Cities: The Birth of Modern London*, London, Macmillan, 2005.

Jennings, T. W., *Good News to the Poor: John Wesley's Evangelical Economics*, Nashville, Abingdon, 1990.

Lynch, K., *The Image of the City*, Cambridge, Mass., MIT Press, 1960. (A classic text on urban planning.)

Meeks, M. D., ed., *The Portion of the Poor: Good News to the Poor in the Wesleyan Tradition*, Nashville, Kingswood Books, 1995.

Merriman, N., ed., *The Peopling of London – 15,000 Years of Settlement from Overseas*, Museum of London, 1993.

Porter, R. S., *London: A Social History*, London, Penguin, 2000.

Rieger, J. and Vincent, J. J., eds, *Methodist and Radical*, Nashville, Abingdon, 2005.

Walker, A., ed., *Spirituality in the City*, London, SPCK, 2005.

Winter, G., *The Suburban Captivity of the Churches*, New York, Doubleday and Co., 1961.